# THE POLITICAL ROLE OF THE COURTS
## JUDICIAL POLICY-MAKING

*a.*
**GLENDON SCHUBERT**
*Michigan State University*

*with an introduction by*
**LEE LOEVINGER**

**SCOTT, FORESMAN AMERICAN GOVERNMENT SERIES**
*Joseph C. Palamountain, Jr., Editor*

**SCOTT, FORESMAN AND COMPANY**
*Chicago • Atlanta • Dallas • Palo Alto • Fair Lawn, N.J.*

*KF*
*8700*
*.S241*

Library of Congress Catalog Card No. 65-17728
Copyright © 1965 by Scott, Foresman and Company
All Rights Reserved
Printed in the United States of America

*K*

*.S367J2*

CANISIUS COLLEGE LIBRARY
BUFFALO. N. Y.

The American system of government strikes a balance between unity and diversity. There is a unity to our system, but it is a unity which tolerates—indeed, requires for its vigor and viability—a broad diversity of institutions, processes, and participants. By organizing the analysis of the sprawling complexity of the American system into smaller, coherent, but interlocking units, the Scott, Foresman American Government Series attempts to reflect this pluralistic balance.

This approach, we believe, has several important advantages over the usual one-volume presentation of analytical and descriptive material. By giving the reader more manageable units, and by introducing him to the underlying and unifying strands of those units, it puts him in a better position to comprehend both the whole and its components. It should enable him to avoid the not-uncommon circumstance of viewing the American system as a morass of interminable and unconnected facts and descriptions.

This approach certainly permits us to tap the expertise and experience of distinguished scholars in the fields of their special competence. Each writes about his specialties, and none is forced to deal with subjects remote from his ken or heart for the sake of "completeness." The unity of the series rests on the interlocking of the various volumes and, in the general emphasis on policy and policy-making, on the method of analysis as opposed to simple description. It does not rest on a unity of approach. The authors vary in their values, their accents, and the questions they ask. To have attempted to impose unity in these matters would have been to water down the series, for the diversity of approach reflects the diversity of the system, its participants, and its commentators. But the final value of this series and its ultimate balance between unity and diversity rest, of course, in the use to which it is put by the reader.

Glendon Schubert's volume forcefully illustrates the desirability of asking experts to write about their fields of special competence for the beginning student. He imparts to the reader the heady joy of new discoveries and the power of new analytical tools in an area often regarded as thoroughly explored and well understood. Casting a cool but sensitive eye on institutions and processes often obscured by myth and presumptions, he paints a clear but fresh picture.

Joseph C. Palamountain, Jr., *Editor*

# INTRODUCTION

It is the history of advance in science that conceptual schemes are successively refined and enlarged to encompass more data and to relate more phenomena. In that sense, this volume represents a scientific contribution to the study of the legal system. It makes a systematic presentation of data, theories, and methods, some of which are so new that they have not previously been related to the traditional body of legal theory or, indeed, even systematically surveyed.

Traditionally the study of the legal process has been concerned with examination and analysis of an abstract general category called "the law." The task which those undertaking such study have set themselves throughout the span of our intellectual history, from Aristotle through Aquinas and John Austin to Roscoe Pound and his contemporary disciples, has been to find the elements of consistency in the logical relationships among legal norms and to state the logical relationships in the form of generally applicable principles. The older, or classical, tradition in jurisprudence assumes an ideal model or order of legal norms which is of transcendent legitimacy and is known as "natural law." This derives its status either directly from divine promulgation and approval or indirectly from being immanent in the general order of nature or in human nature, in either of which it may be discerned or "found" by assiduous reflection and study. The major task of this traditional jurisprudence was to discover the general principles underlying judicial opinions and to harmonize these principles with each other and with the transcendent model of natural law.

In the course of time traditional jurisprudence came to be more concerned with the principles of "positive law"—the commands of sovereigns, including kings, legislators, and judges—than with those of natural law. The first emphasis on the importance of analysis of positive law was in the lectures of John Austin at Oxford early in the nineteenth century; hence, such an approach has come to be known as "analytical positivism," "Austinian jurisprudence," or "Austinism." In the view of this school, the basic judicial task is to examine the correspondence between actual human conduct (or reports of how people have acted) and laws (or statements of how people should act). This school takes its basic data from a limited part of the judicial output, namely the published opinions of appellate courts. This school has a theory of law but no methodology other than ratiocination. Nevertheless, the viewpoint of analytical positivism was dominant in political science and among law professors until World War II and is still largely predominant among the practicing bar.

Two new schools of jurisprudence are products of twentieth-century thinking among lawyers and law professors. These are the schools of "sociological jurisprudence" and "realistic jurisprudence." Both schools have broadened the field of study by observing some elements of judicial input as well as judicial output, and both have assumed a deterministic relationship between input and output, which is generally taken to be a mechanistic cause-and-effect sequence. In other respects there are substantial differences between these schools. Sociological jurisprudence studies the sources of the norms that provide the policy content of judicial decisions and finds them in the needs and demands of society, or "social interests." In the view of this school, of which Pound is probably the leading prophet, law exists to secure social interests, so far as they may be secured by an ordering of men and their relations through organized political society. However, sociological jurisprudence makes no attempt to analyze the operational relationship between the needs and demands of society and the choices of individual judges. On the other hand, realism in jurisprudence shifts attention away from generalizing about law or judicial opinions to the study of individual decisions or particular cases. The great contribution of realism in American legal thinking has been to separate the philosophy of what law should be from the view of what it actually is in individual cases and to emphasize that judges are not merely governmental functionaries but also individuals and human beings. However, with all its emphasis on the specific case and the individual judge, realism has developed no methodology except a naïve and intuitive empiricism. It has attempted no systematic theoretical formulation and so has produced no theory of judicial decision-making.

Since the end of World War II there have been increasing calls for broader and more rigorous methods of studying the legal process. It has been pointed out that reasonably rigorous scientific methods are being used to study various aspects of human behavior in such fields as anthropology, psychology, sociology, and economics and that many of these methods might be found useful in the field of law. The present study by Professor Schubert is based on the analytical framework known in sociology and political science as "systems theory," "structural-functional analysis," or "systems analysis" for short. In this approach we study both the input and the output of the judicial process as well as the conversion process which relates the input to the output. It is in the conversion process that the issues presented by the raw data, or "facts," of an individual case are recognized, individual sets of values are brought to bear, and a judicial decision is determined. This study employs the methods of anthropology, sociology, psychology, and statistical mathematics. It utilizes a sociopsychological conceptualism known as "behavioral theory." This assumes that the conversion structure in the judicial process—the individual judge—is the critical and independent variable in judicial policy-making, and it looks for consistency in the patterning of actions expressing individual sets of values.

Of course, the behavioral theory approach does not blind itself to the views of traditional and conventional jurisprudence. It could not consistently do so, since those viewpoints are still so widely held by professors, lawyers, and judges as to be significant influences in some aspects of judicial behavior. Thus the author here presents the viewpoints of traditional and conventional jurisprudence as well as the more encompassing viewpoint of behavioral theory. More importantly, Professor Schubert presents an overview of the structure of American judicial systems, of judicial functions, of the operation of judicial systems in decision-making procedures, of the relationship between decisions, on the one hand, and policies and ideologies, on the other hand, and, finally, of methodologies actually and potentially employed in examination of judicial structures, functions, and operations.

This book should be of interest to the intelligent and inquiring reader, whether lawyer, social scientist, student, or simply literate citizen. No special training or technical vocabulary is required or assumed. The detail presented should be adequate to satisfy the specialist; the observations ventured should be broad enough to challenge the philosopher. Many prejudices and presuppositions which pass for truisms in popular discussion will have to yield to the contrary evidence presented here.

It is shown that the structural theory which views judicial review as a means whereby the judiciary may impose a conservative check on liberal tendencies in the other branches of government is false. Although it is only in recent years that a majority of the Supreme Court have taken a more liberal position on some policy issues than Congress, it is now clear that judicial review is not restricted to serving as a conservative check on liberal policies. Similarly, the policy orientation of state governments and the national judiciary have changed so that judicial deference to state policy-making no longer has the general effect of upholding liberal values.

The general attitudes of judicial activism and restraint are also reviewed here from the viewpoint of functional theory and empirical data. It is shown that the Supreme Court's basic policies remain stable over long periods of time and that changes which occur reflect fundamental changes in the general political system of which the Court is a component part. So long as the basic goals of the justices are the same as those of political actors in other components of the political system, the Court will accept the policies of other decision-makers and will exercise judicial restraint in dealing with the acts of other branches of government. However, when the majority of the Court disagrees with the fundamental decisions of legislative policy-makers, then it will tend to become judicially activist and to express the conflict through the technical device of judicial review. Thus the Court is activist when its decisions conflict with those of other policy-makers, and the Court exercises judicial restraint when it accepts the policies of other decision-makers. In any event, either course and its characterization is quite independent of whether the Court, Congress, or the executive is serving liberal or conservative values; and, at various times in history, both judicial activism and judicial restraint have served both liberal and conservative goals.

So we are confronted with one of the most significant conclusions to be derived from Professor Schubert's survey. There is no perma-nent or reliable congruence between institutional structures and functions and substantive values. This is of basic importance for theories and studies of legal subjects. It means that static structural theories are likely to be misleading and unlikely to be valid over an extended period of time. This conclusion has even greater significance for political philosophy. It means that there can be no assurance of securing particular social values by innovations in institutional structures. It is the easy and seductive assumption that if some par-ticular institution of government is frustrating an objective that is sought, the remedy must surely lie in abolishing or changing the form of that institution. A companion illusion is that any ideal can be permanently assured by establishing an institution—a specialized agency—to serve that ideal. However, it is demonstrated here that even an institution as stable as the Supreme Court changes in time and comes to serve different values at one time than at another.

This brings us to the principal point of Professor Schubert's book. Mere observation will not suffice to establish the relations between institutional structures and functions and social values. The average person could observe every step in the construction of a com-plicated electronic device without having the slightest idea of how it works or how to replicate the structure. One who knows nothing of legal terminology and procedure is more likely to be confused than instructed by observing courtroom proceedings. But it is also true that one who knows nothing about the contemporary techniques of observing, recording, summarizing, and analyzing behavior is likely to give a very superficial account of judicial behavior, whatever he may know of legal terminology and procedure. That is one of the reasons that much, if not most, of the work currently being done in the scientific investigation of the legal field—jurimetrics—is being done by political scientists and others with scientific training, rather than by lawyers. Science requires both observations and coherent theories to direct and relate the observations. Theories without observations are mere illusion; observations without theories are pure confusion.

In one sense science and the judicial process are similar. Science is man's effort to extend the powers of intellect in observing, describing, and analyzing his environment. It represents man's supreme effort to be rational in viewing the cosmos of which he is a part. The judicial system, on the other hand, is one of the most important institutions society has produced for rationalizing the myriad divergent forces operating within our culture and for reconciling the innumerable conflicts arising among them. As Professor Schubert observes (in Chapter Three), "By thus reducing relative chaos to relative order, the most basic function of judicial systems is to extend the bounds of rationality in human behavior." To extend the bounds of rationality in human behavior is surely one of the most important, if not the most important, objectives of organized society. It is at once one of the principal prerequisites and high ideals of civilized living. Yet, after centuries of pursuit, man still finds rationality an elusive goal.

The approach represented here is a new path toward rationality regarding judicial behavior. It brings to bear upon the study of judicial behavior the techniques and data of what have been called the behavioral sciences. To put it in a way that only seems tautological, this means that we are proceeding rationally to examine our efforts to act rationally in public affairs. This is not a mere academic exercise. The operation of the judicial system is at least in part an expression of the view that judges take of their function; and this, in turn, is largely a reflection of the view that society takes of their function. If our judicial systems are to extend the bounds of rationality in human behavior, then they must themselves be studied and regarded rationally.

Lee Loevinger
Federal Communications Commission

# TABLE OF CONTENTS

# The Judiciary
# in the
# American Polity

### THE POLITICAL SYSTEM

#### PUBLIC POLICY

Judges share with legislatures, chief executives, and heads of major administrative departments the political power and responsibility to make policy decisions that reflect certain priorities of values. Public policy reflects those values that are preferred, for the time being, by such decision-makers. Although public decisions may be enforced by coercion, the coercive aspects are not their most distinctive feature. Rather, public systems of decision-making are best distinguished from private systems by the relative heterogeneity of their constituencies and affected clienteles. The greater generality of governmental systems provides some justification for labeling as "public" decisions that usually are directly advantageous only to minorities of the relevant populace.

Governments have no monopoly of either authority or power. Authority is the consensually recognized right to make certain decisions; power is the ability to control the behavior of others through decisions. Authority and power frequently, but not necessarily, coincide; but even when they do, there is wide variation in the proportions of each that may be associated with particular decision-making roles or with specific decision-makers, either public or private. With regard to one type of question, such as the establishment of a national policy of racial integration in public schools, most courts in the United States have little authority *or* power. The federal Supreme Court has considerably more authority than power in this matter: almost a decade after its basic decision in *Brown* v. *Board of Education*, not a single Negro child attended white public schools in one of the school districts that had been a party to the *Brown* case. On the other hand, courts (like other decision-making systems) may exercise more power than authority; note the federal Supreme Court's abortive attempt in *Dred Scott* v. *Sanford* to resolve the national conflict over slavery. There are some kinds of decisions, such as that to impose capital punishment, which in this country governments have a monopoly of authority (but not of power) to make; there are many others, such as excommunication, which American governments have neither the authority nor the power to make.

Certain functions and facilities, such as taxation and armies, often are suggested as examples of characteristically governmental activities. But only one of the thousands of public governments in the United States maintains armed forces in the form of an army, navy, and air force; and if we turn to armed forces designated as police, capable of undertaking offensive action only against individuals and very small social groups, then many private "governments" (such as the Ford Motor Corporation) also maintain police forces. Public police differ from private police in the broader scope of their responsibility and authority. Most public governments collect taxes, but many private organizations also exact compulsory fees and assessments from their membership. In either case, citizens and members must either pay, suffer pains and penalties for nonpayment, or withdraw from affiliation with the community. Again, the difference is that voluntary expatriation usually involves almost total withdrawal from the normal relationships within a complex society, because it entails a shift in one's physical residence as well as in his psychological allegiance, while the impact upon one's life that results from the resignation of membership in a fraternity or professional society is much more selective and usually is perceived to be so. Many examples can be given, however, of activities that are sponsored jointly or concurrently by public and private governments; the differences among public universities and among private universities certainly are much greater than the differences between them.

When we study policy-making by judges, we focus upon a type of activity that is by no means peculiarly governmental. Adjudication takes place in a wide variety of social groups, including the family. It is in governmental systems, however, that courts are most sharply differentiated in structure from other decision-making agencies; this high specialization of judicial structure and function both justifies and necessitates the analysis of judicial behavior as one focal point in the study of public policy-making. Since judges play particularly critical roles in the formulation of United States governmental policy, the study of the judiciary is an essential and fundamental part of the study of American government.

## SYSTEMS THEORY

This study of the judiciary is based upon an analytical framework known in sociology and political science as "systems theory" or "structural-functional analysis." This basis is chosen in preference to the legal, historical, and institutional categories that in the past have dominated inquiry into the policy-making processes of American government. A major advantage of this strategy is that it diverts attention both from a preoccupation with the substance of judicial policy and from a description of the legal structure of courts in isolation from the rest of the political system. Both of these subjects are relevant to an understanding of judicial policy-making; but the use of systems theory can, it is hoped, expand the relevant field of inquiry to the processes and sources of judicial policy-making as well as to its results. Thus this mode of analysis should facilitate a more general and more comprehensive examination of American judicial institutions and behavior than would be produced by a less inclusive and less consistent conceptual framework.

Systems analysis focuses upon political behavior and upon empirically observable action. Norms and institutions are relevant only to the extent that they affect the behavior of actors within a system under analysis. A "system" consists of the structure or pattern of interaction among the actors. "Interaction" consists of the ways in which two or more people affect each other's behavior; the participants are called "actors" because we are interested not primarily in their individual idiosyncrasies but rather in the extent to which they conform to their socially defined roles. A "role" is socially defined because it consists of the combined expectations, of both what he *ought* to do and what he is *likely* to do, of an individual actor and of those people with whom he interacts; in a reciprocal manner, the complementary expectations of the individual actor help to define the roles of those other persons with whom he interacts. In sociopsychological terms, an actor's role is his orientation toward political action. The limits that define the universe of data deemed relevant for the examination of a particular system are called "boundaries"; the boundaries, in other words, enclose the variables directly related to the making of decisions within the system. The demands and support that function as stimuli to which the actors within the system react are called "inputs," and the policy-making decisions of the actors are called "outputs." Outputs from one system may be inputs for other systems; when the outputs of a system affect the systems that are its sources of demands and support, the process is known as "feedback." In sum, "political institutions or persons performing political roles are viewed in terms of what it is that they do, why they do it, and how what they do is related to and affects what others do."[1]

One major qualification is in order, however, concerning our use of the systems model. The fundamental metaphor upon which systems theory is based is biological, and it thus reflects the impact of the work of Charles Darwin upon nineteenth-century scientific thinking.[2] It is one thing to hypothesize homeostasis—the tendency for a set of interacting systems to maintain equilibrium—in a living and healthy organism. It is quite another matter to assume that patterns of social organization and behavior, which we analogize to living organisms when we adopt the Darwinian metaphor and speak of social systems, necessarily will seek to maintain a natural balance and remain in some state of equilibrium.[3] Although some form of homeostasis usually is explicitly assumed by social scientists who have adopted systems theory to guide their analyses, we make no such assumption here. We shall, however, seek to discover the kinds of influences that both shape and lead to changes in judicial systems, and the correlative kinds of influences that judicial systems bring to bear upon other systems, both public and private, with which they interact.

STRUCTURE OF THE AMERICAN POLITY

The American system of government is characterized by a great deal of pluralism and exceptional fragmentation of both authority and power. The Constitution of the United States recognizes no less than fifty-one different governmental subsystems: those of the fifty states remain largely independent of each other and, to a substantial but diminishing degree, independent of the national government as well. This large measure of constitutional independence has become increasingly sublimated in practice, however, by a vast network of policy interaction in such major fields as agriculture, highways, welfare, education, law enforcement, utilities regulation, and taxation. Each of the fifty-one governments accepts the constitutional principle of the "separation of powers": the Constitution of the United States explicitly provides for differentiated legislative, executive, and judicial organizational structures, and all of the state constitutions do likewise. Most of the states substitute what is in effect a plural executive for the unitary executive system authorized by the national Constitution. Most of the institutional patterns that link the national government with the states and the states with each other involve policy interaction among executive systems. Since the adoption in 1913 of the Seventeenth Amendment (which provided for direct election of United States senators by the people rather than by state legislatures), the communication channels linking national and state legislative systems have been minimal, as the direct communication channels among state legislative systems always have been. Judicial (like executive) interaction is relatively extensive between the national and state systems, while interaction among state judicial systems is relatively slight, thus resembling the relationships among state legislatures.

In a similar mode, we can discuss the patterns of policy-making that obtain within each state. Both the constitutional and the operating relationships between a state government and its multitudinous units of local government are even more complex that the national-state and interstate relationships summarized above. It is generally true that, except among geographically contiguous units of local government, the horizontal patterns of interaction among either local legislative, executive, or judicial systems are not extensive. The same is true of interaction between the state and local legislative systems. But interaction between the state and local executive and judicial systems is even greater than that between national and state executive systems and between national and state judicial systems.

Legislative systems—national, state, and local—operate in terms of certain common assumptions and attributes. Individuals or small groups of legislators are elected for fixed terms from particular geographic areas defined in constitutions or in statutes, by executive commissions, or by judicial decision. The national legislative system, and that of all but one of the states, includes two independent "houses" of legislators with largely duplicating functions; but local legislative systems usually include only a single structure. Inputs to the system consist of what usually are described as "interests" and "pressures" from other governmental systems (such as executive, judicial, or municipal systems) and from constituents, lobbyists, and political parties (as well as the outputs of other governmental sub-systems within the individual legislative districts). On the basis of the estimated support for legislative action from the same sources, the legislature transforms such demands into outputs such as substantive statutory norms, appropriations, taxes, committee and subcommittee investigations, resolutions, and the approval of executive and judicial appointments. Thus the outputs of the legislative system serve as inputs for executive and judicial systems, for non-governmental systems of decision-making (such as those of political parties, corporations, and labor unions), and for other legislative systems.

There is considerably more diversity in the structuring of national and state executive systems and still more in the structuring of local executive systems. The Constitution of the United States provides for a single executive system, whose most conspicuous decision-maker is a President who is now selected, in effect, by a national constituency whose votes are tabulated on the basis of fifty-one electoral districts (consisting of the states plus the District of Columbia). From an operational point of view, however, the executive system of the national government is a vast congeries of largely autonomous subsystems with many overlapping functions. Each subsystem depends in fact upon very complex processes of group decision-making, although legal authority to "make decisions" typically is vested in individual officials with such status designations as "secretary" (department head), "director" (bureau chief), or "commissioner" (board member). If we inquire concerning the source of outputs to which these various types of administrative subsystems are most responsive, we discover that the constitutional principle of "separation of powers" is a most misleading basis for understanding the primary articulations of administrative subsystems for policy-making purposes. *Departmental* subsystems do interact most closely with each other and with the executive subsystems (e.g., the Executive Office of the President) that function in the name of the President; but many bureau subsystems interact more intimately with their counterpart legislative subsystems (congressional subcommittees) than with the departmental systems of which they are—from a legal point of view—components; and, similarly, the source of policy guidance for many boards (particularly for several of the "regulatory commissions") is first legislative, second judicial, and least executive subsystems. This brief sketch of some of the most salient aspects of the public policy-making process in the United States makes it evident that judicial systems are structured and function in an environment that is extremely complex and dynamic and that is itself the product of a highly pluralistic political universe.

## BOUNDARIES OF THE JUDICIAL SYSTEM

Interaction is extensive and pervasive between the judicial system and the legislative and executive systems, as well as between the judicial system and a vast array of private systems of policy-making. The conventional conception of judicial action as consisting of a judge or small group of judges sitting at a bench and presiding over a trial in a courtroom portrays judicial behavior as essentially static, like a still-life portrait. Thereby it sacrifices a concern for what is most significant to a preoccupation with the manifest elements of a ritual which—though not unimportant—is only the most conspicuous scene of a drama with many other acts. As in Shakespearian tragedy, the soliloquies, which are easy to present, occur on-stage; the great and decisive battles are fought off-stage, and we learn of them only through an occasional clamor from the wings and through the formal announcements of heralds, replete with fanfare and flourishes. Likewise, most politically significant governmental action takes place outside the courtroom. It occurs in the establishment of courts and the selection of judges; in the interplay between judicial, legislative, and executive systems, and between national and state judicial systems; and in the effect of judicial decisions upon society and the economy, and vice versa. It is not possible to learn much about legislative policy-making by observing the chamber of the United States Senate from the gallery or to understand presidential decision-making by attending press conferences conducted by the President—or even the usual meetings of the cabinet, for that matter. Yet the predominant tendency, until recently, has been to study judges as though they performed their roles in splendid isolation not only from the rest of the political system but from each other as well.[4]

If we are to extend the relevant boundaries of the judicial system beyond the confines of the courtroom, then we must observe the interaction of constituent assemblies, chief executives, and legislatures with political parties and other private groups in actions that establish the legal bases of organization for courts. The "establishment" characteristically takes the form of reorganization of an ongoing judicial structure whose official incumbents invariably evince the most profound interest in such proceedings and claim to be the most expert witnesses available on the subject. The judges themselves, therefore, are either protagonists or major lobbyists in the consideration of any proposals to change their authority and power.

Judges acquire office either by appointment (as in the national system) or by election (as in most of the state systems). To be appointed, a judicial candidate usually must be sponsored by party officials, bar organizations, and legislators in order to receive serious consideration by a chief executive; in subsequent legislative committee hearings on confirmation, private groups frequently lobby to support or to oppose nominations. Similarly, candidates for elective judicial office must be sponsored by political parties and private groups, and frequently by chief executives and legislators as well. Where there are "nonpartisan" systems of election, similar sponsorship usually is worked out covertly, behind the facade of "citizens' committees for good government."

Once selected, judges like other public officials have a continuing need for legislative support in the form of appropriations. Legislative-executive norms in the form of statutes provide a constantly shifting redefinition of the substantive content of the public policy framework that generally delimits the field within which judicial policy-making takes place. Criminal cases involve continuing inter-action between executive and judicial systems at all levels of govern-ment; the more specialized the jurisdiction (such as that of tax courts or courts that handle juvenile delinquency), the more intricate and informal become the processes of boundary interchange between the executive and judicial systems. (An example of "boundary inter-change" would be outputs of the executive system functioning as inputs for the judicial system, or vice versa; thus the arrest of a defendant is an executive system output, and it frequently becomes also an input for the judicial system.) Similar complexity of executive-judicial interaction is found also in many civil cases, in which "the government" appears as a direct party litigant, particularly in cases involving commercial, labor, or utilities regulation. Many admin-istrative agencies appear in the dual roles of judge and prosecutor in such cases. Some agencies which exercise initial jurisdiction over such cases function in practice as a part of the judicial system as much as of the executive system. The staffing of nonjudicial positions in judicial systems typically involves direct brokerage with political parties. Civil service reform has had relatively little effect upon judi-cial patronage, even in those states that established court admin-istrator's offices during and since the 1950's.

These are but selected examples from a broad range of inter-actions between judicial and other systems. They are, however, suf-ficient to support the proposition that judicial behavior is best studied in the context of the manifold relationships between judicial and other decision-makers. Chapter Five discusses in considerably more detail the inputs and outputs of judicial systems.

## THE POLITICAL ENVIRONMENT

### CONSTITUTIONAL

The Constitution of the United States specifies that there shall be both a national government and an unstipulated number of state governments; the Constitution has been interpreted to mean that governmental authority shall be in part exercised exclusively by the national government, in part reserved to the state governments for whatever implementation may be authorized by their own individual constitutions, and in part shared by both the national and state governments. In addition, certain authority is denied to either the national or state governments, primarily by means of guarantees of personal and property rights. The procedure for the implementation of such guarantees, which are usually called "civil rights and liberties," is not specified in the Constitution, but traditional expectation and practice has been that it is the function of judges—ultimately of the justices of the Supreme Court of the United States—to determine the meaning of such guarantees by their decisions in specific cases. This was apparently the original understanding of the political generation that adopted the Constitution, and the consistent trend in recent decades has been toward greater judicial assumption of responsibility for the making of policy regarding civil rights and liberties. Certainly the Supreme Court has defined this as its primary role for the past quarter of a century.

The federal "division of powers" between the national and state governments has in times past provided the basis for another major function of the judiciary, although in this instance primarily of the national courts and of the Supreme Court in particular. Since the national Constitution provides for no other means to resolve conflicts of authority between national and state governments, this role was assumed by the Supreme Court relatively early in the nineteenth century, through its decisions in such cases as *McCulloch* v. *Maryland* and *Gibbons* v. *Ogden*. Another result of the federal structure of American government has been the establishment of separate judicial systems in each state, in addition to the national judiciary. Such a result is by no means a necessary consequence of a federal constitutional structure; for example, in Canadian federalism there is one system of courts, all of whose judges (except in local governments) are appointed by the central government. The United States Constitution explicitly recognizes only the Supreme Court; the establishment of "inferior" national courts depends upon legislation. Conceivably, Congress and the President might have decided in favor of having no inferior national courts, and the American judicial system might have consisted of one Supreme Court exercising appellate authority over the decisions of state judicial systems, which is the kind of judicial structure found today in Australian federalism. But the decision to establish inferior national courts was made in the first session of the First Congress, and the historical evidence supports the conclusion that this establishment was a part of the initial constitutional consensus.[5]

The Constitution partitions the authority of the national government among three sets of decision-makers: a Congress, a President, and "one Supreme Court, and in such inferior Courts as the Congress may from time to time ordain and establish." Although a system of decision-making has developed around each of these nuclei, there is considerably more interaction and less autonomy among the legislative, executive, and judicial systems than appears to have obtained when our general system of national government was first established. The basic constitutional assumption about national policy-making, in particular, appears to be a vast oversimplification of contemporary practice. Policy-making was a function assigned to the legislative system, while the executive and judicial systems were assigned complementary enforcement roles. Laws made "by the Congress" were to be "faithfully executed" under the supervision of the President, and disputes about the meaning and administration of the laws were to be resolved by the judiciary.

There were ambiguities—many of which were intentional—even in the constitutional model of the policy-making process, however, and this ambivalence soon resulted in a much more complicated structuring of national policy-making than the pristine linearity of the abstract principle of separation of powers. The requirement of presidential assent to statutes has eventuated, for example, in a contemporary practice under which a de facto inversion of roles already is well advanced: the President presents his program, subject to congressional veto. On the other hand, the "faithful execution" of many laws now is supervised either by congressional subcommittees or by federal judges. It also soon developed that there was a major policy-making function inherent in the judiciary's role of interpreting the Constitution in relation to the guarantees of personal and property rights and to the federal division of powers. And it has now been well over a century and a half since the Supreme Court, in *Marbury* v. *Madison* (1803), first staked out its claim of authority to lay down the constitutional policy—again, by interpreting the Constitution—relating to the boundary interchanges between the judicial, and the executive and legislative systems. In such subsequent decisions as *The Brig Aurora* (1813) and *Panama Refining Co.* v. *Ryan* (1935), the Supreme Court claimed further authority to define the boundary interchanges between the executive and legislative systems—an issue of constitutional policy in which the judiciary was not directly involved. Judicial review of executive and legislative decision-making, in terms of their consonance with constitutional norms (as interpreted by the courts), by no means exhausts the scope of judicial policy-making, however. Of increasing importance during the present century has been the policy-making role of the national judiciary in the interpretation of national statutes, including not only such well-known examples as the antitrust and labor-management relations acts, but also a vast array of many others, such as the internal revenue and criminal codes.[6]

POLITICAL

The American two-party political system has exerted a major influence upon the judicial system since the days of the Federalists. The use of judicial posts as a source of political patronage began with the appointments by George Washington in the initial staffing of the Supreme Court and of the lower courts under the Judiciary Act of 1789. Particularly during the administration of John Adams, Federalist judges were notorious for the conversion of their court-rooms to forums for political harangues, as in their many charges to juries under the Sedition Act of 1798. Because of such partisan activities, one justice of the United States Supreme Court, Samuel Chase, was impeached when the Republicans gained control of the House of Representatives, although he was acquitted in the Senate, where the Federalists retained sufficient strength to block his removal.

The most celebrated case in American constitutional law, *Marbury* v. *Madison,* grew out of Federalist attempts to pack the national judiciary through John Adams' appointment of "midnight judges"— so called because their commissions of appointment were rushed through in the waning hours of the outgoing administration. The justices of the Supreme Court, who were solidly Federalist, unani-mously declared unconstitutional the Republican attempt to inter-fere with the Federalist appointments.

The size of the Supreme Court was manipulated no less than seven times in less than seven decades (1801–1869); invariably, the purpose of these manipulations was to retain or to gain majority control over the Court. Throughout our political history the parties have waged a continuing battle over the national judiciary, as exem-plified by the most recent expansion in the number of federal district judges in 1961, after eight years of Republican staffing under Eisenhower. There are two major reasons for the strong and per-sistent desire of parties to influence the judicial system: (1) the national judiciary has always been an important source of patron-age, and this consideration has become increasingly important as the proportion of patronage positions in the executive system has dimin-ished due to the expansion of the classified civil service; and (2) the federal courts have always (and correctly) been perceived by party leaders as a major instrument for control over the substantive content of public policy.

The structure of the American party system is directly related to the articulation of the political and judicial systems. The structure of each party on a national basis is both incomplete and highly decentralized. National political leadership is dispersed among the executive, legislative, and political party systems. For state and local governments, lack of integration generally is even greater, although some of the elected judges of the judicial systems are included among the party leaders. Indeed, in many units of local government (par-ticularly in rural counties and townships) the judges hold the most important public offices available; they *are* the political leaders of their communities.

Because of this decentralization of the party system, men selected for federal judgeships vary widely in their value orientations. Candidates for federal district judgeships must receive state and local party clearance, and the rule of "senatorial courtesy" in the confirmation process means that any senator of the same party as the President can veto any nomination to a district judgeship within his state. For appointments to the Supreme Court, sectional considerations are not as important as they were during the nineteenth century, but neither are they completely ignored. The crossing of party lines in appointments to the Supreme Court remains exceptional and usually has reflected a presidential judgment that ideological congruity between the President and his appointee was a more important consideration than party affiliation. Taft's appointments of Edward White and Joseph Lamar, Wilson's of Louis Brandeis, and Truman's of Harold Burton have been the norm, while an appointment like that of the liberal Benjamin Cardozo by the conservative Hoover is unique. It has been suggested that the recent trend toward promoting lower federal court judges to the Supreme Court betokens not so much a desire to create a career federal judiciary as it does an attempt to identify safe partisans whose ideological positions have been tried and proven in the minor leagues. Many federal judges have maintained a high level of personal interaction with the party system, as exemplified by Chief Justice William Howard Taft's unabated efforts to influence appointments not only to the Supreme Court but to the federal district and circuit courts throughout the country as well.[8]

SOCIOECONOMIC

The need for courts is a direct function of the concentration of people and wealth. In primitive societies, such as that of the nomadic Cheyenne Indians who followed the buffalo herds across the great plains a century ago, the need for organized courts was minimal. Disputes involved primarily obligations arising out of war, hunting, and sexual relationships; these were generally settled by mediation, arbitration, and vendetta without recourse to specialized judicial institutions.[9] But the Barotse of Northern Rhodesia, who practice subsistence farming in the flood plain of the Zambezi River, have a well-developed judicial system and process. The most common types of disputes requiring judicial disposition among the Barotse are those relating to the obligations to each other of members of the most basic primary group, the family, or to obligations arising out of sexual relationships between members of different families.[10] Questions of property rights, however, arise more frequently among the relatively civilized Barotse farmers than they did among the Cheyenne huntsmen. Patently, the complexity of legal relationships involving property rights is vastly greater for Manhattan Island today than for Hannibal, Missouri, in antebellum days; although the difference is not *simply* a matter of either population size or density, the correlation between the complexity of judicial institutions and the concentration of persons and wealth undoubtedly is positive and high. The nineteenth-century pattern of judicial organization was suited to the needs of a rural, agricultural society and economy. The county courthouse with its acolyte corps of lay justices of the peace could and did resolve most disputes of most people, and a single appellate court completed the judicial system in most states. Throughout the century following *Marbury v. Madison,* the United States Supreme Court infrequently decided cases involving claims of personal rights (such as that of Dred Scott). The typical antebellum litigant was a ship, a bridge, a land or canal company, a bank, or, after the Civil War, a railroad, a coal or oil or mining company, or a trust. The subsequent shift to the kinds of questions and litigants now found in the Supreme Court and changes in the structure of judicial systems have been in substantial measure responses to the great changes that have taken place in the American society and economy during the twentieth century.

The major factors to which we can attribute the extent of these changes are industrialization and urbanization. A related factor that has affected judicial organization has been population dispersion. The geographic center of the population of the United States has moved consistently westward every decade since 1790; in the year in which the Supreme Court of the United States was first convened —but made no decisions because no cases were presented—the center of the national population was in Chesapeake Bay and thus quite literally not only along the coast of but *in* the Atlantic Ocean. In 1960, the center was in south-central Illinois, only fifty miles east of the Mississippi River, which it seemed certain to cross before the close of the century.

The trend toward urbanization was no simple linear progression from the farm to the central cities of metropolitan areas, however. Among the conspicuous developments of the post-World War II period was the evacuation of the metropolitan cores, with both residents and retail trade and supporting commercial facilities moving into suburbia and shopping center communities. As was soon demonstrated by the rash of apportionment studies that followed in the wake of the 1960 Census and the decision of the Supreme Court in *Baker v. Carr,* it was the Republican residents of the suburbs, rather than the Democratic dwellers in the core cities, who were most discriminated against in legislative representation; these same persons were also the ones who were least adequately served by the existing structure of judicial services. The lag between judicial reorganization and changing needs due to shifts in population and industry is even greater than the much more publicized lag in legislative reapportionment. Another demographic factor of significant implications relates to the rise of the megalopolis. The metropolis is distinguished by a surrounding hinterland of rural territory, but already emergent in the United States are giant urban complexes which extend for hundreds of miles, as from Arlington to beyond Boston, from Milwaukee to Rochester, or from San Diego to San Francisco.

The adequacy of the fifty relatively static, independent state judicial systems to meet the needs of dynamic population growth and shifts increasingly has been challenged by the concentration of the national population into these interstate urban complexes. One immediate consequence is that the workload of the federal courts is increased, which in turn increases both the pressures upon and the difficulty of access to the Supreme Court. The Court now dockets over two thousand cases in each term; it can decide on the merits of only about a tenth of these cases, given its present basis of organization and operational procedures. The seventy-three new federal judgeships established in May 1962 expanded the national judiciary by about one fourth. Such a rapid expansion was certain to result in changes in the national judicial system, and a few of these already are apparent. All but a dozen of the 119 new federal judges appointed by President Kennedy during his first year in office were Democrats. Because the new judges were added to district courts and courts of appeals in the metropolitan areas of rapid population growth, litigants in federal trials henceforth will be more likely to have their cases heard by a Democratic judge—and the trial is the stage of litigation at which most questions in a case are conclusively foreclosed, as we shall discuss in Chapter Four. Moreover, appellants from the decisions of trial courts are now much more likely to draw a court of appeals panel with a Democratic majority, and so are the government agencies which are required to defend their own decisions before such panels.

A major shift in the balance of partisan representation in the federal judiciary results in important qualitative differences in the kinds of socioeconomic values supported by the national judicial system. In Chapter Six we shall discuss in greater detail the kinds of output differentials that have occurred at various times in the history of the Supreme Court, so a few examples will suffice here. The transition to an industrial economy took place during the closing decades of the nineteenth century, and with the lag of about a generation between changes in the social and economic systems and the corresponding accommodations in the legal system, the Supreme Court remade the Constitution in the image of Social Darwinism and in support of the interests of big business.[11] This remained the official policy of the Court until the advent of the Great Depression and the New Deal, which resulted—after a very much shorter lag, as a consequence of F.D.R.'s attack upon the Court—in a dramatic reversal of the values supported by a majority of the justices and in the received meaning of the Constitution. To take a contemporary example, the decision in *Baker* v. *Carr* followed closely on the heels of the 1960 Census, and consequent attention focused upon the implications for political representation in American legislatures of the new patterns of urbanization. There was then sufficient congruity between the values upheld by a majority of the justices and the apparent interests of a preponderant majority of the American people to impel the Court to make a policy decision that it had refused to make as recently as 1946, when the proportion of urban residents was only about 58 per cent instead of 70 per cent.

PROFESSIONAL

The Constitution of the United States does not require that federal judges shall be lawyers, although the more recently adopted constitutions of many states do include such a "closed shop" provision, adopted at the behest of the organized bar. The politics of judicial selection long have made it necessary, however, for a candidate for a federal judgeship to have had legal training, although no previous experience either as a judge or as a practicing lawyer is required. All of the ninety-four men who have been justices of the Supreme Court had legal training, although the kind and quality of such training have changed over time. Almost all of the earlier justices learned their law under the apprenticeship system; the late Robert Jackson, who died in 1954, probably will prove to have been the last person appointed without a law degree, and the trend increasingly has been for justices to be graduates of the prestige law schools, such as Harvard, Yale, Chicago, Michigan, and Northwestern.

Since 1945 the American Bar Association's Standing Committee on the Federal Judiciary has participated actively in evaluating nominees to federal judgeships. This committee rates nominees in terms of their "legal qualifications"—that is, their status in the legal guild. The committee's reports are considered by the Deputy Attorney General who chairs the Department of Justice committee on judicial selection and who also receives the reports of field investigations, conducted by the Federal Bureau of Investigation, of the nominees' loyalty, sobriety, and sexual orthodoxy. On a four-point scale ranging from 4 (not qualified) to 1 (exceptionally well qualified), 15 per cent of a recent group of one hundred newly appointed federal district and circuit court judges received scores of 1 from the ABA; 50 per cent scored 2; 28 per cent scored 3; and 7 per cent received the lowest score. The average score for all one hundred judges was 2.27, which means that the ABA evaluated their average competence as between "qualified" and "well qualified." Translated into the familiar symbols of academic evaluation, this was a *B–* group—from the point of view of the ABA. Clearly, other considerations than professional status were instrumental in the selection of these men; but clearly also, the institutionalization of the advice of the organized bar makes it improbable that persons who are *persona non grata* to the legal guild will receive appointments to the federal judiciary.

The interest of the bar in the selection of one of the key groups of decision-makers with whom lawyers must interact is both substantial and understandable. Obviously, it is important for the bar to screen the selection of judges to assure that judges will meet at least minimal standards of technical expertise and personal morality; and it is quite rational that the bar should seek to exclude the incompetents, drunks, and crooks (from among its own membership) from positions of authority and power in the judicial system. There are, however, other and perhaps less obvious reasons that reinforce the bar's interest in judicial selection.

There is always explicit consideration, in hearings of subcommittees of the Senate Judiciary Committee on the confirmation of presidential nominations to federal judgeships, of the "judicial temperament" of the nominees. But it is difficult to give concrete meaning to this vague concept; it becomes apparent that from the viewpoint of an individual who is a member of or a witness before the subcommittee passing upon the qualifications of a nominee, persons with whom he is in fundamental ideological agreement are blessed with "judicial temperament," and those with whom he disagrees lack it. In particular, spokesmen for the bar—whether in the role of witness, of co-opted member of the subcommittee, or of built-in (through committee membership as senators) institutional advocate—are in a position to manipulate the notion of "temperament" so as to attempt to minimize the selection of liberals for the federal bench.

Since its organization in 1878, the American Bar Association, in the speeches of its leaders and in the opinions expressed in its *Journal*, consistently has supported the most conservative ideas of the times. During the 1880's and 1890's, doctrinaire laissez-faire ideology was the "party line" of the ABA, as exemplified both by direct representation by ABA leaders before the United States Supreme Court and by the principal speeches at the national meetings of the Association.[12] In particular, the ABA was a bulwark of support for the United States Supreme Court until 1937; but since that

time, while the Court has played a much more liberal role, the ABA
has become its persistent and virulent critic, leading to the resignation in 1959 by Chief Justice Earl Warren of his membership in the
organization, after twenty years of affiliation.

A necessary consequence of the conservatism of the ABA has
been the tendency of its Standing Committee on the Federal Judiciary to equate "judicial temperament" with ideological conservatism
as an attribute of candidates whom it deems qualified to become
federal judges.[13]

### TRADITIONAL

The traditions of his court constitute one of the most pervasive
aspects of the environment in which a judge makes policy. These
traditions are unwritten social norms that have an important influence upon how a judge makes his decisions, for they control many
of the specific applications of the procedures that are employed in
judicial policy-making. They also tend to vary considerably from
court to court; for this reason, we shall focus our discussion upon the
court whose traditions are probably of longest standing and best
understood.

Even such a seemingly basic aspect of judicial behavior as the
public reporting of voting disagreement among Supreme Court justices depends upon custom that has varied throughout the history
of the Court. Initially, the Court followed the English practice, and
each justice delivered his own individual opinion in each decision.
Then, under John Marshall's influence, the general practice was to
"mass the Court" in support of unanimous opinions, read by the
Chief Justice in important cases, although William Johnson (Jefferson's first appointee) often insisted upon making an "independent
expression" of his own views. Since the days of Roger B. Taney,
the custom has been for justices to join in the opinion (usually,
for the majority) that announces the decision of the Court; to write
or to join in independent concurring opinions if they vote with the
majority but wish to articulate a different or an additional rationale;
or to write or to join in dissenting opinions if they vote against the
majority decision of the Court. The writing of the opinion that
announces the decision of the Court is assigned by the Chief Justice,
if he votes with the majority; otherwise, the senior associate justice
voting with the majority makes the assignment. Each justice decides
for himself whether he will join in the opinion of the Court or in a
concurring or dissenting opinion written by another justice, or whether
he will write an independent opinion of his own—in which other
justices might then decide to join. Many other appellate courts follow
quite different practices. In the Michigan Supreme Court, for instance, cases are assigned among the justices by rotation, but any

other justice may write an independent opinion; then, at the conference at which a vote is taken, all opinions that have been prepared are circulated for signature, and the opinion that attracts the largest number of signers becomes the opinion of the Court, assuming that a majority are agreed upon the disposition of the case.

In the United States Supreme Court, the voting division in each decision can be determined only inferentially. That is, reports of the Court's decisions do not explicitly state the vote of each justice; instead, the reports show who wrote the opinion of the Court, who concurred and who dissented, and who failed to participate in the decision. Given the known membership of the Court at any particular time, the justices who joined in the opinion of the Court can be inferred. The decisions of almost all other American appellate courts explicitly specify the votes of individual judges.

Six is now the statutory quorum for decision-making by the United States Supreme Court, and decisions are determined by the vote of a majority of the participating justices. Thus the size of majority voting groups can vary from four to nine, depending upon the number of participants, while the size of dissenting voting groups never can exceed four justices. Ties of three-to-three and four-to-four can occur, if the number of nonparticipants is odd, in which event the Court announces no opinion and the decision of the court that last handled the case is affirmed automatically.

Each Supreme Court justice decides for himself whether to disqualify himself from participating in any decision. The presumption is that all justices will participate in all decisions; but illness may prevent a justice from hearing the oral argument or from attending the conference at which a vote is taken, and a justice customarily disqualifies himself from participating in the decision under either of these circumstances. Similarly, a recently appointed justice may disqualify himself from the substantive decisions in cases on which arguments and conferences were held before he joined the Court. Throughout most of the last eleven (and busiest) weeks of the 1961 term, for instance, there were only seven participating justices, because of Justice Frankfurter's illness and because Justice White's recent appointment prevented him from participating in more than a dozen of the forty-four decisions on the merits during this period. Justices also may disqualify themselves on grounds of constructive bias; that is, a justice who has had any personal relationship to a case during its previous litigation usually will refuse to participate in its decision by the Supreme Court. In recent decades, for example, many justices who earlier had served as Attorney (or Solicitor) General have disqualified themselves in cases to which the national government was a party and for which they had had official responsibility during earlier stages of litigation. Yet another example is Justice

Stewart's decision to disqualify himself in *Ohio ex rel. Eaton* v. *Price,* in the decision of which the remaining eight justices divided equally; the reason for Stewart's nonparticipation was that his father had participated in an earlier decision on the case as Chief Justice of the Ohio Supreme Court. But justices of the federal Supreme Court have not always adhered to such rigorous criteria of putative bias; it was common in the early days of the Court for justices to participate in the decision of cases in which they had direct and sometimes large financial interests. In what is usually considered to be the leading case in American constitutional law, *Marbury* v. *Madison,* the Secretary of State whose negligence initially resulted in Marbury's failure to receive his commission as a justice of the peace was none other than John Marshall himself, the Chief Justice who wrote the unanimous decision of the Supreme Court in the case. Indeed, Marshall had held both posts simultaneously during the closing weeks of the Adams administration.

Many courts have given up the ancient practice of reading in full all opinions written in cases decided on the merits. The Supreme Court continues to allocate several days each month to the ceremony of opinion-reading, although some justices have not agreed with the custom; Justice Frankfurter, for instance, preferred to present oral summaries of his often lengthy opinions. This procedure has led to some public controversy among the justices, while they have been sitting at the bench in open court. Chief Justice Warren once accused Frankfurter of including in his oral presentation arguments that had not appeared in his written opinion. Warren's concern was that other justices could have no opportunity to consider and—if they so chose— to rebut arguments that were withheld from the written opinions (which are circulated among all of the justices prior to the announcement of decisions); a justice who departed from the custom thus would have an unfair advantage.

In many other ways tradition has a very important bearing on the decision-making process of the Court. The secrecy of the conference forces the justices to engage in petty clerical activities that few decision-making groups of similar responsibility and authority— and there are few—continue to tolerate. The most recently appointed justice, for instance, serves as the doorkeeper for the conference, and any information that goes into or out of the conference room while the court is in session there requires his personal attention; thus Oliver Wendell Holmes, as a freshman justice at the age of sixty-one, served for a year as the messenger boy for the group. The decisions themselves are generally a well-kept secret, although a few celebrated "leaks" occurred during the nineteenth century.

The judges of the federal and of most of the state supreme courts wear robes while on the bench, but in several states they appear in business garb. There has been some speculation that the wearing of judicial robes encourages the laity to believe that judges are able to suppress their personal attitudes, thus permitting judges to indulge their biases with less fear of being detected.[14] There is, however, little scientific evidence yet available concerning psychological and other effects that the wearing of robes may have upon judicial decisions.[15]

No written rule defines the extent to which the justices of the United States Supreme Court give reasons in support of their decisions. It is customary for the Court to report an assigned opinion to justify the decisions in most of the cases for which the justices have heard oral argument, although in several such cases each term only brief and anonymous (per curiam) opinions are reported. Either stereotyped reasons that communicate little or nothing (viz., "want of jurisdiction" or "lack of a substantial federal question") or (most of the time) no reasons at all are reported for the Court's decisions to refuse to decide cases on the merits. Many other appellate courts follow the same practice. The new constitution adopted by Michigan in 1963 requires, however, that "Decisions of the supreme court, including all [jurisdictional] decisions on prerogative writs, shall be in writing and shall contain a concise statement of the facts and reasons for each decision and reasons for each denial of leave to appeal." The new constitution also requires that "When a judge dissents in whole or in part he shall give in writing the reasons for his dissent." Such provisions betoken no great popular unrest, of course, but rather represent attempts by lawyers to acquire a better understanding of the motives that underlie the voting behavior of Michigan Supreme Court justices, so that the lawyers will be in a better position to predict probable decisions of the court in cases that the attorneys might seek to bring to the court for review.

The postulated norm of *stare decisis* (i.e., that a court shall follow its own previous decisions, or those of higher courts in the same system, on the same policy issue) presumably is a fundamental aspect of the judicial decision-making process. But for justices of the United States Supreme Court, *stare decisis* does not have even the status of the customary norms discussed thus far.[16] The Court's practice is that each justice decides for himself the extent to which he believes there should be consistency between the Court's past and present policy-making. As we shall discuss in Chapter Six, individual decisions are much less apt to be based upon an undefined and abstract obligation to follow precedents than they are likely to be a function of the considerations relevant to judicial activism and restraint.[17] But the manipulation of precedents in support of decisions is an indispensable judicial skill, since it is the basic tool for the process of rationalization in opinion-writing.

### CHAPTER TWO

# Judicial Systems

## GENERAL STRUCTURE

In the formal or constitutional view, there are fifty-one different judicial systems within the American polity: a separate system for each of the states, and a national system. This view is more formal than real because of the high positive correlation, discussed in Chapter One, between the population of a governmental unit and the complexity of its judicial system. The judicial systems of many of the less populous states are smaller and show less differentiation of both structure and function than do the judiciaries of the more than twenty metropolises with populations of over half a million persons. Indeed, in 1960 the dozen largest cities plus the District of Columbia all had populations in excess of seven hundred thousand, while there were almost as many whole states—eleven—with smaller populations. Many of these municipal judicial systems are almost as autonomous within the state judicial systems as the latter are within the federal system. From a functional point of view, it would be more correct to say that there are over a hundred different major judicial systems in the United States, including those of all of the states, those of the fifty largest cities, and that of the national government.

At this point we must take note of the terminological ambiguity inherent in the term "federal judicial system." Formerly, the central government was described as the "federal" government; hence, we find in the late eighteenth century a political party favoring a stronger central government and soon designated as the Federalist party. In the twentieth century, however, political scientists have tended to appropriate the word "federal" as a label for a concept to describe the conjoint relationships between central and regional units of government in political systems that are characterized by a substantial degree of decentralization. Under this usage, for example, it would be correct to speak of the "American federal system" of public roads or of agricultural education; but it would be possible to speak only to a very limited extent of the "federal system" of either legal or medical education, and it would be equally inappropriate to speak of the "federal" navy. It is traditional to refer to the judiciary of the central government as the "federal system of courts." But these are not federal courts in the analytical sense any more than the F.B.I. is a part of the state police system in Mississippi—or vice versa. We could, of course, follow modern statutory language and refer to the "United States courts," but this seems awkward. Instead, we use the word "national," reserving the term "federal" for use as an analytical concept to refer to conjoint national-state (or state-municipal) relationships. Such federal relationships occur when there is overlap between the national-state, state-state, or state-municipal judicial systems.[1] We shall, however, defer to common usage whereby the national judiciary are called "federal judges," because to do otherwise doubtless would compound the confusion.

## STATE JUDICIAL SYSTEMS

The judicial systems of the American states are poorly designed to cope with the politico-legal problems that arise in metropolitan areas, to say nothing of megalopolitan complexes, and this is why other supplementary judicial systems have had to be established for such urban groupings. The state systems were designed to meet the needs of a predominantly rural populace, thinly spread over an extensive geographic area. The basic pattern—even in states admitted during the twentieth century—reflects the colonial experience of the Atlantic seaboard states, and their judicial organization in turn was modeled after that of preindustrial England. We shall describe first this pattern and then the changes that have taken place in it, particularly during the past quarter century.

In the classic pattern, the structure of state judicial systems is hierarchical and pyramidal. There are three strata: a broad base of nonsalaried, locally chosen, lay magistrates, of whom there might be literally scores in each county (in those states in which counties are subdivided into towns or townships); next, a set of county courts, each comprised of one locally selected judge—who usually has some legal training; and finally, a single state supreme court, convened at the state capitol, consisting of five judges who are qualified as attorneys and selected from among those with experience as county judges. Such a structure is pyramidal because it has a very broad base and a very small apex; it is hierarchical because, at least in legal *theory*, policy-making power is concentrated in the supreme court and is virtually nonexistent at the base. (In the typical state, there are less than a hundred judges at the top two levels, and not all of them are professionally qualified lawyers; in fact, this relatively small group of lawyer-politicians, dispersed throughout the state, is an elite that exercises great influence upon policy-making in local governments, upon many administrative agencies of the state government, and to a lesser extent upon the state legislature and the governor as well. Let us not forget the American tradition of "courthouse politics.") The basic function of the much larger mass of unskilled magistrates (frequently called "justices of the peace") is to settle neighborhood disputes, including the punishment of offenses defined as criminal but not perceived to be heinous.

From a functional point of view, the reason for the pyramidal structure is apparent. County courts are needed only to resolve the relatively small proportion of disputes that cannot be settled by the magistrates; a supreme court is needed only to settle the few cases—typically, an average of only about one or two per county per year—that the county courts either are unable to resolve to the satisfaction of both parties or have resolved in various and mutually inconsistent ways. Thus the state supreme court establishes uniformity in policy-making for the state judicial system, subject to certain exceptions that we shall note below. But this policy-making system, in the classic pattern, consists only of the supreme court and the county court judges; the magistrates, although part of the state judicial system for decision-making purposes, constitute (in theory) a mass of autonomous foci for *local* policy-making, and they supposedly contribute little to the policy-making function for the state system.

These disparate functions, which are performed at the three levels of the system, are reflected in the kinds of records kept by the respective types of courts. Records of judicial decision-making are important, for without them there is rarely any effective way in which one can challenge successfully, through an appeal to a higher court, the decision of a lower court. No transcript is made of the proceedings that take place in magisterial courts, and hence lawyers say that these are not "courts of record." Consequently, an appeal from the decision of a justice court usually takes the form of a "trial *de novo*," which means that a completely new trial is held before the county court, almost as though the justice court had made no earlier decision in the case. Although the county court is called a court of record, what this usually means is that a single transcript of trial proceedings is kept in the files of the clerk of the county court. One who seeks to appeal a decision must pay to have a copy of the transcript made for examination by the supreme court, and there is no systematic procedure for reporting to the public the decisions of the county judges, most of whose opinions, in any event, are oral. The supreme court *is* a court of record, and those of its decisions for which its judges write opinions usually are published, together with the associated opinions.

In many respects, the model we have described would not have fit precisely the actual practice in most of the present fifty states at any time during their history. For example, this model assumes that judges follow the procedures for decision-making known as "common law," but in many of the older states there was a competing and parallel system of decision-making procedures known as "equity jurisprudence." In some of these states, there was a structurally differentiated equity court (or system of courts) called the "chancery," after the English practice. In others, the English pattern was modified by the establishment of only the single state judicial system of our model but required the county and supreme court justices to employ alternative sets of decision-making procedures (legal and equitable). Another example is the separate structures and alternative systems that were established in some states for decision-making in what are termed "civil cases," on the one hand, and "criminal cases," on the other; this distinction persists much more strongly today in the municipal court systems than in state judicial systems. A third example is the separate structure of courts usually labeled "probate" or "surrogate," which frequently were differentiated from the state court system or systems of more "general jurisdiction" (as they usually were called) in order to constitute a specialized system with exclusive decision-making authority to settle wills and estates and to arrange for the custody of certain persons (such as orphan minors) who in earlier American societies were placed under the guardianship of judges. On the other hand, there are still more than half a dozen state judicial systems that *do* fit the model precisely, if we disregard insignificant differences in nomenclature, such as that of calling magistrates "justices of the peace" in rural areas and "police judges" in cities. Indeed, Wyoming, a rural state that ranks forty-eighth in population, has only three classes of courts in its state judicial system: a supreme court of four judges, district courts of general jurisdiction and justice (of the peace) courts.

The clear trend in the evolution of state judicial systems throughout the nineteenth century and during the first half of the twentieth century was in the direction of greater complexity in the differentiation of both structure and function. Recent efforts toward the reform of judicial administration, to employ the customary descriptive phrase, have been directed in part toward designing more simple and more generalized—and therefore, it is presumed, more flexible—judicial structures. Another major objective of reform programs has been to establish specialized offices of "court administrators" to function as agencies of the state supreme court in order to centralize control over budgeting, accounting, personnel, both the quality and the quantity of production in terms of case disposition, and related matters throughout the entire state judicial system. Another objective has been to improve the quality of both judicial decision-makers and their supporting staffs. To improve the competence of judges, attempts have been made to limit access to the office to lawyers, to increase salaries and the length of terms of office, and to substitute appointment for election as the method of selection. To improve the quality of subordinate personnel, some slight advances have been made in the substitution of civil service status for selection through partisan political patronage, the method that long has characterized the selection of judicial personnel at all levels in almost all American judicial systems—national, state, and metropolitan. Reformers also have sought to establish intermediate appellate courts, which would occupy a level in our pyramidal model between the county courts and the supreme court. They have tried to increase the number of judges at all levels except that of the rural magistrates, where they have moved in the opposite direction, seeking generally to abolish the office of justice of the peace.[2]

By the early 1960's, each of the fifty state judicial systems had centralized policy-making authority for the system in a single supreme court, although other labels of historic import (such as "Court of Appeals" in New York, or "Supreme Court of Errors" in Connecticut) are retained in half a dozen states. All fifty systems include courts of general jurisdiction, both original and appellate, and the territory of each state is partitioned into county or multicounty districts. In about one third of the states, such subsystems of the state structure are designated as "circuit" courts, reflecting the practice—which still persists in underpopulated rural areas of many states—of having the judge move around at terms to preside in locations convenient to suitors; in another third of the states, these general subsystems are called "superior" courts; and in the remaining third (approximately) of the states, they are labeled "district" courts. In New York, they bear the quite misleading designation "The Supreme Court of the State of New York." Established in 1846 as the fruit of the reform movement of an earlier day (the Jacksonian democracy), New York's "Supreme Court" is divided, in part for the purpose of electing over two hundred judges, into eleven mostly multicounty districts; for the purpose of establishing intermediate appellate courts, these districts are grouped into four departments, each of which contains an "Appellate Division" court (staffed by Supreme Court justices who function in this capacity by designation of the governor) and from one to four districts.[3]

All except seven of the states retain the magisterial level of courts, although these are variously designated as "justice," "justice of the peace," "magistrate," or "police" courts. A majority of the state systems include a distinctive level of municipal courts, and most of the remaining state systems resort to *ad hoc* arrangements for a few of the larger cities. Only a minority of the state systems (twenty-one in 1962) retain the county court structure of our model, and in every one of these systems the county court is a substructure of the courts of general jurisdiction (circuit, superior, district) described above. Thus one major respect in which the original model of state judicial systems no longer fits the facts is that the general subsystems now are multicounty in scope. There are also probate court subsystems in twenty-one of the state judicial systems, but in a majority of the state systems the specialized surrogate's function has been assimilated by the broad jurisdiction of the general subsystems. Similarly, distinctive equity structures remained in only five states in 1962, and only Texas and Oklahoma still had one intermediate appellate structure for criminal appeals and a separate one for civil appeals. This tendency toward the elimination of probate, chancery, and criminal appeals courts confirms our earlier observation concerning the move toward simplifying the general structure of state judicial systems as a key feature of contemporary reform proposals. On the other hand, several state systems still retain the structural differentiation between criminal and civil courts, at the level of the general subsystem (trial) courts, and a variety of new specialized subsystems has evolved in many states. The most common of the new judicial structures are juvenile courts, in over a third of the state systems; but there are also domestic relations courts, family courts, courts of claims, courts of small claims, and traffic courts; and in addition there are unique structures such as Oregon's Tax Court, and the Court of Industrial Relations and the Workmen's Compensation Court of Nebraska.

By 1962, a majority of the state systems had a "court administrator's office," although initially most of these lacked the budgetary, personnel, and political support to function other than as agencies for the collection and distribution of information about the activities of their respective judicial systems. Even this, however, was an important step in the direction desired by reformers, since such information generally had not been available previously. By 1964, less than a third of the state judicial systems included an intermediate structure of appellate courts; of these fifteen, that of New York had been established seventy years earlier, while Michigan's was brand new. Intermediate appellate subsystems vary considerably in size, ranging from three judges (in Alabama) to thirty-three (in Texas), but they are included in the state judicial systems of ten of the eleven most populous states, with Massachusetts constituting the exception.

In the model system, the higher status of supreme court judges is signified in various ways: the office itself is a relatively scarce commodity, since there are fewer positions on the supreme court than in the lower courts; supreme court judges are paid higher salaries, serve for longer terms, and frequently are selected by a different method than are judges of the "lower" courts. Such distinctions increasingly are tending to disappear for judges of courts above the magisterial level. Therefore, it is possible now to generalize with substantial accuracy about state judicial systems by focusing upon the status similarities and differences among judges of the state supreme courts.

The most common method of selection, employed in two thirds of the states, is popular election, with about half of them using partisan and the other half nonpartisan ballots. The remaining states can be partitioned into seven in which judges are chosen by gubernatorial appointment, five in which judges are elected by the legislature, and four which have adopted the widely touted but rarely followed "Missouri Plan,"[4] according to which the effective selection of judges is made by what amounts to guild control through organizations run by lawyers. However, in a majority of the states in which judges nominally are selected by popular election, the effective power of choice is exercised by the governor through appointments to fill interim vacancies; gubernatorial domination of the selection process by this means is highest in states where nonpartisan elections are used, because incumbency provides a decisive edge in elections that are noncompetitive in fact.[5]

About half of the state supreme courts have seven judges; in another third of the states, there are five judges on the highest court; the remainder range in size from three to nine, although only three states have an even number of judges (four or six), because of the possibility that such a group might divide equally and be unable to agree upon policy outcomes. (Such care to avoid deadlocks reflects a well-known aphorism of the common law: it is more important that a case should be settled than that it should be settled correctly.) The tenure of state supreme court judges ranges from a minimum of two years in Vermont to life in neighboring Massachusetts and Rhode Island and also (in effect) in New Jersey; in a majority of states, however, the term is either six or eight years.

Salaries range from a minimum—again, in Vermont—of $10,500; but only a little over a hundred miles from Montpelier, in Albany, the judges of the New York Court of Appeals receive salaries of $36,500. Appellate judges in the New York City subsystem of the state system are compensated at about the same level—a few even get up to $2500 more, while until the adoption of the 1964 federal salary act (78 *Stat.* 434) the justices of the United States Supreme Court received from $1000 to $1500 *less*. There was also recently a proposal before the Judicial Conference of the United States to permit states to supplement the salaries of federal judges in order to equalize them with those of state appellate judges whose courts are located in the same part of the state. It is a very common practice in many states (including New York) for counties and municipalities so to supplement the salaries of judges paid by the state. For federal judges assigned to courts in the New York City metropolitan area, such supplements would range from $4500 to $6000. The Judicial Conference, however, opposed the proposal as representing "an undesirable policy" raising "serious constitutional questions."[6]

METROPOLITAN JUDICIAL SYSTEMS

Although part of a formally independent—the national—system of courts, the federal judges assigned to the New York metropolitan area are functionally a part of the metropolitan judicial system. There are forty-one federal judges in this area, thirty-three of them in Manhattan. Twenty-four are members of the United States District Court for the Southern District of New York, eight are members of the court for the Eastern District, and the other nine are members of the United States Court of Appeals for the Second Circuit. Moreover, the metropolitan area extends demographically, socially, and economically—in fact, in just about every significant way except politically and legally—over a multistate area that includes much of New Jersey and Connecticut, as well as many New York counties outside of New York City.

A comprehensive functional description and analysis of the judicial system of the metropolitan area would have to include all of these structures. To the best of our knowledge, no such inventory has been made.[7] Neither does there appear to be any systematic reporting of data, on a comparative basis, for metropolitan judicial systems, such as there has been since 1951 for state judicial systems.[8] We can, however, illustrate our earlier statement that metropolitan systems are more important and complex than state systems by summarizing a few of the most rudimentary structural characteristics of the *municipal* judicial system in New York City (bearing in mind that the municipal system is but a part, albeit a major one, of the total metropolitan system). Included in this system are all of the courts (save the two national courts) located in the five county-boroughs of New York City, regardless of whether they are labeled "state," "county," or "city" courts. Most of the people, most of the judges, and most of the government in New York State are located within New York City, and the significant distinction, from a functional point of view, is between what is in the city and what is upstate. For example, what for years had been called the "City of New York Domestic Relations Court" recently was redesignated, by amendment of the New York State Constitution, as the "New York State Family Court Within the City of New York," but the personnel and basic functions of this court remained the same.

The courts in New York City for some time have comprised the second largest, the second most expensive, and structurally one of the most complicated judicial systems ever known. About 350 judges form the cadre of this system, which is almost the same size as the entire federal judiciary, excluding only the five federal judges of territorial courts and about three dozen other judges assigned to specialized national courts. A decade ago the cost of the city system ran a close second to that of the national system, but, as Table I shows, fiscal support for the national judiciary has grown more rapidly in recent years. The municipal system, however, is notorious for its failure to grow rapidly enough to accommodate the increasing demands made upon it. The chronic time lag between the filing and deciding of cases in these courts, particularly in civil cases requiring juries, was greater than anywhere else in the country. For example, in 1953 there was an *average* delay of four and a half years before a negligence case (with jury) could be reached by the Kings County (Brooklyn) City Court; in the following year, the average delay for the same type of case in the equivalent court in each of the five counties ranged from over two to over four years.[9] The size and complexity of metropolitan judicial systems raise questions not only of administrative efficiency but even of their ability to perform their basic functions. Particularly for poorer litigants, "justice delayed is justice denied."

Before the latest reorganization in 1962, the municipal judicial system had grown to include some sixty-nine structural units.[10] It will simplify generalization if we distinguish between general and special functions and if we further subdivide the general into civil and criminal adjudication. It also is necessary to distinguish among three degrees of importance: "most important," corresponding to felonies in criminal cases, and property valued at more than $6000 in civil cases; "more important," corresponding to misdemeanors in criminal cases, and property valued at more than $3000 but less than $6000 in civil cases; and "less important," corresponding to violations of ordi-

TABLE I

Budgetary Support for New York City and United States Courts, 1953–1963
(in millions of dollars)

|  | 1953 | 1963 | % change |
|---|---|---|---|
| New York City courts (including the Supreme Court and Appellate Divisions) | 21.8 | 35.3 | +62 |
| United States courts | 27.6 | 63.3 | +229 |

nances and other offenses, such as parking violations, which are proscribed but not perceived to be reprehensible—not really "criminal" acts—and property valued at less than $3000 in civil cases.

The "less important" criminal cases were tried in five City Magistrates' Courts, one for each of the boroughs—Manhattan, Bronx, Brooklyn, Queens, and Richmond. The group of fifty-odd appointed magistrates was partitioned among about a dozen functional subdivisions for each court, including Girl's Term, Home Term, Narcotics Term, Municipal Term Court, Night Court, Felony Court, Homicide Court, Traffic Court, Probation Court, Commercial Frauds Court, Women's Court, Bail Court, and Adolescent Court. The "more important" criminal cases were decided by the two dozen appointed judges of the Court of Special Sessions, which really was five courts, one for each borough. Cases were decided by three-judge panels without juries, and these courts also reviewed on appeal the decisions of the Magistrates' Courts. The "most important" criminal cases were decided by the twenty-two elective judges of the County Courts (called the "Court of General Sessions" in New York County[11]), who presided individually over petit (trial) jury actions consequent to grand jury indictments of the defendant.

The "less important" civil cases were decided by the sixty-eight judges of the twenty-eight districts of the Municipal Court. The districts were subdivisions of the five counties, and appeals from the decisions of the district judges went to the respective Appellate Term of the judicial district of the Supreme Court (to be discussed below) of which the county was a part. The "more important" civil cases were decided by the twenty-seven elective judges of the five divisions of the City Court, with appeals (as above) to the appropriate Appellate Term of the Supreme Court. In each county there was a Surrogates' Court of one or two judges to decide cases involving estates and the guardianship and adoption of children. The twenty-three appointed judges of the Domestic Relations Court were divided among children's divisions and family divisions, one each to each of the five counties. The "most important" civil cases were decided by the four judicial districts of the Supreme Court: the First (New York and Bronx Counties), Second (Kings and Richmond Counties), Ninth (Dutchess, Orange, Putnam, Rockland, and Westchester Counties), and Tenth (Queens, Nassau, and Suffolk Counties). Immediately prior to the reorganization of 1962, there were some ninety-odd elective judges assigned to these four district courts, which were in turn grouped into two departments: the First Judicial Department included only the First Judicial District, while the Second, Ninth, and Tenth Judicial Districts were grouped under the Second Judicial Department. Each department contained a seven-judge court called the "Appellate Division of the Supreme Court" and was staffed by judges of the Supreme Court. The Appellate Divisions decided appeals in both criminal cases (from the Court of Special Sessions and from the Court of General Sessions and the County Courts) and civil cases (from the Supreme Court and from the Surrogates' Court and the Domestic Relations Court).

Altogether, the municipal court subsystem included about 325 judges divided among about seventy courts (if we disregard labels and observe the political realities of physical structure). After the reorganization of 1962, there were about 340 judges divided among some thirty-five courts; thus the principal result of the "reform" of the system was to cut in half the number of structural units. But the same 100 appointed judges remained appointed, and the same 220-odd elected judges (plus a few new ones) remained elected—in almost all instances to the same terms of office as before the reshuffle. What had the change accomplished? The twenty-eight Municipal District Courts had been eliminated, and their personnel had been transferred (along with the judges and staff of the five City Courts) to what was called a Civil Court but what amounted to five Civil Courts—one for each borough, of course. The five Magistrates' Courts and the five Courts of Special Sessions had been combined into a Criminal Court, which was physically located in each of the five boroughs; combining the two courts in each borough resulted in a reduction of five courts. The Court of General Sessions and the four County Courts were abolished, and their judges— together with their new function of conducting jury trials in the "most important" criminal cases—were transferred to the appropriate judicial districts of the Supreme Court; this resulted in a reduction of five courts. On the other hand, the Tenth Judicial District of the Supreme Court was divided by transferring Queens County into a new Eleventh District, which added one court. Also, the restructuring of the former city Domestic Relations Court into the New York

State Family Court, which now had six "terms" (in effect, the ten courts as before, two to each county, plus three new centralized courts), resulted in a net gain of three courts. So thirty-eight courts were eliminated and four were added, and the net result was a reduction of thirty-four, or about half of the pre-reorganization total of sixty-nine. There were now sixty-three appointive judges concerned exclusively with the criminal decision-making function, and all were associated with the new Criminal Court. There were about a hundred elective judges who were exclusively concerned with civil cases, and except for the half dozen surrogates these judges were assigned to the new Civil Court. The two dozen appointed judges of the restructured Family Court continued their primarily civil decision-making function. The one hundred fifty-odd remaining elective judges were divided among the five districts and two appellate divisions of the Supreme Court, with the function of deciding both trials and appeals in both civil and criminal cases.

The structure of the New York municipal judicial system had been somewhat simplified, primarily by (1) eliminating the relatively highly decentralized district courts that formerly decided the "less important" civil cases; (2) combining into one set of courts the function of deciding both the "less" and the "more important" criminal cases; and (3) adding the function of deciding the "most important" criminal cases to what for many years had been the almost exclusively civil function of the Supreme Court, so that the Supreme Court districts became courts of original and general jurisdiction, in both law and equity, for the decision of the "most important" cases, both civil and criminal. The effect of these changes upon the functioning of the system can be determined only by an analysis of its policy outputs, and it is still too early for such analysis; but the seeming superficiality of the structural changes may remind skeptical readers of the proverb *"Tout ça change, tout c'est le même chose."*

### THE NATIONAL JUDICIAL SYSTEM

When Lyndon Baines Johnson became President, there were about 440 judges in the national judicial system. They included a Chief Justice of the United States and eight associate justices of the United States Supreme Court; 78 chief judges and circuit judges of the eleven courts of appeals; and 291 chief judges and district judges of the eighty-eight district courts.[12] These federal judges constituted the principal cadre of the "regular" or "constitutional" federal judiciary, so-called because of the legal presumption that in establishing them Congress had acted under the authority of Article III (the judiciary article) of the Constitution. Another sixty-odd federal judges were members of what lawyers long have called "non-

Article III" or "legislative" courts, reflecting the legal presumption that Congress had established such specialized courts not in order to provide for the exercise of "the judicial power" discussed in Article III but rather as convenient and optional instruments for the carrying out of other functions, such as providing systems of government for the national territories, making regulations for the administration of the armed forces, collecting taxes, and settling claims against the United States. The legal theory was that since Congress does not have to use courts to implement these other functions, such courts as it does choose to establish need not be staffed by judges whose tenure and salary are the same as those of "regular" federal judges.

Three decades ago the Supreme Court announced a series of decisions that had the general effect of denigrating and obfuscating the status of the national "legislative" courts, making their judges the second-class citizens, if not the pariahs, of the federal judiciary.[13] The Court also had cast the national courts for the District of Columbia into a temporary limbo, but the District of Columbia judges soon were restored to the fold.[14]

Congress then enacted legislation during the middle 1950's which in effect overruled the Supreme Court by declaring that three of the specialized courts were really constitutional courts;[15] and in 1962, a majority of the Supreme Court agreed that whatever they may have been prior to that legislation, the Court of Claims, the Customs Court, and the Court of Customs and Patent Appeals now were constitutional courts and their judges were part of the regular federal judiciary.[16] This left only the two dozen judges of the Tax Court, the Court of Military Appeals, and the four territorial courts with the ambiguous status of being federal judges who were exercising a judicial function, but not the one that Article III defines.[17] Historically, this peculiar status was a *modus vivendi* during the transition from territorial government to statehood, but that problem is no longer with us. Since the justification has disappeared, and since there are administrative advantages in having a single status, floor for all federal judges,[18] it seems likely that John Marshall's distinction between constitutional and legislative courts,[19] having outlived its purpose, will disappear. More meaningful now is the distinction between national courts with a diversified and those with a specialized policy-making function.

*Courts with a Diversified Function.* The United States district courts are the trial courts of general jurisdiction in the national judicial system. There is at least one district court in each state, and there is one in each of the five more important of the remaining national territories. The number of courts assigned to each state reflects past partisan choices of Congress more than it does present needs. The correlation between state population and the number of district *courts* is much higher for the years immediately prior to the Civil War than it is now, but the same comment does not apply for the correlation between the number of federal *judges* and state population. New York and Texas each are divided into four judicial districts; eight states (Alabama, Florida, Georgia, Illinois, North Carolina, Oklahoma, Pennsylvania, and Tennessee) are divided into three each; sixteen states have two districts; and the remaining twenty-four states have one each. However, the ten most populous states, ranked according to 1960 populations, were assigned federal district judges as follows: New York, 35; California, 22; Pennsylvania, 21; Illinois, 14; Ohio, 10; Texas, 14; Michigan, 10; New Jersey, 8; Massachusetts, 5; Florida, 8. Evidently, the correlation between population and number of federal judges is high and positive, but it would be even better if three of the judgeships in Texas (which ranks second among the states in area) were transferred to Massachusetts (which ranks forty-fifth.).

The number of judges assigned to district courts ranged from one to twenty-four. Less than a dozen districts had only a single judge, and only four districts had ten or more judges: New York, Southern (New York City), 24; California, Southern (Los Angeles), 13; Pennsylvania, Eastern (Philadelphia), 11; and Illinois, Northern (Chicago), 10. Most common were districts with two judges, and there were thirty-two such districts in 1962. Because of its specialized functions, which we shall discuss below, there were fifteen judges assigned to the District Court for the District of Columbia; Puerto Rico had two; and the Canal Zone, Guam, and the Virgin Islands had one judge each. In many of the less populous states which, nevertheless, included more than one district, at least one of the judges is assigned to two, or even to three, different districts, in an attempt to equalize workload differentials within the state. Moreover, temporary transfers are frequent. During the fiscal year 1961–1962, for example, eighty-four judges undertook 128 visiting assignments involving a total of about 3000 days of participation. Over three fourths of such temporary assignments were between courts within the same "circuit."

The term "circuit" is a semantic vestige of the earlier appellate system, under which there was a circuit court for each state, usually composed of a specially designated circuit judge and one of the district judges participating together. They were joined during part of each year by the Supreme Court justice who was assigned to the regional grouping of states—the circuit—of which the state was a part. Supreme Court justices and circuit judges alike "rode the circuit" until the 1890's, although by then no longer on horse-

TABLE II

States and Territories in Each of the Federal Circuits

| | |
|---|---|
| **First:** | Maine, Massachusetts, New Hampshire, Rhode Island, Puerto Rico |
| **Second:** | Connecticut, New York, Vermont |
| **Third:** | Deleware, New Jersey, Pennsylvania, Virgin Islands |
| **Fourth:** | Maryland, North Carolina, South Carolina, Virginia, West Virginia |
| **Fifth:** | Alabama, Florida, Georgia, Louisiana, Mississippi, Texas, Canal Zone |
| **Sixth:** | Kentucky, Michigan, Ohio, Tennessee |
| **Seventh:** | Illinois, Indiana, Wisconsin |
| **Eighth:** | Arkansas, Iowa, Minnesota, Missouri, Nebraska, North Dakota, South Dakota |
| **Ninth:** | Alaska, Arizona, California, Hawaii, Idaho, Montana, Nevada, Oregon, Washington, Guam |
| **Tenth:** | Colorado, Kansas, New Mexico, Oklahoma, Utah, Wyoming |
| **D.C.:** | District of Columbia |

back. Just before the turn of the century, the present system of permanent (and fixed) courts of appeals was substituted. Although each Supreme Court justice still is assigned to one or more circuits, his major duty today consists of hearing emergency motions that arise during the Court's summer vacation.

All of the circuit courts of appeals decide cases that are (in effect) appealed from the so-called "independent federal regulatory commissions" (particularly the National Labor Relations Board) and from the Tax Court of the United States, as well as from the district courts in the included states and territories. There is also a Court of Appeals for the District of Columbia circuit, which supervises the decision-making of the district court, and a Court of Municipal Appeals of this circuit. Although this court of appeals gets fewer appeals from the Tax Court and the N.L.R.B. than do the courts of appeals for the numbered circuits, it reviews a larger proportion of the decisions from the other administrative regulatory agencies.

In both the courts of appeals and the district courts, the chief judge is the judge under the age of seventy with the greatest seniority. There are from three to nine circuit judges assigned to each court of appeals, and there were a total of seventy-eight circuit judges in 1964, plus several who had retired but were available for part-time work. However, with few exceptions, the decisions of courts of appeals are made by "panels" (subgroups) of three judges. Such panels vary in composition from case to case, so that in the larger courts of appeals there are many different subgroups that might make the decision in the name of the court. Since subgroups do not always agree on what should be the policy position of the court, it is from time to time necessary to resolve intracourt (interpanel) conflicts.

This is done by having all of the judges assigned to the court decide the issue by majority vote in what is called an *en banc* decision. Individual circuit judges do not make decisions for their court except in procedural matters, similar to the occasional decisions of Supreme Court justices (in their role as circuit judges) described above. In the district courts, to the contrary, almost all decisions are made by individual judges, who act in the name of their respective courts. Out of some 230,000-odd decisions made by the district courts in the fiscal year ending June 30, 1962, only 105 were made by so-called "three-judge" district courts—and this was twice as many as had been usual in recent years. Such panels, consisting (usually) of two district judges and one circuit judge, are part of a special procedure established by a few statutes, originally in order to expedite judicial review of certain decisions of the Interstate Commerce Commission. It was assumed that there was a particular public interest in settling policy in such matters, so the statutes provide that cases will be tried by specially convened three-judge courts, with appeals direct to the Supreme Court—thus by-passing, of course, the courts of appeals. In recent years, there has been relatively frequent use of such special district courts in equity cases where the policy issue has been racial integration or state legislative reapportionment.

The circuit judges and the judges of the eighty-eight district courts in the fifty states and in the District of Columbia are appointed for terms of life. Their commissions of appointment read "for good behavior," but the chances of any federal judge's being removed by impeachment, the only authorized means, are very remote. No circuit judge ever has been impeached; of the six district judges who have been, three were acquitted, an insane and alcoholic Federalist was removed in 1803 by a Congress dominated by Jeffersonians, a border-state supporter of the Confederacy was removed on grounds of sedition by the Union Congress in 1862, and Judge Ritter of the Southern District of Florida was removed in 1936. About eight judges have resigned under threat of impeachment. A judge appointed for good behavior cannot successfully be removed merely for partisan reasons, for simple neglect of duty, or for incompetence.

The formal method for appointing federal judges is for the President to present nominations to the Senate. If the Senate "confirms" (concurs) by a majority vote, the President directs that a "commission" (certificate of appointment) be issued to the candidate, who accepts his appointment by his oath at a "swearing in" ceremony. The functional considerations channeled through the formal conduit are these: the senator (or senators) of the President's party —or, if there are none, those representatives of the President's party from districts within the jurisdiction of the court to which the appointment is to be made—suggests candidates. Other suggestions are received from a wide variety of other sources, including national, state, and local political party leaders. As described in Chapter One, there is now an institutionalized clearance process under which the Deputy Attorney General functions as a clearing house for the collection and evaluation of information concerning the qualifications of all proposed appointments of legal personnel to the Department of Justice, including United States attorneys and marshals as well as federal judges. The Deputy Attorney General receives investigative reports from the F.B.I., as well as from the American Bar Association, and this information is pooled so that a supporting "record" accompanies nominations submitted to the Senate. The Senate Judiciary Committee then conducts hearings upon the nominations, at which witnesses testify for or against the candidate. The Senate almost always follows the recommendation of its committee. However, the influence that a single senior senator can have in the appointment of a federal judge is suggested by the case of Sarah T. Hughes, a Dallas lawyer who was appointed to the Northern District of Texas in 1962. At the time of her confirmation, Judge Hughes was sixty-six years of age and was rated as "not qualified" by the ABA,[20] but she had the support of the Texan who presided over the Senate and who for years had been its most influential leader. When President Kennedy was assassinated in Dallas on November 22, 1963, it was Judge Hughes who administered the presidential oath of office to her long-time personal and political friend, Lyndon Johnson.

The district judges in four of the five national territories have even more diversified functions to perform than do the federal district judges in the states, because to a greater or lesser extent these territorial courts exercise judisdiction equivalent to that of a state court, in addition to the ordinary jurisdiction of a national district court. This is maximally so for the district courts in the Canal Zone, in Guam, and in the Virgin Islands, where there is no other court of record than that of the federal district judge. In the District of Columbia, there is a municipal (but not a state) court system. There are sixteen judges of a District of Columbia Court of General Sessions, which consists of a Criminal Division and a Civil Division (including Small Claims and Conciliation, Domestic Relations, and Landlord and Tenant Branches); three judges of a District of Columbia Court of Appeals; and three judges of a Juvenile Court of the District of Columbia. All twenty-two of these judges are appointed for ten-year terms by the President with senatorial confirmation. The commissioners of the District of Columbia appoint one judge for a ten-year term to constitute the Tax Court for the District. In terms of our earlier definition, however, the "more important" civil and criminal cases—those handled by state courts in the states

—are decided by the United States District Court for the District of Columbia. In the Commonwealth of Puerto Rico, however, there is a state judicial system, with one supreme court (consisting of five judges appointed for life terms by the governor with the consent of the commonwealth senate) provided for by the commonwealth constitution, and with other lower courts established by the legislature. Accordingly, the federal district court in Puerto Rico is limited to the same functions as the federal district courts in the states. All of the territorial district judges are appointed in the same way and are paid the same salary as other federal district judges. However, only those in the District of Columbia are appointed for life terms; the tenure for the others is now eight years.

*Courts with a Specialized Function.* There are also five other adjudicative agencies that Congress has seen fit to designate as courts, each of which works in a special area of public policy. The judges of three of these agencies (the Court of Claims, the Court of Customs and Patent Appeals, and the Customs Court) are appointed for life terms; the judges of the Court of Military Appeals have terms of fifteen years and those of the Tax Court of the United States have twelve-year terms. All are appointed by the President, with confirmation by the Senate. The judges of the Customs Court and those of the Tax Court are at the same status level as district judges (and are paid the same salary), since appeals from the former go to the Court of Customs and Patent Appeals while appeals from the latter go to the courts of appeals. The judges of the Court of Claims, the Court of Customs and Patent Appeals, and the Court of Military Appeals are at the status level of the courts of appeals and receive the same salaries as circuit judges. However, Supreme Court review of the decisions of the courts of appeals, though discretionary, does occur on a regular if limited basis; but the Supreme Court relatively infrequently reviews decisions of the Court of Claims, rarely reviews decisions of the Court of Customs and Patent Appeals, and there is no provision for direct review by the Supreme Court of the decisions of the Court of Military Appeals.[21] In terms of our earlier distinction between civil and criminal law, the Court of Military Appeals is exclusively concerned with questions of criminal law, and the other four courts are exclusively concerned with questions of civil law. Indeed, they so specialize in particular kinds of property rights that Supreme Court Justices Douglas and Black recently argued that it was a denial of the constitutional rights of the accused for a retired judge of the Court of Customs and Patent Appeals to have presided by special assignment over the trial by the District Court for the District of Columbia of a defendant who was convicted of armed robbery.[22]

Three of these courts are concerned with the administration of the collection of taxes: the Tax Court specializes in internal revenue, and the Customs Court and the Court of Customs and Patent Appeals in external revenue. Only a part of the internal revenue code comes within the purview of the Tax Court, whose jurisdiction is particularly defined by and in terms of specific statutes. The court functions through sixteen divisions, one for each of its judges, and it works in the field, establishing terms and dockets in the larger cities where taxpayers have claims (against the Bureau of Internal Revenue and vice versa) that remain unresolved after the extensive processes of administrative adjudication within the Treasury Department have been exhausted. The Customs Court has its headquarters in New York City, but its nine judges are divided among three divisions which conduct trials there and in other major ports. It is concerned primarily with reviewing appeals from administrative appeals of the decisions of customs collectors in regard to the amount of taxes due on imported merchandise. The Customs Court decided almost 50,000 cases in 1962; 71 per cent of these protested administrative decisions classifying goods (i.e., specifying the applicable tax rates), while 28 per cent protested appraisals (i.e., administrative assessments of the economic value of goods). The extent to which the Customs Court succeeded in performing its basic function—to settle the conflicting claims of taxpayers and the government—is best suggested by examining how many of its decisions were appealed to the Court of Customs and Patent Appeals. In 1962, the five judges of the latter court decided thirty-five cases on appeal from the Customs Court and about three times as many on appeal from the Board of Appeals (which acts for the commissioner) of the Patent Office of the Commerce Department. The latter cases take the form of claims by inventors that the Patent Office wrongfully refused to issue to them the legally approved monopolies that they sought; like the customs cases, they reach the Court of Customs and Patent Appeals only after extensive prior administrative adjudication. The District Court of the District of Columbia provides an alternative forum for appeals on the question of patentability; and in addition, there were scattered among the district courts in 1962 over 850 other patent litigations—conflicts over infringement in which the question of patentability often was raised as a defense, thus constituting what lawyers call a "collateral attack" upon the patent.

There are many claims against the national government which allege that plaintiffs have suffered wrongs either (1) due to injuries, called "torts" (usually caused by the carelessness of governmental employees), or (2) due to the failure of governmental employees to carry out obligations to which the government previously had agreed in (usually, written) contracts. Under present legislation, most of the claims for property damages of less than $10,000 are settled by administrative adjudication by the executive departments most directly involved, while the district courts and the Court of Claims have concurrent jurisdiction to decide claims involving larger amounts and also appeals from the departmental adjudications. In 1962, the five judges of the Court of Claims decided over three thousand cases, 78 per cent of which were claims of government employees for overtime pay. Notwithstanding the relatively wide publicity given to the handful of cases that the *Supreme* Court has decided during the past generation, relating to the claims of Indian tribes for fair compensation for their long-lost hunting grounds, in 1962 the Court of Claims decided only a dozen such cases—which was less than one half of 1 per cent of the total of its decisions for the year.

The three civilian judges of the Court of Military Appeals were largely substituted, after World War II, for what used to be (at least in principle) appeals to the President who, in his capacity as Commander in Chief, remains the "court of last resort" of the system of military courts (of the army, navy, air force, and coast guard). The court hears appeals—on questions of "law" (policy) only— in all cases involving either (1) persons with the rank of brigadier general (or its equivalent) or higher, or (2) any person sentenced to execution. It also hears cases which the chief legal officer of each of the armed services wants reviewed, as well as cases it chooses from among petitions filed by defendants who have been sentenced by military courts to more than one year of imprisonment.

*The United States Supreme Court.* The Chief Justice of the United States and the eight associate justices of the United States Supreme Court are appointed for life terms, by the President with confirmation by the Senate, at salaries about seven thousand dollars higher than those of circuit judges. The Court convenes, exclusively *en banc*, from early October through the middle of June, in the District of Columbia. In recent terms, it has refused to review, by denying certiorari or by dismissing appeals, an average of two thousand cases. A majority of the cases in which its review is sought come on petition for certiorari from the courts of appeals, but well over 40 per cent come from the state supreme courts, with most of the remainder being direct appeals from the United States district courts. Both "certiorari" and "appeal" are technical terms for the discretionary procedures by which the Court selects the relatively much smaller number of cases—usually less than two hundred per term—that it chooses to review; of these, about half are decided unanimously. The Court occasionally decides a case under what is called its "original" jurisdiction, and sometimes—as in the Tidelands Oil Cases of 1947 and 1950—such decisions are of considerable importance for the public policies at issue; but they constitute only a fraction of 1 per cent of the cases on the Court's dockets in any term. There are also other procedures (certification and extraordinary writs) under which cases quite rarely—on the average, less than one per term—are reviewed.

The overwhelming majority of the Court's decisions consist of denials of certiorari to review the decisions of the courts of appeals or of state supreme courts. Most of these denials are in cases from the Miscellaneous Docket, which the Court established in 1945 in order to segregate the cases—now averaging a thousand per term— in which prisoners in national (and in recent years, to an even greater extent, in state) penal institutions seek to be released on the claim of illegalities in their trials. The late Caryl Chessman exemplifies the latter type of litigant. He was executed by California in 1960 only after eight stays of execution and a dozen years of post-conviction maneuvering in the courts of both that state and the United States. There were fourteen appeals in the California courts, twelve in the United States District Court and the Court of Appeals for the Ninth Circuit, and sixteen to the United States Supreme Court. Several of the latter were granted in order to review various of his claims on the merits of the substantive issues that he sought to raise. Chessman is doubtless the most publicized of such petitioners *in forma pauperis*, primarily because he was talented both as a lawyer and as an author, but more successful in the latter role.

### SUPPORTING ADMINISTRATIVE STRUCTURES

It is evident to anyone who visits the sumptuous marble palace in which the Supreme Court has worked since 1935, located on "the Hill" only a little more than the length of a football field from the Capitol, that there are many supporting players in addition to the nine stars who fill the most conspicuous public roles. Each justice is assigned (on the average) two administrative assistants; in most instances these are young honor graduates of the leading law schools, and they are called "law clerks." The principal administrative officer is the Clerk of the Supreme Court. Each justice has a secretary; there is a librarian, a marshal, a reporter, and their staffs; messengers; bailiffs; and custodial employees. The custodial staff has remained constant at about 150 since the move into the new building, but the administrative staff of the Court more than doubled during the two decades (from 30 in 1937 to 63 by 1957) following the move. It would be impossible for each of the nine justices to participate in the decision of over two thousand cases each year without the assistance of the administrative staff and the physical facilities made available with the help of the custodial staff. For each justice, there are on the average about 21 persons in the supporting administrative structure.

For the other national courts, there are over 6000 supporting personnel in the administrative category alone. In 1962 there were 375 active judges and 91 who had retired or resigned. They were assigned some 350 law clerks and over 400 secretaries. There were over 1300 persons working in the offices of the court clerks, and there were about 900 probation officers and their clerks. Then there were some 230 court criers, almost 300 reporters, and almost 200 law clerks to court reporters. The 190 bankruptcy referees were assisted by 700 clerks. The 691 United States commissioners had only 7 clerks, although this is readily explained by the fact that only half a dozen worked full time as commissioners; about 10 per cent doubled in one of the other positions listed above (e.g., 50 were deputy district court clerks). The commissioners are the functional equivalents (for the national judicial system) of the justices of the peace and magistrates of the state judicial systems, and only about two thirds of them are lawyers. Only the larger courts had full-time messengers or librarians; there were only 40 of the former and 30 of the latter. Finally, there were some 90 persons listed simply as "District of Columbia miscellaneous" and the 165 members of the staff of the Office of the Administrative Director of United States Courts (described below), the organization that exercises administrative supervision over all of the persons mentioned above in this paragraph. But these are not the only relevant supporting staff; others are primarily subject to the administrative control of the Department of Justice, including the United States attorney and marshal assigned to each district court, and their own staffs, which are extensive in the larger cities.

In a broader sense, the entire Department of Justice provides a supporting administrative structure for the national courts. The department's professional staff consists almost entirely of lawyers, and most of what they do is directly related to the functioning of the national judiciary. Beyond that, there are thousands of private attorneys throughout the country who, having been admitted to practice before the national courts, technically are considered to be "officers of the court." Certainly the judges could not perform the functions presently assigned to them without the interactions of these private attorneys, who (together with the United States attorneys) assume most of the initiative in the process of judicial decision-making, particularly in the trial courts. The bar, of course, tends to specialize, *inter alia*, on a subject matter and/or a geographical basis (for practice in the district courts and courts of appeals) and on a functional basis (for practice before the courts with specialized functions). Thus there are lawyer-specialists, who comprise the tax bar, the customs bar, the claims bar, and the patent bar—although many of the practitioners of the patent bar are formally educated as engineers rather than as lawyers. Finally, the even larger number of laymen who enter into court proceedings in the roles of litigant, witness, juror, and audience also perform essential functions, and they should be considered a part of the supporting administrative structure for judicial decision-making.

## THE JUDICIAL CONFERENCE OF THE UNITED STATES

The principal policy-making group for the national judiciary is the Judicial Conference of the United States, which was authorized by statute in 1922 and has met at least once a year since then. The conference is composed of both ex-officio and elected members: (1) the fourteen chief judges of the Supreme Court, the courts of appeals, the Court of Claims, and the Court of Customs and Patent Appeals; and (2) eleven district judges, one of whom is elected by each of the analogous circuit judicial councils. The Chief Justice of the Supreme Court chairs the conference in his capacity as Chief Justice of the United States. Most of the other ex-officio members of the conference are in effect selected on the basis of seniority, since the chief circuit judges are so selected. Conferences typically last for one or two days and are held in the District of Columbia; in some years (e.g., 1962) there is more than one conference. Their agenda range from the broadest questions of policy to the minutiae of judicial administration. Verbatim transcripts of proceedings are not published; instead, there is a summary of the decisions, which tends to suggest— doubtless quite falsely—that all decisions are reached not only consensually but also unanimously. These summaries, together with a transmittal statement from the Chief Justice to the Congress, emphasizing the conference's policy recommendations for legislation, are published in the same volume with the annual report of the Director of the Administrative Office of the United States Courts. One example of a conference policy recommendation appeared early in this chapter: the disapproval of the suggestion that Congress permit federal judges to receive fiscal grants from states.

A more general legislative function of the conference is its role in the formulation of rules of procedure for the national courts. The conference is a major decision-making group but has been since 1958 only one among many in the widespread process of consultation that is associated with this particular policy-making function. The formulation or revision of such "rules" (which is the term lawyers use to describe the legal norms, analogous to statutes, that are made by judges or executive agencies) is preceded by the establishment of study groups consisting of committees of technical specialists. These specialists include practicing attorneys, judges, and law professors;

such professional organizations as the Association of American Law Schools, the American Judicature Society, and the American Bar Association and its state affiliates cooperate with the conference in staffing the study groups. Of course, the Administrative Office of the United States Courts, the Department of Justice, and state attorneys general present their views to the study groups. The latter's recommendations to the conference are published as reports, which are given broad circulation among the legal and related professions prior to action by the conference. After the conference has approved a set of rules, they are sent to the Supreme Court—which is the statutory rule-making agency—for its (*pro forma*) approval and then transmitted to the Congress. Initially, the rules of civil procedure and of criminal procedure were transmitted through the Attorney General, but now this is done directly by the Chief Justice. If Congress fails to act, presumably by adopting a resolution disapproving of the draft rules in whole or in part, they become effective at the end of ninety days.[23] Congress has not yet adopted any such disapproving resolution, and in view of the widespread process of antecedent professional consultation, it seems very unlikely that the conference would recommend a rule so controversial that it would be politically possible to get Congress to nullify it. Moreover, lawyers constitute the principal occupational group in the Congress, and there is immense prestige (at least among lawyers) associated with the work of the conference. Both that prestige and the factors of inertia that make it difficult to get any kind of resolution through two houses of Congress within ninety days make such disapproval most unlikely, quite apart from the substantive merits of any particular rule.

The rules of procedure for both the lower federal courts and the Supreme Court are published along with the decisions of the Supreme Court in the *United States Reports* and with the statutes of Congress in the *United States Code*. This arrangement suggests the ambivalent status of the rules—structurally, an output of the judicial system, but functionally, most analogous to the acts of Congress which (in terms of their substantive content) they have tended to displace. The most recent general revision of the Supreme Court's rules was made in 1954, although the Court from the outset has made its own rules of procedure under a delegation of authority in the Judiciary Act of 1789. The areas of policy-making for the lower federal courts and the dates in which the Supreme Court first exercised the powers transferred to it by Congress are as follows: "Rules of Practice in Admiralty and Maritime Cases" (1854); "General Orders and Forms in Bankruptcy" (1898); "Rules of Civil Procedure for the United States District Courts" (1938); and "Rules of Criminal Procedure for the United States District Courts" (1945).

There is convened at least twice a year in each circuit a judicial council, which discusses many of the same policy questions that come before the national conference, as well as matters of primary interest to a particular circuit. Such councils are presided over by the chief circuit judge and consist of the district and circuit judges assigned to the circuit, and sometimes also selected members of the bar.

## THE ADMINISTRATIVE OFFICE OF THE UNITED STATES COURTS

The Administrative Office was established by Congress in 1939 as a direct consequence of President Franklin Roosevelt's political attack upon the Supreme Court in 1937, in which he accused the Court of administrative inefficiency and the justices of superannuation—indeed, he stated that the latter caused the former. Congress also soon adopted legislation that liberalized the retirement system for federal judges and that was intended (among other things) to encourage the "Nine Old Men" of the Supreme Court to make way for younger men of Roosevelt's choice. A majority of five of the Supreme Court justices obligingly had retired or died by 1939.

The Supreme Court appoints the Director and the Deputy Director of the Administrative Office. This provision of the statute is intended to assure that the justices will be able to maintain policy control over the Administrative Office, which is designated by the statute to be an agency of the Judicial Conference of the United States. The question of who exercises policy control over whom is of some interest, considering the scope and depth of the "housekeeping functions" that the Administrative Office has come to exercise for the courts of appeals and district courts. Except for the Supreme Court, for which similar functions are performed by its own clerk's office, the Administrative Office centrally directs and manages many court operations. It controls the hiring and compensation of subordinate personnel, i.e., all except the judges. It collects and analyzes information concerning dockets and workload. It compiles and distributes to the chief circuit judges reports for purposes of statistical control over decision-making activities. It supervises the pay of both judges and subordinate personnel and provides office facilities and supplies for the lower national courts. It administers an annuity system for judicial retirees, supervises the preparation of budgets by court clerks, and audits their accounts. It also supervises the accounts of federal probation officers and of federal "administrators" appointed under the Bankruptcy Act. (The federal district judges act, in effect, as foremen for the administration of the national probation and bankruptcy systems.) It submits an annual public report to the Judicial Conference, the Congress, and the Attorney General; and it publishes, in cooperation with the Bureau of Prisons of the Department of Justice, the journal *Federal Probation*, which is devoted to "correctional philosophy and practice." It has also arranged seminars in which experienced federal judges orient newly appointed judges. These seminars were in addition to sentencing institutes, which the Administrative Office helped to arrange in 1961 and 1962 on an individual or a joint-circuit basis. In effect, the Administrative Office has come to perform the general function of a brain for the national judicial system.

## THE DEPARTMENT OF JUSTICE

The Attorney General of the United States is the political administrator of a large organization, most of whose activities are indispensable to the functioning of the national courts. In 1962, the department included over 32,000 people whose activities involved the expenditure of over $300 million. Its organization chart depicts, in the usual hierarchical manner, three levels of administrative structure: (1) a primary level, consisting of the Attorney General and Deputy Attorney General and their offices, the Solicitor General, the Legal Counsel, the Administrative Division, the Pardon Attorney and Pardon Board, and the Board of Immigration Appeals; (2) a secondary level, consisting of seven divisions (Tax, Civil, Lands, Antitrust, Criminal, Civil Rights, and Internal Security), each headed by an assistant attorney general; and (3) a tertiary level, consisting of three bureaus (Investigation, Prisons, and the Immigration and Naturalization Service) and the United States marshals and attorneys.

From a functional point of view, however, the department is better conceptualized as three subsystem structures. The major function of one of these subsystems is political; that of the second is direct police operations; and that of the third is interaction with the national courts. The political subsystem can be further subdivided in terms of external and internal orientation. Thus the assistant attorney general in charge of the Office of Legal Counsel is almost exclusively oriented outside of the department, while the Administrative Division is primarily concerned with intradepartmental activities, and both the Attorney General and the Deputy Attorney General have dual responsibilities. The police subsystem is concerned with the surveillance, apprehension, and custody of persons who, as suspects in cases of either ordinary or political crime, are deemed to constitute an actual or potential danger to the national order and security. This subsystem consists of the three bureaus that conduct direct—primarily field—operations; the Criminal and Internal Security Divisions; and the two appeals boards (Parole and Immigration) and the Pardon Attorney. The courts subsystem includes the Solicitor General, five divisions whose job is litigation management in behalf of the national government (Tax, Antitrust, Lands, Civil, and Civil

Rights), and the United States attorneys and marshals (who are officers of the district courts throughout the country).

The relative importance that is attached by Congress to these various functions is suggested by the amounts of their respective budgets. In 1962, the lion's share of the departmental budget, some $129 million or about 42 per cent of the total of $305 million, went to the Federal Bureau of Investigation, whose director, J. Edgar Hoover, was rounding out forty years of continuous service as the sacrosanct chief of the F.B.I. The other two bureaus (the Immigration and Naturalization Service and the Bureau of Prisons) received $65 and $58 million, respectively. These three direct-operations units of the police subsystem received over 82 per cent of the total departmental appropriation, and the remaining one sixth went to pay for the costs of all of the rest of the department: general administration and legal activities, the seven divisions, the attorneys and marshals in the field, the fees and expenses of government witnesses, and the boards and offices that comprise the superstructure in the departmental organization chart. Evidently, the detection of crime and the incarceration of criminals are the costly functions of the department, while those of interaction with the national judicial and administrative systems are relatively inexpensive to support.

The Attorney General's principal function is to symbolize and to represent the Department of Justice in relations with the President, the Congress, the Supreme Court, other political administrators both outside and inside the department, and the public—that is, to represent the department in interactions at the policy level with other actors in the major subsystems of the national political system. In effect, these functions of representation are divided among the Attorney General's principal associates: the assistant attorney general who is Legal Counsel works with the Executive Office of the President and with other administrative agencies; the Solicitor General represents the department before the Supreme Court; the assistant attorney general in charge of the Administrative Division is concerned with interrelationships among the administrative units of the department; and the Deputy Attorney General shares much of the Attorney General's responsibility for interaction with Congress, particularly in regard to interstitial procedures that have become routinized. In a sense, the Deputy Attorney General is the department's chief lobbyist with the national legislative system, just as the Solicitor General is the chief lobbyist with the national judicial system and the Legal Counsel with the national administrative system.

It is the Deputy Attorney General who handles the screening of all nominations for the federal judiciary, and it is he who presents the department's views in the clearance of pending and enrolled bills (of which there were some 2242 requests, for the policy advice of the department, in 1962). He also supervises the activities of the United States attorneys and marshals; there is an attorney and a marshal (plus their staffs) attached to each district court. An example of such supervision is the direction of the activities of the task force of marshals who were assembled and flown to Oxford, Mississippi, in September 1962 to enforce James Meredith's claim of constitutional right to enroll as a student of political science at the University of Mississippi. A quite different and considerably less well publicized responsibility of the Deputy Attorney General is the department's recruitment program for honor law graduates. The 1962 class of seventy-five attorneys was selected from forty-seven law schools, presumably without regard to race or politics or religion, although over half of the recruits did come from the more prestigious schools of the East and over 80 per cent from the East and Midwest combined.

The Legal Counsel prepares formal opinions of the Attorney General and also provides informal opinions and legal advice to the agencies of the national administrative system. He also reviews various kinds of executive legislation, such as Executive Orders, presidential proclamations, and presidential regulations. The Administrative Division conducts the business management operations of the department, including budgeting and auditing, personnel, records control, and the departmental library. Of particular relevance is the Examiners' Section, which acts for both the department and the Administrative Office of the United States Courts as a "fact-finding" agency and as liaison with the field establishment of the national courts and directly associated supporting structures. Specifically, the eleven field examiners attempt to check upon the activities of the United States marshals and attorneys, court reporters, clerks of the district courts and courts of appeals, and United States commissioners, referees, receivers, trustees in bankruptcy, and probation officers in the judicial districts. In 1962, there were 69 special examinations and 120 investigations, but the small staff was able to conduct only 21 surveys; thus each judicial district is subjected to a general fiscal and administrative audit about once every five years.

The courts subsystem of the department interacts primarily with the rest of the national judicial system, of which it must certainly be considered an integral component. The Solicitor General personally argues certain cases before the Supreme Court, in order to emphasize their policy significance, while members of his staff represent the national government in all other Supreme Court cases to which the United States is a party litigant. He also can and does intervene and, through what are called *amicus curiae* (friend of the court) briefs, he presents the administration's policy views in cases between private parties. Moreover, he has an important influence in deciding which private interest groups will be permitted to present their own policy views to the Court through *amicus* briefs and oral argument. Since the national government is a formal party to about half of all of the cases that the Supreme Court decides on the merits of the substantive issues presented, the career staff of the Solicitor General's office has come to acquire a considerable advantage over private counsel in terms of experience, expertise, and prestige. The Solicitor General also is in a much better position than are private counsel to pick and choose the time, place, and circumstances under which he will push a policy issue to decision by the Supreme Court. The latter advantage stems from the Solicitor General's power to manipulate the issues that will be considered by appellate courts; without his approval, no case in which the national government is a party can be appealed to a higher court. In 1962, for example, the Solicitor General's office authorized 930 appeals (of which about a third were granted) from district courts to courts of appeals, while the Supreme Court granted 10 of the 23 appeals that the Solicitor General approved from lower federal courts. Similarly, a recent study has shown that in the much larger volume of cases in which review by the Supreme Court is sought on certiorari, the Court grants only about 6 per cent of the petitions filed by private litigants, while approving over half of those petitions supported by the Solicitor General.[24] In a typical recent term, the Solicitor General's staff (1) participated in over a third of *all* cases docketed by the Supreme Court; (2) participated in over half of the cases that went to oral argument; and (3) were successful in over two thirds of the cases decided on the merits. Thus the Solicitor General is by far the most frequent, as well as one of the most successful, of the lobbyists with the Supreme Court. The details of his current record of wins and losses are reported in the latest issue of the Attorney General's *Annual Report*.

Of the divisions in this subsystem of the department, the Antitrust Division deals primarily with the control of monopolistic business organizational structures and practices, partly through litigation but to an even greater extent through negotiated settlements. Many, but by no means all, of the antitrust prosecutions that do go to litigation result in policy decisions at the level of the Supreme Court. In February 1961, for example, the District Court for the Pennsylvania Eastern District (Philadelphia) made an unreported decision approving an antitrust decree against the heavy electrical equipment industry for conspiracy to combine to fix prices. In the following year, over 1700 private suits for treble damages were filed by customers against the industry, in thirty-three different national judicial districts located in twenty-four states and the District of Columbia. The Civil Division deals with a miscellany of policy issues, including the following categories of cases: admiralty and shipping; tort and contract claims against the government; fraud; patents; veterans affairs; customs; and alien property. The Tax Division employs about two hundred lawyers (of whom half were new in 1962), and its primary function is to represent the Internal Revenue Service of the Treasury Department in both civil and criminal litigation in both the state and national courts (except for the United States Tax Court, in which attorneys of the Treasury Department's Office of General Counsel represent the I.R.S.). The Lands Division is concerned with the very slow and very complicated litigation relating to claims for and against government ownership of real property, Indian lands, water rights, and other natural resources. The national government claims title to some 768 million acres of land, about a third of all of the land in the United States, and each year the aggregate of funds which the national government pays in settlements and judgments in land condemnation cases *exceeds* what it expends for *all* other settlements and judgments in federal courts. To protect the government's large financial interest in this field of policy and litigation, the Lands Division employs a hundred lawyers in Washington and seven in the field (where the land is located).

The other division in the courts subsystem is the Civil Rights Division, which has initiated and sponsored the litigation of many of the most important Supreme Court decisions in the two decades since the end of World War II. Among the components of judicial policy that the Civil Rights Division has helped to shape are (1) elections and the right to vote, as this relates both to legislative reapportionment and to racial integration, and (2) other aspects of racial integration (e.g., schools and hospitals receiving funds from the national government; interstate transportation facilities such as airports and railroad and bus terminals; sit-ins; employment discrimination). An example of this division's work is its activities under the Civil Rights Acts of 1957 and 1960. There are some two hundred counties, mostly in the states of the former Confederacy, where public officials in charge of voting registration discriminate against Negroes. In 1962, the Civil Rights Division initiated fifteen cases against such registrars, with results typified by those in Bullock County, Alabama, where the number of registered Negro voters was increased from 5 to 915.

The police subsystem, which preëmpts the greater part of the department's fiscal and personnel resources, is built around the activities of the three large operating bureaus. The 6000 special agents and 8000 supporting personnel of the F.B.I. are mostly decentralized among over fifty field offices. The substantive concerns of the F.B.I. range from organized racketeering, certain ordinary crimes (bank robbery, interstate transportation of stolen motor vehicles, income tax evasion, etc.), investigation of the Communist party and subversion, and the protection of civil rights, to the training of state

. . . . . . . . . . . . . . . . . . . .

and local police employees, a national laboratory for scientific crime detection (which maintains a nation-wide fingerprint identification clearing house, sponsors research in the "forensic sciences," etc.), and such publications as *Uniform Crime Reports*, a national compilation of statistics on the detection of crime and the arrest of defendants. In its crime detection work, the F.B.I. places considerable reliance upon a network of mostly paid but undercover agents; the F.B.I. credits these confidential informants with the apprehension in a recent year of over 2500 federal defendants, with the detection of almost as many others who were arrested by local and state police, and with the recovery by the F.B.I. of property worth $4,200,000 and by local and state police of property worth $24,500,000.

The Bureau of Prisons has almost 3000 custodial employees and about the same number of supporting personnel, who are responsible for the custody of about 24,000 prisoners in six penitentiaries, five reformatories, five youth and juvenile institutions, eight correctional institutions, six camps, one medical center, and one new psychiatric hospital. Of these prisoners, about 75 per cent are white, and most of the remainder are Negro. The most common offense in recent years has been auto theft, for which 25 per cent of these prisoners were convicted. The social sciences, sociology and psychology in particular, have had considerable influence upon the Bureau of Prisons, as exemplified by the bureau's participation in the sentencing institute for judges. The bureau has advocated increasing use of the clinical psychology approach to sentencing, and it has made available to federal district judges, on a voluntary basis, the use of a diagnostic commitment procedure (oriented to the rehabilitation of the criminal rather than toward punishment for his offense). The new approach has been used in about 5 per cent of the cases since 1958.

The third bureau, the Immigration and Naturalization Service, deals with the admission, exclusion, and deportation of non-resident aliens and with the naturalization of resident aliens. It, too, functions through a highly decentralized structure, with thirty-four field districts grouped into five regions. An example of its recent work is the screening of the large influx of political refugees from Cuba and from Hong Kong.

The two divisions in the police subsystem are Criminal and Internal Security, which specialize in the prosecution of "ordinary" and of "political" crime, respectively. The Criminal Division enforces national criminal law, including acts of Congress and administrative regulations and decisions of the national courts relating to interstate commerce, the postal business, government officials (viz., bribery), national territories and maritime jurisdiction, frauds against the government, national banks, stock exchanges, and taxation. The Internal Security Division is concerned with espionage, seditious ac-

CANISIUS COLLEGE LIBRARY
BUFFALO. N. Y

tivity, the Communist party and its various "front" organizations, and other organizations with extremist political goals or methods of operations.

The other units in the police subsystem are the Office of the Pardon Attorney and the two appellate boards, for parole and for immigration cases. The Pardon Attorney receives, investigates, and recommends to the President action for "executive clemency" in regard to about five hundred applications each year from national prisoners. The attorney recommends approval of about a third and disapproval of the remainder. The Board of Parole's activities are closely articulated with those of both the federal district judges and the Bureau of Prisons, of which it is, in effect, a component structure. Its function is to grant, modify, or revoke parole for federal prisoners. The board has given full support to the bureau's advocacy of the new—for the national government, at least—procedure of indeterminate sentencing, first authorized by statute in 1958. The board conducts annually about 14,000 hearings at approximately thirty-five field locations, and in 1962 it approved about a third of the requests for parole in the 9000 nonjuvenile cases that it heard.

Like the Board of Parole, the Board of Immigration Appeals is in effect an administrative court, composed of persons who do not have the formal status of judges but whose function—and, increasingly, procedures—are very similar to those of courts. In 1962, for example, the Board of Immigration Appeals decided some 1200 cases, of which about 300 were heard in oral argument. These were cases relating to the status of aliens, and the typical question was whether a specific nonresident alien should be deported from the country. In all such cases, there were extensive hearings and investigations undertaken by the Immigration and Naturalization Service before this relatively small proportion of the total caseload of the bureau was appealed to the board. Thus the function of the board is hardly distinguishable from that of such specialized national courts as the Customs Court or the Tax Court. We might well infer that the Board of Parole and the Board of Immigration Appeals represent an intermediate evolutionary stage, and the Tax Court of the United States a later stage, of a process of institutional development, which at a still later stage is recognized as having culminated in a full-fledged court such as the Customs Court. Certainly such an inference is perfectly compatible with the known natural history of these and other adjudicatory subcomponents of the national judicial system.

# Judicial Functions

## INTERCHANGE BETWEEN THE NATIONAL AND STATE JUDICIAL SYSTEM BOUNDARIES

The continuously expanding scope of the policy-making by the national courts, particularly during the present century, has been primarily a reflection of the expansion in the policy-making responsibilities of the legislative and administrative systems of the national government. It was probably inevitable that, once the other two major subsystems of the national political system were committed to a course of big government, with substantially greater public management of both the economy and society, then the judicial system would be forced to accept and accommodate to such major changes. It was not inevitable, however, that the national judiciary in general, and the Supreme Court in particular, should have emerged in mid-century as the most dynamic force for socio-politico-economic change—in such major policy fields as racial integration and legislative reapportionment—to which the national legislative and executive-administrative systems as well as the state political systems would have to accommodate *their* own actions.

Notwithstanding this sharp increase in policy-making by the national judiciary, it remains true that in terms of both qualitative and quantitative criteria, an even greater amount of policy is made by the fifty state judicial systems. The volume of decisions made by the state courts is many times greater than the output of the national courts, and it is the state judicial systems—not the national—which have the function of resolving most of the litigational problems that arise in the lives of most of the people in the United States. These problems include (but are by no means limited to) conflicts involving marriage, divorce, the custody of children and the mentally ill, and other legal aspects of domestic relations; petty and grand theft, embezzlement, assault, robbery, breaking and entry, homicide, rape, forgery, auto theft, disorderly conduct, and other common crimes and misdemeanors; real property, negotiable instruments, sales, torts, contracts, and other business relationships; vagrancy, inebriation, sexual deviance, gambling, narcotics, and other "morals" offenses; industrial accidents, workmen's compensation, motor vehicle accidents, and other kinds of personal injury and property damage; and labor-management relations, corporate organization, competitive practices, and other aspects of business practice.

The subject categories of the cases typically decided by the national judicial system will be analyzed later in this chapter. Some of the categories relate to conflicts that rarely if ever are decided in state judicial systems; they constitute what lawyers call the "exclusive jurisdiction" of the national courts. Examples are suits between two or more states, or between a state and the United States, or a petition of a federal regulatory commission asking a court to decree the enforcement of the commission's decision, or a prosecution for a violation of the national criminal law. Except occasionally through what lawyers call "collateral attack" (in cases over which a state court otherwise has jurisdiction), state courts do not decide questions of "exclusive national jurisdiction."

The converse of this proposition, however, is not true. Almost any question of "exclusive state jurisdiction" can—and a small proportion do—become redefined as a matter of national jurisdiction, because of the overlapping bases of national jurisdiction. The jurisdiction of the national courts is defined partly in terms of "parties" (i.e., who is suing or being sued by whom), and partly in terms of "subjects" (i.e., maritime, bankruptcy, taxation, etc.). Moreover, as Congress, the Presidency, and the Supreme Court have redefined the boundaries between the national and the state constitutional systems, the jurisdiction of the national judicial system has expanded. The scope of state policy-making responsibility has increased considerably on an absolute scale, despite the transfers (either wholly or in part) of many formerly state functions to the national government; but the policy functions of the national system have increased to an even greater extent, both absolutely and in relation to the states. Moreover, the United States Constitution has been interpreted to mean that Congress can manipulate most, if not all, of the jurisdiction of the national judicial system (including that of the Supreme Court). As a consequence, many types of cases can be shunted into state judicial systems, depending upon how Congress or the national courts (by statutory interpretation) define the minimal jurisdictional amounts or the prerequisite status of parties litigant for suits in the national courts. The Constitution states that "The Judicial Power of the United States . . . shall extend to all Cases . . . between Citizens of different states" but "in such inferior Courts as the Congress may from time to time ordain and establish" and with the Supreme Court's appellate jurisdiction subject to "such Exceptions, and under such Regulations as the Congress shall make." The subject-matter scope of "diversity jurisdiction" extends to most of the civil categories described above as characteristic problems resolved by state judicial systems, since the primary test of diversity jurisdiction is that the parties to a case be resident in different states—irrespective of the substance of their conflict. Congress has added specific requirements that must be met before the federal district courts can accept a case in diversity jurisdiction. Among these is the prerequisite that the economic value involved in the dispute must be at least $10,000.

Let us assume, for example, two cases raising an identical question relating to a widow's claim against the out-of-state life insurance company that had insured her deceased husband. In one case, the claim is based on a policy of $5000; in the other case, the amount of the policy is $15,000. The first case would be decided by a state court, while the second case might be decided by either a state or a national court, depending upon the plaintiff widow's choice.[1] Under the current procedural policy of the United States Supreme Court, it is presumed that either the national district court or the state trial court would follow the same substantive norms of judicial policy, since the federal judges are supposed to invoke the norms that they think would be followed by the appropriate state court if it were deciding the case.[2] There would still be differences in the rules of procedure followed, for purposes of decision-making, by the national and the state court, however. There might also be significant differences in the location of the two courts or in the probable bias of the jury composition in the state as compared to the national court. The ideological values held by the state judge or the federal judge who would be most likely to preside at the trial might also vary significantly: one might be an economic liberal and the other an economic conservative—perhaps the one had been a labor union lawyer and the other an attorney on the legal staff of an insurance corporation, before they became judges. For these and similar reasons, it may make a considerable difference to the parties (or to their respective counsel) whether a case is to be tried in a state or national court, notwithstanding the legal presumption that the "law" is the same in both of these courts.

Consequently, plaintiffs are free to elect whether to begin a diversity suit involving $10,000 or more in a state or a national court. If a plaintiff chooses a national court, then the defendant usually has no recourse but to litigate the issue in that court; if a plaintiff chooses a state court, however, then the defendant can file a petition at any time before the trial begins, requesting that the case be "removed" to the United States district court that has territorial jurisdiction. Such a right of transfer obtains in diversity cases only if none of the defendants are citizens of the state in which the suit is brought in the state court. The right, however, is "absolute," as the statute puts it, in either diversity or nondiversity cases if the legal question is civil (rather than criminal) and if the defendant's claim is based upon the "laws or Constitution of the United States"—that is, if the defendant's claim raises what lawyers call a "federal question." Examples of federal questions include: either a civil or a criminal prosecution, commenced in a state court, against a federal officer acting under color of his office; cases involving defendants who are members of the armed forces of the United States; and certain civil rights cases that involve claims of the denial of equal protection of the laws.

Litigants also have a choice between state and national systems of adjudication in those areas of policy-making in which the functions of courts and administrative agencies substantially overlap. For example, many states have enacted labor legislation that purports to regulate aspects of labor-management relations over which the National Labor Relations Board has inchoate jurisdiction—that is, the N.L.R.B. has not chosen to exercise the authority to regulate certain industries or relationships which it might claim to control but which remain in the meantime under state jurisdiction. In states that provide for judicial rather than for administrative enforcement of such state labor acts, the plaintiff might have a choice between initiating action in a state court or trying to persuade the N.L.R.B. to accept jurisdiction. Conversely, the choice may lie between a national district court and a state administrative agency. Louisiana and other Southern states, for instance, have established elaborate systems of administrative adjudication—designed, apparently, to exhaust litigants who are supposed to "exhaust their administrative remedies" before taking their cases to court—in such aspects of racial integration as pupil placement and voter registration. Typically, it is futile to pursue the state "remedy" in such cases, because by the time the plaintiff has gone through the several stages of state appellate administrative review and then three or four levels of the state judicial system, his child has grown up or the election is long past. Yet attempts to invoke the jurisdiction of a national district court may be rejected as premature if no effort has been made to use the state system of administrative adjudication to challenge the adverse administrative decision. Such situations present difficult questions of legal-political tactics.

The other way in which the national and state judicial systems most commonly articulate is through Supreme Court appellate review of the decisions of state judicial systems. Usually, such decisions are those of the state supreme courts. In many states where there is an intermediate appellate court, appeals to the state supreme court are almost completely discretionary with that court, and in some cases state law makes no provision for appeal of any kind. In such instances, the Supreme Court will sometimes directly review whatever purports to be the final decision made within the state judicial system. Thus in a recent case the United States Supreme Court was the only court to review a misdemeanor case that had been tried by a municipal court in Kentucky.[3]

There are two principal methods by which the Supreme Court exercises jurisdiction to review the decisions of lower courts, including state courts. These methods are the statutory procedures for appeal and for certiorari. In legal theory, a party to a case has a right to have the United States Supreme Court review his appeal from a state court decision which either (1) declares unconstitutional some provision of national law or (2) upholds the validity of some provision of state law against a claim that it is contrary to the Constitution of the United States. In practice, however, the Supreme Court notes probable jurisdiction in (i.e., accepts) only about a fourth of such cases, dismissing the others because of "want of a substantial federal question" or simply "for lack of jurisdiction."[4] Of course, such reasons are worthless, and the Supreme Court as a matter of policy chooses to refuse to explain why it accepts some appeals from state courts and rejects others.

The other procedure, certiorari, is used in those cases where a petitioner seeks review by the United States Supreme Court of a state court judgment but can invoke neither of the two grounds for appeal mentioned above. His counsel can file a petition with the Supreme Court which should—although it frequently does not—focus upon *why* it is a matter of substantial public importance that the Court should decide the question of public policy that his case raises, instead of focusing on the claim that the court below erred in its disposition of his case. The Supreme Court typically denies certiorari—it refuses, that is, to hear oral argument or to consider a more lengthy written brief which *would* focus upon the merits of the petitioner's side in the case—in about 97 per cent of these state cases. Consequently, both processes of review of the decisions of state judicial systems are discretionary with the United States Supreme

Court; the Court is free to pick those few cases that raise the policy issues it wishes to consider, when it wishes to consider them, and the particular factual contexts in which it wishes to decide the issues. The "legal right" of appeal, as distinguished from the avowedly discretionary certiorari process, is not without significance, however. The odds against a litigant's getting the Supreme Court to reconsider a state court decision are about 30 to 1 in certiorari, but they drop sharply to only about 4 to 1 if his counsel has been able to import into the record of his case either of the two constitutional grounds to make at least a *prima facie* showing of the right to appeal. Once he gets there, however, it makes little difference which route he took; the odds then shift to his favor, since in decisions on the merits the Supreme Court tends to reverse state courts in about two thirds of the cases.

### FUNCTIONS OF THE NATIONAL JUDICIAL SYSTEM

Many discussions of the national courts in general, and of the United States Supreme Court in particular, tend to create the impression that the primary function of federal judges is to consider the constitutionality of acts of the Congress, state legislatures, national administrative agencies, and, from time to time, even of the President himself. Judicial review, thus defined, is said to uphold the constitutional principles of separation of powers and of federalism by keeping within their assigned systemic orbits the two "political branches of the national government" and the states. As the overseer of the "judicial branch" of the national government, the Supreme Court also sees that lower court judges keep within their assigned rotations and revolutions around the axis that constitutes The Law, as defined in the decisions of the Supreme Court. The Supreme Court thus emerges as something more than the superego (to use a modern idiom) of the American constitutional polity; its role is even more majestic, since the Court is expected to play God for the American political universe by preventing tyranny, upholding the union, preserving democracy, and (incidentally) righting all legal wrongs—or at least all those that rise to constitutional stature—to boot.

A principal difficulty with such an idealized conception of the function of the Supreme Court is not so much what it says but what it leaves unsaid. Judges would have to be demigods to live up to the expectations of the stated ideal, which demands that they function like Plato's philosopher-kings; but American judges are only too human.[5] To take as an example those who scintillate as the "most dazzling jewel in the judicial crown of the United States," as one writer puts it,[6] Supreme Court justices sometimes bicker with each other at oral argument or when opinions are being read (to say nothing of what they say in their written opinions, for posterity to read); several of them have looked upon the Court as merely a stepping stone to higher political office—and have guided their behavior as justices accordingly; others have clung to the office, long after blindness, senility, or terminal and incapacitating illnesses have rendered them unfit to continue, for a variety of very human reasons, ranging from the felt responsibility for the support of relatives (in either an economic or a psychological sense) to the fear that the incumbent President might appoint an extremist from the other political party as one's successor; and still others have perished, in Byronesque fashion, quite literally in the arms of their mistresses. Such human failings, however, are not well known among the general public, and the general standard of deportment of the justices has been very high. Consequently, the United States Supreme Court is the model that much of the rest of the civilized world—including most of the new political societies of Africa and Asia—seeks to emulate in their own judicial systems.

The Supreme Court does occasionally argue on constitutional grounds its disagreement with statutory policies of the Congress, but such decisions declaring acts of Congress invalid have averaged considerably less than one per term during the past quarter of a century, and their policy impact has been confined almost entirely to the status and rights of national citizenship, especially in the context of civil-military and foreign relations.[7] Decisions announcing the unconstitutionality of national statutes constitute an almost imperceptible fragment of the function of the lower national courts and have considerably less effect upon the political system—in part because the Supreme Court's decisions since 1937 have been based exclusively upon civil liberties grounds, and the generally more conservative judges of the lower national courts have tended to uphold the military (and therefore the constitutionality of the challenged legislation); in part because of the limited territorial jurisdiction of the lower courts; but most importantly because the lower court decisions are almost always subject to Supreme Court review. Cases such as the Steel Seizure decision of 1952 (in which David Pine, a United States District Judge for the District of Columbia, ruled [with the subsequent approval of a Supreme Court majority] that President Truman had violated the Constitution by placing certain steel mills under paper government control to prevent a labor strike which would have crippled defense production during the Korean War) are few and far between, in any courts, national or state. Nor does the evidence suggest that the rare decision in which a majority of Supreme Court justices shout "Check!" at the President has had the presumably salutary effect of keeping the Presidency in rein, to say nothing of rendering it mated. The most effective restraints upon both the Presidency and the Congress have been those imposed by other components of the national political system.[8] Judicial review of administrative action is primarily a function of the lower national courts, and the Supreme Court at least purports to intervene primarily in order to lay down new policy guidelines for the courts of appeals.[9] On the other hand, it has been the Supreme Court itself that has been most active in making policy for the states in cases raising claims of civil liberties under the national Constitution. Civil liberties questions less frequently reach the Supreme Court through the lower national courts, usually when plaintiffs ask a United States district court to follow equity procedure (which we shall explain below) and enjoin state officials from acting in a manner that is claimed to violate national civil rights. In the major policy fields of racial integration and legislative reapportionment, cases raising the most important questions have reached the Supreme Court through both channels, directly from the state courts and indirectly through the lower national courts. Frequently, the latter channel involves "direct appeals" from three-judge district courts. The enforcement of such policies, however, quite clearly has been a function of neither the Supreme Court nor the state judicial systems but, rather, has been a major job of the national courts of appeals and district courts.[10] In many other relatively less well publicized components of national civil liberties policy, the Supreme Court has been equally active in reviewing state court decisions to persuade the states to liberalize their policies in regard to such varied questions as police methods of search and seizure; the rights of indigent criminal defendants to counsel and to appellate review of trial court decisions; and the disintegration of religious influence in the public schools. (These substantive policy questions are discussed in some detail in Chapters Five and Six.) It is in the review of civil liberties claims against the states that the Supreme Court has come closest to living up to the ideal portrait with which we introduced the present discussion.

By far the larger function of the national courts, certainly in terms of the number of decisions and perhaps in terms of impact upon the American polity as well, lies not in "constitutional interpretation" but in the judicial interpretation of national statutes, administrative regulations and decisions, judicial regulations (such as the procedural rules for the national courts), and judicial decisions. In legal theory, the analogous forms of state lawmaking are interpreted by the state's own courts, not by the national courts. This may help to explain, in part, why the Supreme Court employs constitutional interpretation actively in regard to state law but rarely in regard to national law. The various forms of national law all can be reinterpreted by the Supreme Court to have a meaning consistent with the policy views of a majority of the justices. This obviates the necessity for the more open and direct clash between the Court and other major national decision-makers, while at the same time accomplishing the same result as judicial review: the substitution of the Court's policy for the one initially made by another decision-maker.

## A QUANTITATIVE ANALYSIS

Both district courts and courts of appeals decide civil and criminal cases, and this constitutes, in one sense, their most important function. In addition, the courts of appeals have a specialized function of administrative supervision. The district courts have a different function of administrative supervision, as well as many primarily administrative tasks.

Table III shows the number of cases, in each of these categories, that were docketed in a recent year. The naturalization of aliens and the approval of passport applications, which constitute the largest number of items for the district courts, are direct administrative functions that require only a small amount of judicial time for their accomplishment. Bankruptcy and parole are next most numerous, and together they constitute about half as many cases (approximately 175,000) as are in the direct administrative category. Bankruptcy and parole cases require administrative supervision by the district courts and consume, relatively, considerably more judicial time. The judges must appoint referees to supervise the management of estates in bankruptcy, and approve their decisions. Parole supervision is closely related to the sentencing of convicted criminals, either under the more traditional system in which the judge determines sentences or under the newer "flexible" procedures of indeterminate sentencing through which the judge delegates much of his discretion to the parole (administrative) officials. Very few of either these direct or these supervisory administrative functions of the district courts are reviewed by the courts of appeals. Even in the bankruptcy cases, which are among the exclusive functions of the national court system, less than a tenth of 1 per cent are appealed beyond the district court level.

The district courts docket almost thirty times as many civil and criminal cases as do the courts of appeals, but only about 11 per cent in each category go to trial; the remainder are resolved by negotiation and agreement between the parties. There were 6260 civil trials in 1962, about half of which were tried with a jury. Almost three fourths of the 3788 criminal cases that went to trial, however, involved the participation of petit juries (we shall discuss in the next chapter the difference between grand and petit juries). The average allocation of the time of the district courts is about 3 to 1 in favor of the

TABLE III

Major Components of Decision-Making of Lower National Courts (1962)

| Type of case | District courts | Courts of Appeals |
|---|---|---|
| United States civil | 19,793 | 936 |
| Private civil | 38,203 | 1,508 |
| Total civil | 57,996 | 2,444 |
| Criminal | 34,392 | 622 |
| Total, civil and criminal | 92,388 | 3,066 |
| Administrative appeals | —— | 1,024 |
| Bankruptcy | 137,709 | 128 |
| Parole | 36,663 | —— |
| Aliens naturalization | 98,573 | —— |
| Passport application | 249,655 | —— |

civil cases. Moreover, the courts of appeals review proportionately almost two and a half times more civil cases tried by the district courts: about 40 per cent of the civil cases (2444 out of about 6200) but only about 16 per cent (622 out of about 3800) of the criminal cases. Therefore, the ratio of civil to criminal cases docketed by the courts of appeals is about 4 to 1 (2444 to 622), but criminal appeals constitute less than a sixth of the total caseload of the courts of appeals, and their disposition requires an even smaller proportion of the time of these appellate courts. The point is that both the district courts and the courts of appeals give most of their time and attention to civil cases—i.e., to what are predominantly questions of property rights rather than personal rights.

About three fourths of the cases reviewed by the courts of appeals come from the district courts, but the remaining quarter constitute many of the most complicated and important policy questions. The latter come under the rubric of what lawyers call "administrative law," and they are appealed directly from the so-called regulatory commissions, from one of the specialized national courts, or from the executive departments. For example, almost 10 per cent of all the cases docketed with the courts of appeals come from the National Labor Relations Board, either as Board petitions to have a court order the enforcement of the Board's decision or as petitions from private litigants who seek to have a court declare invalid an order or proposed action of the Board. Only about 5 per cent of these N.L.R.B. cases come before the Court of Appeals of the District of Columbia; the remainder are divided among the courts of appeals for the ten numbered circuits. About 5 per cent of the cases docketed with the courts of appeals consist of attempts, either by the Tax Division of the Department of Justice or by counsel for taxpayers, to overturn decisions of the Tax Court of the United States. Practically none of these cases come before the District of Columbia Court of Appeals. This court does, however, somewhat specialize in the supervision of administrative decision-making, in addition to its special function in relation to the municipal courts of the District of Columbia and its general function in relation to the usual jurisdiction of United States district courts. About 7 to 8 per cent of the cases docketed with the courts of appeals consist of appeals from a large variety of regulatory commissions and administrative agencies, including the Civil Aeronautics Board, the Federal Communications Commission, the Federal Power Commission, the Federal Trade Commission, the Secretary of Agriculture, the Securities and Exchange Commission, the Immigration and Naturalization Service of the Department of Justice, and the Court of Tax Appeals of the District of Columbia. Of these, about a third go to the Court of Appeals of the District of Columbia, while another third go to the Courts of Appeals for the Ninth (Far West) and the Fifth (Deep South) Circuits. Most appeals from the Interstate Commerce Commission (it will be recalled) do not come to the courts of appeals at all but go instead to special three-judge district courts, which has the nominal effect of "expediting" the disposition of such cases and the practical effect of maximizing the probability that the Supreme Court will review the trial courts' decisions in such cases. Since the Supreme Court, at the present time, has a more liberal orientation than the great majority of the panels of the courts of appeals, the effect of by-passing the courts of appeals in most I.C.C. (and other three-judge district court) cases is to provide a more liberal base for policy-making in appellate review than obtains generally for cases that must be filtered through the courts of appeals.

The "United States" (viz., the five divisions of the courts subsystem of the Department of Justice) was the plaintiff in about two thirds and the defendant in the remaining cases classified as "United States civil" in Table III. Of the "private civil" cases in that table, almost half are diversity-of-citizenship cases, over a third raise "federal questions," and the remaining sixth are "local" cases. We have already explained what lawyers mean by "diversity" and "federal question" jurisdiction; for present purposes, we shall simply summarize by stating that "diversity" cases—the most numerous subcategory of the "private civil" cases—require that the national courts apply what they understand to be public policy of the various states in regard to questions that are conceptualized, for substantive purpose, as being matters of "state law"; while, quite to the contrary, in "federal question" cases the national courts are asked to interpret the Constitution, statutes, administrative orders and regulations, and the judicial decisions that embody the policies of the national political system. In deciding diversity cases, the United States district courts are supposed to follow the policy guidance of the state courts, while in deciding federal question cases, the district courts are supposed to follow the policy guidance of the Supreme Court and of the courts of appeals for their own circuit. The third subcategory of "local" cases we have not previously discussed. These "local" cases arise exclusively in the national territories, and they consist (like the diversity cases) of policy questions that are decided, in the states, by state courts. They differ from the diversity cases in two respects: (1) they include many types of questions that rarely can involve diversity of citizenship among the parties; and (2) in terms of policy guidance for United States district courts, they are like federal question rather than diversity cases, since there is no relevant "state law" and the national political system, in combination with the local political system in each territory, makes the policy norms that are supposed to guide the territorial district courts.

The largest subcategory of the diversity category consists of tort cases, and the most frequent type of tort, about 7000 in 1962, was "motor vehicle, personal injury" claims. The major subcategories of the federal question cases were "marine, tort, personal injury," about 3700; "marine, contract," about 2200; "antitrust, electrical equipment industry," about 1700; and Federal Employers' Liability Act, about 1100.

There were over 7000 local cases in 1962, of which over 50 per cent arose in the District of Columbia. The largest subcategory of local cases—2750—consisted of insanity commitments; 96 per cent of these were in the District of Columbia. Second were about 1200 "motor vehicle, personal injury" claims, and third were some 466 domestic relations cases. These three together comprised over 60 per cent of all local cases in the national courts.

Approximately 35,000 criminal cases were docketed by the district courts in 1962, and a majority of these were sufficiently serious to have been based upon indictment by a grand jury. About four fifths of the total were classified among the following eight categories: embezzlement and fraud; liquor and internal revenue; forgery and counterfeiting; auto theft; larceny; immigration; narcotics; and juvenile delinquency.

Of the approximately 35,000 criminal defendants in 1962, some 86 per cent were convicted either of the offenses with which they were charged or of lesser offenses. The highest rates of conviction were for violations of the immigration laws (96 per cent of 2349) and for forgery (94 per cent of 2887); the lowest rates were for the defendants in antitrust prosecutions (61 per cent of 114) and for defendants charged with perjury (50 per cent of 32). Of the 28,511 persons who were sentenced, half received jail terms that averaged two and two-thirds years, and 40 per cent were placed on probation; the remaining 9 per cent received fines only. Analyses of trial time indicate that antitrust and robbery cases require, on the average, about the same amount of time in court. But analyses of the types of sentence, in relation to the types of crime, suggest a consistent relationship between judicial leniency and the social status of the defendants: businessmen convicted of violations of economic regulatory legislation simply do not go to jail.[11] None of the sixty-nine businessmen sentenced for violation of the antitrust laws were imprisoned or even put on probation, sixty-six were fined, and three received "other" punishment. Similarly, none of the businessman defendants convicted of violations of the Motor Carrier Act went to jail, although 86 per cent were fined, 11 per cent were put on probation, and 3 per cent received "other" punishment. Of the 283 bank robbers, however, 83 per cent were sentenced to five or more years in jail, and, similarly, 82 per cent of the 875 violators of the narcotics acts (other than the Marihuana Tax Act and the border registration legislation) were sent to jail for five or more years.

A QUALITATIVE ANALYSIS

In the most general sense, both the national and the state judicial systems have the function of resolving conflicts of interest between persons. The parties to cases decided by the courts range in numbers from the solitary individual, who frequently is the *in forma pauperis* defendant in a criminal case, to the complex bureaucracy such as the Department of Justice which, in the name of an even more huge and diffuse and complex aggregate called "the United States," prosecutes him. But armies and policemen and psychiatrists also resolve conflicts; the peculiar and characteristic function of courts is to legitimatize proposed solutions to conflicts so that acceptance is consensual among observers as well as parties to judicial proceedings. In the latter sense, all of society is indirectly an "observer of the proceedings." As the next two chapters will show, a judicial system transforms a heterogeneous aggregate of demands and interests into a much more homogeneous and stereotyped set of responses. By a process that results in immense oversimplification, a court substitutes limited and feasible goals—cast as imperative modes of behavior—for the much more extreme (and sometimes unlimited) demands that the opposing parties have made upon each other. By thus reducing relative chaos to relative order, the most basic function of judicial systems is to extend the bounds of rationality in human behavior.

The national judicial system has the particular function of legitimizing acts of the other subsystems of the national political system, and the Supreme Court has the additional function of legitimizing the acts of the lower courts in the national judicial subsystem. The Supreme Court's most difficult function, however, is to attempt to legitimize its own acts; this is why the robes and ritual, the formality of oral argument and opinion reading, the secrecy of discussion, and especially the writing and content of opinions are so important in the Court's decision-making process. Necessarily, the public image of the legitimacy of the Supreme Court is affected by the communications about the Court that are disseminated through the mass media.[12] Suggestions by Southern senators that the Chief Justice ought to be impeached because of his "softness" toward Communism, or addresses to the nation by the President charging (as Franklin Roosevelt did) members of the Court with being too old to hold down their jobs have the effect, and are intended to have the effect, of impairing the Court's ability to legitimize what the Court's critics perceive to be the undesirable policies that it has been sponsoring. The Supreme Court's own legitimacy, upon which hinges its capacity to legitimize the policies of the national political system, is therefore a question of fundamental political significance.

Sometimes a lag occurs in the restructuring of the values of a majority of the Supreme Court. The Court's values may then deviate more or less sharply from those of most of the other major actors in the national political system, who are more directly responsive to electoral changes. The restructuring of the values of the Court is a continuing process, produced primarily by personnel changes among the justices. When a lag persists or when it conspicuously exists during a time of national crisis, then tension between the judicial subsystem and the rest of the political system occurs, as exemplified by *Marbury* v. *Madison* (1803), *Dred Scott* v. *Sanford* (1857), *Pollock* v. *Farmers' Loan and Trust Co.* (1895), or *Schechter Poultry Corp.* v. *United States* (1935). A less important kind of lag occurs when the values of a majority of the Supreme Court have been brought into line with those of the current national majority but the values of a majority of the circuit and district judges remain unchanged. The obvious short-range solution to such a problem, since federal judges have life tenure, is the same as Lincoln's and Franklin Roosevelt's solution for lag on the Supreme Court: create a new majority by adding new judges. This is what the Kennedy administration did with the seventy-three new circuit and district federal judgeships created in 1961, and this is what the Eisenhower administration had done in 1954, after two long decades of a Democratic Presidency. It should be noted that what the Federalists attempted in 1801 was the opposite: they tried to reinforce an existing lag by packing the lower national courts with Federalists, thus *increasing* the gap between the value orientation of the judicial subsystem and that of the rest of the national political system.

The structure of the American polity is such, however, that even when the national judicial subsystem has been brought into accord with the rest of the national political system, substantial disequilibrium can occur between the national courts and state political systems because of the gross disjunction between the values of a majority of Supreme Court justices, on the one hand, and, on the other, of the local majorities (present or past) who dominate state policies on such issues as racial integration or legislative apportionment. Here, too, there is lag, but with the substantial difference that the lag lies in the traditional values accepted by discrete local popular pluralities—not necessarily majorities—rather than in the Supreme Court. Moreover, the political structure of Congress and of the American political party system and the method of electing the President are such that on issues such as racial integration and legislative reapportionment, national decision-makers whose own acts are indirectly but frequently subject to the legitimizing popular audit of the electoral process cannot assume the initiative in national policy-making. This does not mean that the Presidency and congressional majorities, or the popular pluralities whom they represent, are opposed to the Court's policies regarding race relations and political representation; to the contrary, it means that the rest of the political system can perform the indispensable function of legitimizing the policies of the Supreme Court, when the Court is the only national decision-maker in a position to assume the initiative in such policy-making. When President Eisenhower sent the National Guard to Little Rock in 1958, when President Kennedy sent United States marshals into Mississippi in 1962, and when Congress enacted the Civil Rights Acts of 1957, 1960, and 1964—the first such national legislation since the days of Reconstruction—the rest of the political system was legitimizing the fundamental national policy of racial integration in education, which the Supreme Court had assumed the initiative to make for the nation. But even more fundamental, in its implications, is the Court's policy in regard to political representation, for by insisting upon legislative reapportionment in the states and upon redistricting for Congress, on the basis of substantial equality among district populations, the Court is so restructuring the national and state political systems that these systems (1) will be more likely to continue to legitimize the Court's policy-making in other fields—to the extent, at least, that the Court itself represents majoritarian values—and (2) even more importantly, will be more in a position themselves to assume the initiative in policy-making and thereby tend to constrain the Court to its more usual function of legitimizing the decisions of other major actors in American political systems.

On the basis of our entire federal experience to date, however, it can be anticipated that there probably will continue to be policy problems that are national in scope but federal in their resolution, because of conflict between national and local majorities, which in turn frequently will lead to conflict between national and state political systems. We can expect that in such policy fields the Supreme Court will act in response to widespread political demands that the rest of the national political system is unable to satisfy. The classic statement of this point of view comes from Holmes who, speaking explicitly of his experience on (and with) the Supreme Court, remarked:

> I do not think the United States would come to an end if we lost our power to declare an Act of Congress void. I do think the Union would be imperiled if we could not make that declaration as to the laws of the several States. For one in my place sees how often a local policy prevails with those who are not trained to national views. . . .[13]

We have said that the basic function of any court is to resolve conflicts, that a particular function of the national courts is to legitimize the policies of the rest of the national political system, and that it is a particular function of the Supreme Court to illegitimize policies that are favored by local but opposed by national majorities. In the performance of all three of these mutually reinforcing functions, the national courts make the many decisions that were quantitatively summarized in the preceding section of this chapter. *In addition to* their obvious impact on the immediate parties to cases, such decisions are, in effect, policy directives to other political actors. And even when the national courts are legitimizing the policies of other actors, the judges charge a toll for their imprimatur: their price is the reformulation, sometimes in major respects and sometimes in detail, of the *others'* policies which *they* interpret. The Supreme Court, for example, issues policy directives to Congress and to state legislatures; occasionally to the Presidency or to governors but more often to national or to state administrative agencies; and frequently to local police officials (in regard to issues of search and seizure and of coerced confessions) and to local school boards (as in "released time" and "school prayer" as well as in racial integration cases). The Court also issues policy directives to guide the behavior of lawyers in their handling of future cases at both trial and appellate levels within the judicial system. Evidently, too, the Court's decisions (on such issues as school integration or Sunday closing) function as policy directives to the American public as well.

### HOW THE SUPREME COURT SUPERVISES LOWER COURTS

Technically, all of the Supreme Court's decisions (except for the fraction of 1 per cent decided in original jurisdiction)[14] take the form of orders *to lower courts*. The Court gives directions only indirectly, through the intervening action of lower courts, to administrators, legislators, school boards, and special interest groups; even the Court's orders to the immediate parties to a given case are given indirectly through lower courts. Typically, the Supreme Court's policy directives to lower courts assume one of three forms. The first two of these are overtly legislative in function, and they apply only within the national system.

#### FORMAL RULE-MAKING

The first category consists of rules of procedure, which are formulated largely by professional working groups of lower court judges, lawyers, and law professors and which are promulgated by the Supreme Court under statutory delegations of authority. (This process was described in greater detail in the preceding chapter.) These rules are intended to guide the process of decision-making in the trial (district) courts, and they are clustered under such major substantive legal categories as "civil law," "criminal law," "bankruptcy law," and "maritime and admiralty law." Such rules are subject to interpretation by the lower courts and by the Supreme Court in the same manner as are acts of Congress or administrative regulations.[15] In a statement protesting some amendments that accompanied the Chief Justice's report to Congress early in 1963 of draft *Rules of Civil Procedure* for the United States district courts, Justices Black and Douglas argued that the Supreme Court's participation in the rule-making process was unconstitutional:

> MR. JUSTICE BLACK and MR. JUSTICE DOUGLAS are opposed to the submission of these rules to the Congress under a statute which permits them to "take effect" and to repeal "all laws in conflict with such rules" without requiring any

affirmative consideration, action, or approval of the rules by Congress or by the President. We believe that while some of the Rules of Civil Procedure are simply housekeeping details, many determine matters so substantially affecting the rights of litigants in lawsuits that in practical effect they are the equivalent of new legislation which, in our judgment, the Constitution requires to be initiated in and enacted by the Congress and approved by the President. The Constitution, as we read it, provides that all laws shall be enacted by the House, the Senate, and the President, not by the mere failure of Congress to reject proposals of an outside agency. Even were there not this constitutional limitation, the authorizing statute itself qualifies this Court's power by imposing upon it a solemn responsibility not to submit rules that "abridge, enlarge or modify any substantive right" and by specifically charging the Court with the duty to "preserve the right of trial by jury as at common law and as declared by the Seventh Amendment to the Constitution." Our chief objections to the rules relate essentially to the fact that many of their provisions do "abridge, enlarge or modify" substantive rights and do not "preserve the right of trial by jury" but actually encroach upon it.[16]

After exemplifying their argument with several pages of more detailed specifications, Justices Black and Douglas concluded that the Supreme Court's participation was also dysfunctional:

> The present rules . . . are not prepared by us but by Committees of the Judicial Conference designated by THE CHIEF JUSTICE, and before coming to us they are approved by the Judicial Conference. . . . The Committees and the Conference are composed of able and distinguished members and they render a high public service. It is they, however, who do the work, not we, and the rules have only our imprimatur. The only contribution that we actually make is an occasional exercise of a veto power. If the rule-making for Federal District Courts is to continue under the present plan, we believe that the Supreme Court should not have any part in the task; rather, the statute should be amended to substitute the Judicial Conference. The Judicial Conference can participate more actively in fashioning the rules and affirmatively contribute to their content and design better than we can. Transfer of the function to the Judicial Conference would relieve us of the embarrassment of having to sit in judgment on the constitutionality of rules which we have approved and

which as applied in given situations might have to be declared invalid.[17]

In addition, there are the procedural rules that each national court, including the Supreme Court, makes for itself under a statutory delegation of authority that began in the Judiciary Act of 1789.[18]

INFORMAL RULE-MAKING

The second category arises from a much more recent practice of the Court, begun barely two decades ago,[19] of announcing procedural rules in the opinions of the Court's majorities. These rules are intended to regulate the national police in their treatment of criminal defendants during investigations of crimes. The sanction behind these procedural rules is the Court's directive to the district courts not to receive as evidence information obtained from defendants in violation of the rules. Thus the Court uses what are in effect direct orders to lower court judges in order to extend its policy control over the national police. The purported power base for such policy directives is the Supreme Court's claim to "inherent" supervisory authority over lower national courts. In order to attempt to accomplish similar policy control over state and local police, the Supreme Court must infer analogous procedural norms to be a "requirement of the Constitution"—usually, as a part of the revealed meaning of the Fourteenth Amendment's due process clause.[20]

DECISIONAL RULE-MAKING

The third category of Supreme Court rule-making consists of the *ad hoc* and discrete orders that accompany the disposition of particular cases. From what they perceive to be logically related sets of decisional "rules," judges and law professors infer principles of "decisional law." In a few instances, quite elaborate attempts have been made to specify the precise, internally consistent content of the "decisional rules" associated with particular (and presumably homogeneous) sets of decisions, of which the work done on the "right to counsel" cases affords an example.[21] These so-called principles of law are not to be confused with the orders that direct lower courts in the disposition of particular cases; the latter are called the "mandates" of the Court.

There is a jurisdictional decision for almost every case that is docketed with the Supreme Court. Certiorari petitions are by far the most common type of review process, and denials of certiorari are by far the most common type of jurisdictional decision. If the Court accepts jurisdiction, then it grants the writ of certiorari and sched-

ules the case for oral argument, unless the case is decided summarily on the merits at the same time that the jurisdictional decision
is announced. Technically, the writ is an order to a lower court
directing that it transmit to the Supreme Court the record of the
proceeding before the lower court. A summary decision of the Court,
on the merits of the question or questions that the Court was asked
to decide in the certiorari petition, is one in which the Court acts
on the basis of the information in the certiorari briefs (pro and
con) plus the record of antecedent court action, without the benefit
(as the phrase goes) of having heard oral argument; presumably,
the issues presented in cases decided summarily are so clear that
oral argument would not change the voting alignment of the justices.
The most usual function of the certiorari grant with summary affirmance or reversal is to decide satellite cases by per curiam order
(i.e., by an anonymous statement of the decision for "the whole
Court"). The "satellites" are cases docketed at about the same
time and raising the same policy issue as some other case that the
Court has decided formally (i.e., on the merits after oral argument
and with an assigned opinion for the Court written by a designated
justice).

Other than certiorari, the most common process for review by
the Court is the jurisdictional statement (with accompanying brief)
for an appeal. As we discussed earlier, appeals from state courts
are now handled by the Court much as if they were certiorari petitions. In certiorari cases, the Court "grants" the writ, while if the
Court decides to accept an appeal or decision on the merits, the
jurisdictional decision that it announces is to "note probable jurisdiction" in the case, which means that the case then is scheduled
for oral argument. Most appeals from state courts, however, are
"dismissed" (not "denied," as are certiorari petitions) with a stereotyped reason that is no more informative than the silence that
accompanies certiorari denials.

Almost all appeals from the national courts come directly from
three-judge district courts. In order to appear to adhere to the principle that there shall be at least one stage of appellate review for
all cases, the Supreme Court must seem to make decisions "on the
merits" in all such cases. Most such decisions, however, are summarily made and most are summary affirmances; that is, the Court
notes probable jurisdiction and then proceeds, without hearing oral
argument or entertaining briefs from the parties on the substantive
merits of the issues, to announce its affirmance of the decision below.

The Court has available and utilizes three alternative forms of
mandate in order to signify summarily its agreement with the decisions of lower courts. Which form it invokes depends upon the
type of review process (certiorari or appeal) and the type of lower

court (state or national) associated with the case. In certiorari cases, the Court frequently expresses summary agreement by denying the writ; in appeals from state courts, the Court accomplishes the same purpose by dismissing the jurisdictional statement; and in appeals from United States district courts, the Court summarily affirms, on the merits, the decision of the lower court.

There is, however, one manifest difference between the form in which jurisdictional decisions are made, as between certiorari and appeals cases. The certiorari decisions are listed in what is now called the "Orders" category, which means that they are collected at the rear of each volume of the *United States Reports*. It is not customary but neither is it uncommon for certain dissenting justices to announce their voting position, and occasionally a dissenting or concurring opinion may accompany the announcement of such jurisdictional decisions. The per curiam decisions, however, have since 1957 all (instead of selectively, as was true earlier) been reported among the formal decisions; and now per curiams are grouped in clusters which alternate with clusters of the formal decisions that comprise the greater bulk of each volume.

The per curiam decisions generally may be characterized as follows: (1) each is accompanied by an anonymous opinion "for the whole Court," and it seems probable that most per curiam opinions are written either by the Chief Justice or for him by one of his four law clerks; (2) although the per curiam decision sometimes is used for cases that have gone through oral argument, this is unusual, since it is primarily used in order to dismiss state appeals and to affirm appeals from the national district courts; (3) per curiam decisions rather than "orders" are used for jurisdictional and jurisdictional/summary appeals dispositions in order to maintain the fiction that all appeals cases are decided on the merits, since appeals are stated (in the act of Congress authorizing the Supreme Court to exercise such appellate jurisdiction) to be a legal right; (4) summary certiorari decisions are made per curiam, irrespective of whether they come from national or from state courts; and (5) dissenting and concurring opinions are filed in the nonjurisdictional and nonsummary per curiam decisions to about the same extent as in formal decisions.

# Decision-Making Procedures

Judicial decision-making procedure can be regarded as a continuum of behaviors. The series of successive decisions in a single case—the trial decision, the decision at the first stage of appellate review, the decision at the second stage of appellate review, etc.—are the "sections" of the continuum; within each such section, we can identify half a dozen "segments" that correspond to developmental stages in the process of decision-making. The following concepts afford a generalized way of talking about all of the discrete behaviors within any particular segment of a section of the continuum: initiation, accommodation, persuasion, decision, implementation, reconsideration. This set of concepts is sufficiently general to subsume all of the legal categories—many of which are overlapping and logically inconsistent—with which we must deal. Lawyers use some, but not all, of these concepts with meanings similar to ours.

**TRIALS**

INITIATION

Cases are initiated, for potential decision-making by courts, because of conflicts of interests among persons in the political society in the name of which the courts act. From a legal point of view, some persons "injure" others by committing or threatening to commit "wrongs" which are defined (tautologically) as violations of the "rights" of the person injured. The task of courts is to provide remedies—frequently in the form of mandated substitutions for irreparable losses—with the objective of "righting wrongs" or of preventing them, to the extent possible. Under this view, it is clear that the fundamental objective of courts is to maintain, or to restore, the *status quo ante delictum*. This goal is in close accord with the concept of homeostasis which, as stated in Chapter One, usually is associated with systems theory and analysis. It can be and is argued that the primary goal of the judicial system is to protect individual rights.[1] But it also can be and is argued that the primary goal is to settle disputes—to maintain order.[2] Empirically, both points of view tend to be represented, and in competition with each other, in functioning judicial systems. For reasons that we shall discuss in Chapter Six, liberals tend to stress the importance of protecting individual rights, while conservatives emphasize the importance of conflict resolution—of stability.

Both of these perspectives are too narrow, however, from a political point of view which perceives courts as instruments that can be used by persons to aggrandize their own power and influence. The judicial system is seen as merely one among many alternative instrumentalities that may appropriately be invoked—singly, in sequence, or several simultaneously—in order to realize political ends. Consequently, the moralistic overtones of both individual "right and wrong" and societal "good" become displaced by considerations of strategy and tactics for manipulating judicial systems.

The vocabulary used to describe court procedures was developed by lawyers, not by political scientists. Therefore, if we are to stay within a realm of discourse that encompasses practically all of the published work on this subject, we must use concepts that clearly presume the legal point of view, even though our own assumption is that the political perspective is at least equally relevant.

From such a legal point of view, there is a basic distinction between civil and criminal cases. In civil cases, the conflict of interest is between or among individuals or groups of individuals, one or more of whom has a complaint against another or others. If the parties have made an agreement to act in concert in order better to accomplish some common and legal objective, then the failure of one party to carry out his part of the bargain is an offense against the rights of the other party or parties to the contract, and he or they may seek to have the offense redressed by filing a complaint in the appropriate court. Other injuries, which may lead to a judicial finding of private liability in the absence of a contractual relationship, are classified as torts.

Crimes are torts against society. Many local communities still rely upon the older system of private prosecution for many petty offenses. This requires some individual or individuals to assume the initiative in "bringing malefactors to justice" by appearing before a magistrate to swear out a complaint against the particular defendant or defendants who are accused of having committed designated wrongs, which are defined by law to be offenses against the interests of the state—as well as often being private torts against the injured individuals. Once the complaint has been filed, however, the remainder of the function of prosecuting the defendant is assumed by the government of which the court is a part. In regard to most minor offenses and practically all major crimes, however, court action is initiated by the filing of complaints by police officers, with the result that both initiation and the subsequent steps in prosecution are made by the employees of the government. Although in most states the title of criminal cases is "The People of the State of X versus John Doe," the parties whose immediate interests appear to be in conflict in most criminal cases are the police and prosecutor, on the one hand, and the defendant, on the other hand.

There are technical and historical differences between the initiation of complaints, in civil procedure, at law and at equity, but we shall notice in subsequent discussion only such major differences as the use of juries and the form of verdicts. The party who initiates a case, in both civil and criminal procedure, is the "plaintiff"; the opposing party who is required to answer the complaint is the "defendant." The initiation of criminal procedure is more complicated than the relatively simple filing of a complaint, which civil procedure requires. Closely associated with the criminal complaint are supporting administrative procedures. Usually the police investigate the alleged offense. In cases involving serious crimes, either the police alone or they in cooperation with investigators working directly under the prosecuting attorney undertake to apprehend, arrest, temporarily confine, and interrogate various suspects, often including the person who subsequently becomes the defendant in the case. The counterpart in civil procedure of these investigatory activities in criminal procedure consists of the consultation between the plaintiff and his counsel, and the latter's inquiry into the facts alleged by his client and also into the law (the policy norms) that he predicts most likely to be applied by the court or courts in which he might file a complaint on behalf of the plaintiff.

In criminal procedure, the functional equivalent of the civil complaint is the filing of a paper with a court, charging a named person (who thereby becomes a defendant) with explicit offenses. Such a charge must state both the law which allegedly has been violated and also the relevant facts in a general way—that is, the specific acts of the defendant that are presumed to constitute the stated violation of law. There are two principal ways in which such charges are filed. The most common method, used exclusively in about half of the states and for lesser offenses in the remaining states and in the national judicial system, is for the prosecutor and his staff, without recourse to jury proceedings, to decide to file an initiating complaint called an "information." The other common method, used in about half of the states and in the national judicial system to bring charges against defendants accused of serious crimes, requires that a grand jury rather than the prosecutor make the formal decision whether to file a complaint against a suspect.

The grand jury usually consists of from one to two dozen persons who are selected—presumably at random—from a list of qualified citizens maintained by the clerk of the court. There is a presumption that a grand jury represents a cross section of the dominant opinions in a community. This notion long since has been discredited as a legal fiction. The universal practice is to exempt those classes of citizens who would be best qualified (by education, by awareness, and by involvement in the affairs of the community) to serve as jurors. The consequence, for both grand juries and also for the petit juries to be discussed below, is that jury panels are loaded with middle-aged housewives whose children are grown, with semi-professional jurors for whom the juror's fee provides an attractive day's wages, and with "senior citizens" who come out of retirement to serve as jurors. Far from constituting a sample representative of the community, such a grand jury appears (from a political point of view) to be a sample biased toward conservatism and dogmatism[3] relative to whatever would be average on these dimensions for a particular community. The prosecutor appears before such a group, which convenes in the courthouse in secret proceedings, and presents his charges and evidence. If the group votes (by a majority or some other requisite proportion or quantity of jurors) to accept the prosecutor's charges, then a suspect is indicted; otherwise, he is not charged with the crime. The "indictment" is technically the statement of charges that the grand jury directs to be filed in the court. Where the grand jury participates in the initiation of criminal cases, the prosecutor must share part of his decision-making authority with the jury, just as when trial by jury is used, the judge must share part of his decision-making authority with the petit jury.

Another kind of complaint, known as the "presentment," occasionally emanates from grand juries. Here the jury acts on the basis of information "of its own knowledge," which necessarily is acquired by having the jury itself supervise police investigatory activities. Instead of having the prosecutor select what part of his evidence he chooses to put before the grand jury, in support of charges that he has decided upon, the jury (at least in form) draws upon funds and personnel made available to it by the court and conducts its own investigation. The practical difference is that such investigations almost invariably are sallies into local politics as much as, or more than, they are inquisitions into local crime. This is evidenced by the kinds of complaints that are made to the court; often, a presentment will inform the court that gambling and vice are rampant in the community, and instead of charging specific individuals with indictable offenses, the presentment will charge the community at large with "moral laxity" and with "responsibility" for the cited evils. Evidently, the objective is to influence public opinion and political behavior rather than to initiate criminal proceedings in court against any defendant in particular. Presentments are relatively rare in state judicial systems, and they are practically unknown in the national judicial system.

In addition, a few states, of which Michigan is the best example, sometimes employ what is known as the "one-man grand jury."[4] This is not a grand jury at all but, rather, consists of a judge assigned to direct a special investigating staff. In the latter respect, the device resembles the grand jury presentment described above. The judge, in his role as a "one-man grand juror," has witnesses brought before him—and under the earlier Michigan practice, which was held in part unconstitutional by the Supreme Court,[5] witnesses testified in secret, without benefit of counsel, and under physical circumstances (in hotel rooms, bars, and private dwellings) that often resembled a floating crap game more than a courtroom. Under present Michigan practice, the judge-juror no longer can summarily punish witnesses for contempt of court if he disbelieves their testimony. The judicial investigator proceeding has been used primarily as a political instrument when organized crime and official corruption (of the police, of the state legislature, of prosecutors) were so widespread that the usual method of investigation (by local prosecutors, with complaint by information) was ineffective. Some of the inquests, such as one into the unusual fiscal and sexual practices of the House of David and another into the gangster murder of several state legislators during prohibition days, made quite spectacular news at the time.

The ordinary methods for initiating criminal cases, and the only ones used in the national court system, are the information and indictment, under both of which the prosecutor shares only with the police the direction of the precedent investigation. At least in form, the laymen who comprise the grand jury displace the prosecutor in the direction of the investigation when a grand jury makes a presentment. And it is a judge who directs the police investigation when a "one-man grand jury" is used.

ACCOMMODATION

In civil procedure at common law in Shakespeare's day, the issue that the court was asked to decide was precisely defined by a complex (and, as it eventually became, quite stereotyped) series of alternative motions filed by the parties. These motions constituted the "pleadings" in the case. Any error in the prescribed form of such statements could result in a motion by opposing counsel to have the judge "quash" (dismiss) the complaint. Today more importance is attached to the substance than to the form of civil complaints, and auxiliary procedures have been developed to explore the issue further than can be done through the pleadings. One such procedure is that of "discovery," under which an attorney can ascertain, before the trial takes place, what sort of evidence opposing counsel has available for use; thus discovery is a procedure for developing consensus as to the facts of the case. Increasing use also is being made of pre-trial "conference," which brings opposing counsel and the judge together to discuss the "case"—that is, the evidence and the arguments—that each party expects to present, and the result is that greater consensus with regard to the legal issues develops among all of the principal actors in the impending trial. Another consequence of the conference is that the opposing counsel often will agree to "stipulate"—that is, to agree upon a statement, which becomes part of the record— concerning many of the "facts" that initially were in dispute. This reduces the costs of a trial, since most of the time at a trial is devoted to attempts to introduce, or to preclude the introduction of, evidence that is intended to support one set of inferences concerning "the facts" instead of various possible alternative versions. The general effect of these various pre-trial procedures, plus such others as direct negotiation between the opposing counsel, is to bring about a compromise settlement, "out of court" (as the newspaper phrase goes), of most complaints. It will be remembered that about 90 per cent of the civil cases filed in the national court system never go to trial.

About the same proportion of criminal complaints also are accommodated without a trial. In many, the complaint is in effect dismissed by the prosecutor for any of a variety of undisclosed reasons: because he thinks that his evidence, community sentiment, or the attitudes of the judge are such that his own "record" would be impaired if the case went to trial; because of the improbability of securing a conviction; because he believes the defendant to be innocent; because of political influence brought to bear in behalf of the defendant; because he has thereby purchased the cooperation of an undercover agent to assist him in subsequent investigations of more important suspects; etc. Similarly, many defendants who are guilty decide or are advised by counsel that the probabilities of their being convicted are so great that their best bet is to "throw themselves on the mercy of the court" and hope for some leniency in punishment in exchange for having "saved the government the expense of a trial." Most other complaints that do not go to trial are compromised, usually as the result of negotiations between defendant's counsel and the prosecuting attorney: the defendant either pleads guilty to a reduced charge, or he pleads guilty with what he understands to be an informal commitment concerning his sentence.[6]

These accommodations are formalized at a hearing called an "arraignment," which in the national court system is held before a United States commissioner rather than before a judge. At the arraignment, the defendant pleads to the initial or substitute charges that have been filed against him, unless at this time the charges are withdrawn on motion of the prosecutor. Only those cases go to trial in which the defendant's plea is "not guilty" or in which such a plea is entered for him because he "stands mute" (refuses to respond to the charge).

PERSUASION

The trial of a case consists of a public hearing, in a courtroom, at which a judge presides over argument between opposing counsel. In state judicial systems, most cases are decided by the judge alone, acting without a jury. In the national system, about half of the civil cases are decided without juries, as we observed in the preceding chapter, and so also are almost a fourth of the criminal cases. The reason for the decreasing use of juries, in both civil and criminal trials and in both state and the national judicial systems, is their high cost in terms of both time and money. Moreover, a trial before a jury is substantively a quite different kind of proceeding than a trial before a judge alone. A petit jury of twelve men or women (in the national courts, and as few as six in some state courts) consists of lay persons whose average socioeconomic and educational status is at or below the level of mediocrity.

In some states, but not in the national courts, special panels of "blue-ribbon" juries are established, from which particular juries are selected from time to time for criminal cases deemed important by the prosecutor. Such juries are biased to be above average in education and socioeconomic status, since they are packed with upper-middle-class white-collar and professional males. It is believed that such juries will vote for conviction more frequently than will juries drawn from the ordinary lists in the same community. It has been argued also that there is a built-in bias in favor of the United

States, in trials in the District of Columbia courts, because of the high concentration of national civil servants resident in the District, with the result that government employees predominate in the jury panels. Since they tend to identify themselves with the interest of their employer, they therefore (it is presumed) tend to vote pro-government as jurors.

Even when an above-average group of citizens comprise the jury, they are put in their role precisely because they are laymen—that is, because they are generally inexperienced in and ignorant of trial procedure. As a consequence, lawyers must appeal primarily to the beliefs and values of the jurors, and the introduction of evidence is directed not so much to the transcendental notion of trying to establish what "the facts" are, but rather to the much more directly significant question of what the jury will believe the facts to be. In most civil cases, where only a simple or extraordinary majority must agree in order for the jury to reach a decision, counsel can afford to ignore one or two jurors whose values are idiosyncratic and play instead for the majority sentiment; but in a criminal case, where unanimity is required for a decision, the prosecutor must convince every juror of the defendant's guilt, while the defense counsel has only to convince a single juror of his client's innocence. Or so, at least, it seems.

The petit jury has been used in Anglo-American criminal trial procedure for over eight centuries, but relatively little social scientific knowledge is available about jury behavior.[7] We do know that experienced trial lawyers do their best to manipulate, within the relatively narrow limits where choice can move, the value composition of juries by the blackballing procedure known as the examination of jurors *voir dire*: in the recent trial in Dallas of Jack Ruby for the video murder of Lee Oswald, chief defense counsel Melvin Belli so maneuvered that considerably more time was devoted to the selection of the jury than to the trial.

Research in jury decision-making is difficult to carry out because the secrecy of proceedings precludes direct observation of how real juries make decisions. Most work has been done either with simulated jury groups or with anecdotal materials provided by the reminiscences of ex-jurors. Recent experimental research suggests that when a pseudo-jury group is almost consensual on the initial ballot, the lone dissenter soon succumbs, in most instances, to social pressure to defer to what appears quite literally to be overwhelming majority opinion.[8]

In the realm of fiction, the public trial, which constitutes the most conspicuous ceremonial aspect of criminal procedure, is high-lighted, and even the casual viewers of television's Perry Mason might well conclude that the innocence or guilt of most criminal defendants is determined by the histrionic artistry of opposing counsel. Those who followed more closely the activities of Raymond Burr, the actor who portrays Perry and who in real life had become a very popular lecturer on the subject of criminal procedure before both bar and lay groups, might have noted a disillusioning national wire service release in 1963. Perry—that is to say, Mr. Burr—had made the mistake of attempting to defend himself against a civil complaint in an Arizona state court, and his lack of familiarity with the local procedures for accommodation had resulted in a decision for the plaintiff long before the case ever reached the stage where Mr. Burr— Perry, that is—might have had an opportunity to demonstrate his renowned ability to persuade judges and juries.[9] A more realistic fictional view is that presented in the best-selling novel of the late 1950's, *The Anatomy of a Murder* by "Robert Traver" (former Michigan Supreme Court Justice John D. Voelker), in which the drama of a criminal trial is of central importance but most of the action takes place offstage.

We know of no scientific research on the extent to which trial judges are persuaded by the arguments of counsel to modify their attitudes toward the policy issues that are either explicit or implicit in trials. Judges constantly are exposed to the arts of advocacy, and even after making due allowance for differences in personality types, it seems likely that experienced trial judges are influenced by the persuasion of counsel to the extent that the lawyers' arguments function as stimuli to activate responses that reflect the judges' underlying belief systems and accepted values. Of course, the actions that occur in the courtroom and that are directly observed by the trial judge also affect his perceptions of counsel, of witnesses, of parties, and therefore his attitude toward the policy issues with which these actors variously are identified.[10] Undoubtedly, too, the interaction between judges and counsel, both in and out of the courtroom, has an important effect upon the attitudes of judges *toward the lawyers* and therefore indirectly upon their judicial perceptions of the policy views advocated by the attorneys.[11] For example, social psychologists have shown that the *intensity* of interpersonal attitudes is positively correlated with, and probably is a direct function of, the *frequency* of interpersonal contacts.[12] From this general theoretical proposition, one ought logically to infer that the decisions of trial judges in criminal cases will be influenced most by the lawyers who appear most frequently before the court—in most criminal courts, the local prosecuting attorney. This is the kind of hypothesis about judicial behavior that appears to have a high probability of being confirmed by empirical evidence, not only at all levels in the judicial systems of the United States but in judicial systems throughout the world and in cultures that range from the most primitive to the most highly developed Western industrialized societies.[13] If such confirmation proved possible, notwithstanding the great diversity and vast cultural differences among the societies in which courts function,[14] it could only be because our hypothesis derives from a theoretical proposition that describes a very fundamental communality in human behavior—which applies to the relationship between judges and attorneys because they, too, despite their specialized sociopolitical roles, are human.

Of course, a judge influences a jury by his own demeanor, and lawyers are sensitive to the possibility of such influence, as demonstrated by the following brief excerpts from a trial record.[15] Judge Harold J. Medina presided over the trial, in the United States District Court for the Southern District of New York in New York City, of the then national leaders of the Communist party of the United States. Sacher and Gladstein and Isserman and Crockett were among the defense counsel who subsequently were tried and convicted, summarily and without a jury by Judge Medina, at the conclusion of the trial of the nominal defendants, on the basis of conversational exchanges between himself and these lawyers, including and typified by the following:

The Court: You mean that I will take disciplinary measures against you because you said I scratched my head? Don't be absurd, Mr. Sacher. Don't be absurd.

Mr. Sacher: The point I am making is that in every available means your Honor is conveying to the jury your lack of sympathy if not hostility to the defendants, their counsel's presentation of the case, and in these circumstances I want certainly to note on behalf of my clients a vigorous objection to your Honor's conduct and I wish to join Mr. Gladstein in the motion to declare a mistrial by the withdrawal of a juror.

The Court: Motion denied. (Pp. 3316–3317.)

. . . . .

The Court: I wish you would stop talking about nodding my head, scratching my head and pulling my ears. Why don't you leave that all out? What good does that do?

Mr. Isserman: Well, whether your Honor——

Mr. Crockett: Pardon me one minute. I think it is very important because there are some things that are not made a matter of record on the Court——

The Court: You haven't missed any of them.

Mr. Crockett: ——so far as the transcript is concerned. Very frequently I notice in the course of testimony your Honor

makes frequent glances over toward the jury or some facial
expression that gives the impression, to me at least, that the
Court——

The Court: Well, it is funny——

Mr. Crockett: Pardon me. I think that whenever it is so
obvious, as it was a while ago, some mention of it should be
made so that it will be carried in the record.

The Court: If there is something about my winking at
the jury or something of that kind, I am surprised that you
did not mention it at the time.

Mr. Crockett: No, I have not noticed a winking yet. If
I had I would have mentioned it. (Pp. 7269–7270.)

This kind of judicial influence on juries is, of course, a departure
from the official role of judges, even though it probably is to some
extent, intentionally or otherwise, present in all jury trials. (Even
if the judge were capable of preventing the emission of any cues, he
could not prevent individual jurors from imagining that he had
revealed his own attitude by his tone or gesture—as perceived by
the jurors.) However, there is a much more direct and "legitimate"
procedure by which a judge can influence the jury. When both
counsel have completed their introduction of evidence and their concluding speeches, in which they implore the jurors to vote in behalf
of their own respective clients, then the judge presents his "charge"
to the jurors before they retire from the courtroom to begin their
own task of persuading each other to agree. The judge's charge
purports to summarize in "lay language" (viz., English) the legal
jargon in which the relevant decision-making norms find expression
as the "law." The judge defines for the jury the issue or issues
that they are to decide, and in so doing he may comment selectively
on the "facts" as well as on the "law." Although some jurors may
be persuaded while others are antagonized by the judge's remarks,
it is inconceivable that juries generally are not influenced by the
judges who charge them; indeed, it is part of their respective roles
that the jury *should* be influenced by the judge's charge. Needless to
say, the judge's influence is maximal when he "directs" (i.e., orders)
the jury to report back to him a verdict which he specifies to them
and thus (at least in effect) preempts to himself the function of
jury as well as that of judge.

DECISION

The role of juries in judicial decision-making cannot be ignored,
but the right to trial by jury usually is waived by defendants in
both civil and criminal cases. In the state judicial systems, there

are many relatively less important cases for which no right to jury trial exists. In the national system, juries are not used in civil cases tried under either equity procedures or by the three-judge district courts, and juries rarely are used in trials under the admiralty rules of procedure. When juries do share with judges the decision-making function, their role in the United States district courts is restricted to complex inferences concerning the probability of occurrence of events which are alleged to have transpired before the invocation of judicial proceedings: such events are conceptualized as "facts," and the decision of a jury about facts is called a "verdict." The probability of a jury reaching an agreement concerning the facts is maximal when the decisional norm is simple majority rule; the likelihood of jury agreement is least when unanimity is required, as for the conviction of criminal defendants in the national courts. The jury's view of the facts is not the only one, nor is it by any means even the only view to get into the official record of the case; and opposing counsel and the judge and witnesses (among others) no doubt adhere to their own views, notwithstanding the verdict of the jury. But the jury's view of the facts is usually the most important set of perceptions, since the procedures for decision-making are so designed as to give the most weight to the jury's verdict.

Depending upon the demands of counsel and their disposition by the judge, a jury may be asked to bring in a general verdict or a set of special verdicts; that is, the questions that the jury is asked to decide may be cast in a relatively general or in specific form. The more general the issue that the jury is asked to decide, the greater its share in the decision. In many state judicial systems, juries are asked to assume a much larger share of the decision-making authority than are "federal" juries: some state juries are asked to decide the offense, its degree (in a legal sense), and the appropriate punishment if they agree that a defendant is guilty. However, the jury's verdict is subject not only to influence by the judge in all cases but also to his veto in at least some types of civil cases. If the trial judge's own perception of the facts is considerably at variance with that of the jury, he may usually do either or both of two things. In "discharging" (releasing) the jurors from their official roles, the judge may emphasize his disagreement by converting them into a captive audience who must suffer in silence (under threat of summary punishment for contempt of court) while he lectures them on their iniquities. (This kind of judicial behavior is intended, presumably, to deter future juries from pursuing a similar course of action, at least before this same judge; but it also has the incidental effect of getting into the record the *judge's* view of the facts, for whatever weight it may have if the case should be appealed to a higher court. It thus constitutes a covert invitation to the losing counsel to appeal the case.) An even stronger way in which the judge can manifest his disagreement is to substitute his own decision "n.o.v."—*non obstante verdictum*, notwithstanding the verdict—for that of the jury. This action differs from that of the directed verdict primarily in that here the jury is permitted to disagree and to assume the initiative in making the decision—and these are differences of some importance. The legal theory is that the "weight of the evidence" must so overwhelmingly support the judge's position, in the case of either directed verdicts or "n.o.v." judgments, that no rational (honest, unprejudiced, dispassionate, etc.) group of jurors possibly could disagree with him. Nevertheless, Supreme Court majorities not infrequently find themselves in agreement with juries rather than with trial judges. In regard, for example, to Federal Employers' Liability Act cases (where juries often vote that railroads must pay monetary compensation to injured railroad employees), the Supreme Court in 1956 reversed two affirmances, one by a United States court of appeals and the other by a state supreme court, of judgment for the defendant railroad, notwithstanding jury verdicts for the plaintiffs; and in the following term the Court reversed a state supreme court that had affirmed a state trial judge's directed verdict in favor of a railroad.[16]

The judge himself is supposed to decide questions of law; that is, he is supposed to rule upon disputed questions relating to the procedural norms that are presumed to guide the decision-making processes of the trial, and he also is supposed to decide the disputed questions of substantive policy which constitute the issues that purport to bring to a focus the underlying conflict of interests between the parties to the case. The final decision of the trial judge upon the latter issue (or set of issues) constitutes the "judgment" in the case. In the three-judge United States district courts, of course, the judgment depends upon the agreement of at least two of the participating judges. If there has been a jury trial, then there may be a delay after the announcement of the verdict before the judge announces the judgment, except that judgment customarily is pronounced immediately after verdicts of acquittal in criminal cases. If the judge has tried the case without a jury, then both his "statement of the facts" and his "conclusions of law" may be announced at the same time, although the rules for the United States district courts require that these decisions regarding questions of fact and questions of law be stated separately.

Together, the verdict and the judgment constitute what is usually and somewhat loosely called "the decision of the court," although in a more technical legal sense, the court's decision takes the form of an order requiring that some specified action be taken by, or in regard to, one or both of the parties to the case. The most usual (and the classic) forms of a decision are these: (1) in civil cases "at law," the court orders one of the parties to return property belonging to another, to pay the monetary equivalent of the property, or to pay monetary compensation for personal injury; (2) in civil cases in equity, the court's decree orders one party to do—or more often, to refrain from doing—some specified act or set of actions affecting the interests of the other party; and (3) in criminal cases, the defendant is either released from the custody of the court or detained for sentencing, usually at a later time. In many civil cases, the judge will request opposing counsel to agree upon the draft of a decree, after he has announced his judgment. As a result, the opposing counsel usually participate in the preparation of the order which the judge signs to dispose of the case. The legal theory is that once he has "clarified" the relevant legal principles, then the mere application of those principles to the (by now) authoritatively determined facts of the case is only a clerical matter that reasonable men (such as the opposing counsel) who are officers of the court will perform almost mechanically, thus relieving the court of the burden of drafting the decree. More realistically, however, the right of counsel to formulate the specific terms of the settlement is important as an additional means for accommodating and compromising the conflicts of interest that remain after what is thought of as the decision in the case has been made.

Most decisions of trial courts are announced orally, by judges who are talking to lawyers in open court. It is only in a small minority of the trials that written opinions are filed by the presiding judges. Moreover, by no means all of the written opinions of the United States district courts and courts of appeals are published. Rather incongruously, there is no official sponsorship of the printing of the written opinions of the district courts and courts of appeals, although there is official publication of the reports (opinions) of the Customs Court, the Court of Customs and Patent Appeals, the Court of Claims, and the Tax Court of the United States. The reports of the Supreme Court have been published by the government since 1882,[17] and a commercial law book company does publish many of the reports—for the district courts in what is called the *Federal Supplement* series and for the courts of appeals in the *Federal Reporter, Second Series* (F. 2d.).

IMPLEMENTATION

The implementation of the orders of trial courts is a function of the supporting administrative structures described in Chapter Two. The sanction behind orders for the transfer between the parties of money or property is the attachment by the United States marshal of the same or an equivalent amount of the property of the losing party, and if necessary the liquidation of the property through a distress sale. For civil decrees, in equity form, the sanction is the authority of the court summarily to punish disobedience of the order through an ancillary criminal proceeding, in which the judge is the prosecutor and the losing party is cast in the role of defendant against charges of contempt of the court. In criminal cases, convicted defendants are investigated by probation officers, upon whose report—together with whatever recommendations may have been made by the prosecuting attorney or by the petit jury—the judge places as much reliance as he chooses when deciding the sentence. The sentence may take the form of imprisonment, a monetary fine, probation, parole, or a combination of these. It will be recalled that the district judges of the national courts increasingly are being conditioned to utilize the indeterminate procedure for sentencing, which involves the allocation to presumably expert bureaucrats of a larger share, and to presumably inexpert (because they are generalists) judges a smaller share, in the decision-making function for implementing decisions in criminal cases.

Of course, what a United States district court can do to punish and/or rehabilitate a young man who drives a "hot" car across the George Washington Bridge from Manhattan to Fort Lee presents a very different kind of implementation problem than does a civil antitrust decree against one corporate giant (such as DuPont), ordering that it divest its dominating stock interest in another super corporation (such as General Motors). The complex interlocking relationships between two or more such corporations can well involve thousands—perhaps millions—of people over a period of more than forty or fifty years, while the casual theft of the car and its transportation in interstate commerce could be carried out, from inception near the New York end of the bridge to arrest upon arrival at the Jersey shore, by one individual in less than ten minutes. Typically, it takes from one to two *decades* from the early planning of a major antitrust case (such as the example above) through trial(s) and the exhaustion of appellate review to reach the point in the process—usually, the remand to the district court of the Supreme Court's remittitur—at which it is possible to start talking about implementation of the antitrust decree. When the district court finally confronts that problem, considerably more is involved than merely calling in the marshal or a probation officer. The "enforcement" of the court's decree will itself require many complicated decisions to be made by many people over an extended period of time. Implementation may involve not only the Presidency, the Congress, several divisions of the Department of Justice (including, of course, the Antitrust Division), the Treasury Department, the Securities and Exchange Commission, and the Department of Commerce, but many other agencies, both state and private as well as national. The trial court of necessity retains a continuing supervisory role in the proceedings, in order to assure that the monopolistic relationship is not resumed and that the court's orders are carried out. Within five to ten years *after* the "final" decree is approved by the trial court for administrative enforcement, one can expect that there will have been some changes made in the structure of the corporate relationships and in the functioning of the competitive relationships of the major industries involved in the antitrust prosecution.

### RECONSIDERATION

We have discussed implementation before reconsideration because in most cases there is no appeal from the decisions of trial courts. The data in Chapter Two indicate that no more than 5 per cent of the decisions of the district courts, in any of the major categories, are appealed, and the average is only 2 to 3 per cent. We might well, therefore, look upon reconsideration as an auxiliary subsystem into which are diverted a few of the cases that are channeled into the national judicial system for specialized processing before they are fed back into the main system for final processing.

There are three principal types of reconsideration. The first is that in which the counsel for either or both parties—since most decisions constitute a compromise between their conflicting claims—ask the trial judge to change his decision, in whole or in part. Such requests, almost routine in some types of cases, are rejected with equally routine uniformity, and they rarely lead to any change in the court's order. The usual purpose in asking for this type of reconsideration is to "complete the record" by having it show that all possible "remedies" have been exhausted before an appeal is filed. Appeal is the second, and by far the most common, type of reconsideration. The filing of an appeal to a higher court in either a civil or a criminal case constitutes the first step in the initiation procedure for the higher court; thus, in effect, it amounts to a recycling, although in somewhat different form, of the stages in the process just described for the trial courts. The third type of reconsideration, habeas corpus, is available ordinarily only to persons who are confined against their will. In the national judicial system, it applies primarily to prisoners in penitentiaries or jails, to persons held in detention centers by the immigration authorities, and to inmates of mental hospitals.

Originating in common law, habeas corpus is a petition to a judge, filed by the prisoner himself (*pro se*) or by his counsel or his "next friend" or a relative in his behalf, alleging that his detention is contrary to law and asking that the court inquire into the matter. If the judge is satisfied that the petition *prima facie* ("on its face") establishes grounds for reasonable doubt that the detention is legal, he directs the jailer to reply, and thus a suit is joined. As Chapter Two stated, this procedure is used primarily by state prisoners who seek to upset ("attack collaterally" is the legal phrase) their convictions by asking United States district judges to review (in effect) the decisions of the state courts. Of course, the legal theory is that the federal judges are concerned not with the guilt or innocence of the petitioners but only with the "constitutional" question— usually whether the conviction is contrary to the Fourteenth Amendment's guarantee of due process. The inevitable effect of the use of this procedure is that some prisoners are released from state jails on orders of federal district judges, because the policy norms accepted within the national judicial system are more liberal than the equivalent norms within the respective state judicial systems.

The second largest category of habeas corpus petitioners are federal prisoners in the custody of the United States Bureau of Prisons. For several reasons, this is a smaller group. There are far fewer federal than state prisoners. Federal rules of criminal procedure are generally more liberal than are the corresponding norms of most of the states in defining the legal rights of criminal defendants and the limitations upon the investigatory and prosecutory powers of the government. And actual practice seems to correspond more closely to the relevant norms in the national courts than in most state criminal courts.

Habeas corpus petitions must be filed in the district courts that have territorial jurisdiction over the jailers. This means that the dozen or so federal district judges whose bailiwicks happen to include the major national penal institutions become highly specialized in interacting with the sponsors of such petitions. State prison petitioners, on the other hand, are dispersed throughout practically all of the national judicial districts, and almost every United States district judge gets some.

The prisoners of immigration and hospital authorities who invoke habeas corpus use what is for this purpose conceptualized as a "civil" rather than a "criminal" remedy, since the legal theory is that persons detained under these circumstances are not being punished. Most immigration suits are filed against district directors of the Immigration and Naturalization Service, by persons who seek judicial review of administrative deportation or exclusion. One notorious example of 1953 involved a man who, though an alien, had resided in Buffalo, New York, for a quarter of a century; upon his return from a trip abroad for the ostensible purpose of visiting his dying mother, he was denied readmission. Since no other country would accept him, he remained in the then custodial facility upon a small island in New York harbor, apparently under what amounted to a decree of life detention after his efforts to obtain his release through habeas corpus were rejected by the United States District Court for the Southern District of New York, the Court of Appeals for the Second Circuit, and (in 1953) the Supreme Court.[18] The use of habeas corpus to challenge the legality of detention in mental hospitals is less common. From the point of view of defense counsel, a plea of not guilty by reason of insanity often functions as an alternative stratagem to an attempted defense on the merits of the charge. Widespread judicial recognition of this functional equivalence sometimes results, because of judicial refusal to accept pleas of insanity, in the execution of defendants who evidently are insane;[19] and sometimes it results in the insistence, by trial judges, that mental hospitals be used as instruments for the punishment of criminals— although in this latter case, too, habeas corpus can be used as the basis for obtaining reconsideration and appellate review of the trial court's decision.[20]

## PRIMARY APPEALS

In this section, we shall summarize briefly only the major respects in which the procedure for deciding primary appeals differs from trial procedure. In the concluding part of this chapter, we shall discuss in somewhat greater detail the Supreme Court's procedure, which is concerned almost exclusively with secondary appeals.

In the national judicial system, only two stages of appellate review of the decisions of trial courts are possible: (1) primary, from single-judge courts (such as the ordinary district court or a division of the Customs Court), and (2) secondary, from multi-judge courts (the courts of appeals, the three-judge district courts, and the Court of Claims) to the Supreme Court. There are only rare exceptions in which a case (such as one that comes into the Supreme Court via the Court of Appeals of the District of Columbia from the strictly municipal courts of the District) may pass through more than two stages of direct appellate court review. Many conservative judges (such as the late Justice Frankfurter) have argued that only one appeal should be provided, in an efficient judicial system, for the consideration of complaints about the trial court's decision. In Frankfurter's view, the purpose of a second level of appeal is to use cases as instruments for policy-making for the entire system or as instruments for policing the consistency with which courts at the primary appellate level adhere to the Supreme Court's policies. It follows logically (and it is Frankfurter's view) that the Supreme Court should confine its activities exclusively to such functions—which it ought also to monopolize. This is a highly rationalistic model of the national judicial system, and it presumes that efficiency is a primary value of the system. A pluralistic model affords recognition to the substantial influence upon policy-making of judges at all levels in the system. This appears to be in much closer correspondence with the available empirical evidence. But liberal judges (such as Justice Douglas) argue that in addition to the Supreme Court's policy function, it is a proper function of review at the secondary level to be concerned with outcomes in individual cases despite the impossibility of the Court's "righting all wrongs" committed by lower courts and despite the intrusion of such a chari-table function upon the time available for the policy function.

## INITIATION

As stated earlier, to petition a court of appeals to consider an appeal from a district court decision is to recycle the process of decision-making. Accordingly, appellate procedures, also, may be analyzed in terms of the stages of initiation, accommodation, per-suasion, decision, implementation, and reconsideration. But appellate operations tend to be more stereotyped than those of trial courts. Consequently, the description that follows applies to both criminal and civil cases and, among the latter, to both those in which the trial procedures are primarily legal and those in which they are primarily equitable.

Notwithstanding statutes of limitations and doctrines of laches (relating to delay in beginning suits), the plaintiff in a trial has considerably more room for maneuver, in terms of where and when he will commence his suit, than does the appellant (the party—either plaintiff or defendant—who seeks to upset the decision of a trial court). The appellant has no choice concerning the court of appeals in which he will file—there is only one with jurisdiction over his appeal—and the time during which he must file is strictly and nar-rowly defined by rule. Once an appeal has been initiated, then the other party automatically is cast in the role of appellee, unless he chooses to file a cross-appeal of his own, in which event both parties must play the dual roles of appellant and appellee.

## ACCOMMODATION

Accommodation is accomplished by the appellee's answer to the appellant's petition and by direct negotiation between their respective counsel. Often an appeal is taken by a relatively affluent litigant who does not expect to obtain an appellate reversal of the trial court decision but hopes to exhaust the litigative capacity of his opponent. The threat of continuing expenditures of both time and money in combination with the uncertainty that to some extent always characterizes the probable outcome of an appeal—for reasons developed below—induces some appellees to agree to compromise settlements "out of court." Thus large corporations, who maintain legal counsel as a cost of "doing business," can (and not infrequently do) maximize their economic power to attain legal advantage over private litigants of inferior socioeconomic status. The classic example is provided by the insurance company that uses litigation—including the extension of litigation beyond the trial—as a means to harass widows and orphans. The example (like the phrase that describes it) is both trite and true.

## PERSUASION

Persuasion takes the form of the briefs on the merits filed, and the oral arguments presented, by opposing counsel. The audience for both written briefs and oral argument is a panel of three circuit judges. A "brief" is a statement in writing which is addressed to a court and which argues, with supporting citations to "legal authorities," the policy alternatives preferred by the party whose counsel submits the brief. Such alternatives are described as questions of "law" to be decided by the judge. Briefs sometimes are filed in the trial of certain kinds of civil cases (e.g., antitrust) but rarely in most trial proceedings; the use of formal written briefs is, however, an almost universal characteristic of persuasive tactics in appellate courts. Moreover, oral argument is not primarily fragmented and *ad hoc* as it is in trial proceedings; instead, it consists of prepared formal speeches, limited in duration and opportunity to a single appointed occasion. The content of oral argument tends to be more technical in appeals than in trials, in part because of the sharper focus (and the sublimation of dramatic context) afforded by both the administrative and the physical milieu in which arguments are delivered in primary appeals, and in part because there are no roles for laymen to play in the appellate courtroom. There are no jurors, and the proceedings are not sufficiently well publicized to attract the throngs of adolescent pilgrims and other spectators who pass through the portals of the small auditorium in which the Supreme Court entertains oral argument. Consequently, the objective of counsel is to attract the voting support of at least two of the circuit judges, while at the same time losing the vote of no more than one (and preferably none) of them. This kind of game makes the vote of the most moderate judge (in relation to the value constellations of the other two) critical to the outcome of the appeal, and it tends to keep the style as well as the content of argumentation within narrower bounds, since an overly hyperbolic statement may boomerang and alienate the critical middleman.

## DECISION

Since most courts of appeals (nine of the eleven) are composed of from six to nine circuit judges each, many different panels of three judges can be established. From a population of six circuit judges, for example, twenty different samples (i.e., panels) can be drawn, and with a court of appeals composed of nine circuit judges, eighty-four different three-judge panels are possible. Consequently, although we can assume that all possible combinations are unlikely to occur empirically, there is enough variation in panel composition in most courts of appeals that the outcome of any particular appeal may well depend more upon the "luck of the draw" than upon anything else. Assuming that the judges of a nine-man court can be arrayed along a continuum according to their relative degrees of liberalism and conservatism, then many cases might be decided by the "court" in opposite ways, depending upon whether the panel includes the court's three most liberal or most conservative members. Neither combination is likely to occur empirically, however; mixtures of conservatives and liberals with each other and with moderates will be the rule. Nevertheless, panels biased with either liberal or conservative majorities could form a fourth of the time, even on a chance basis—which underscores both the speculative and the manipulative propensities of the panel system. Even in the Fourth Circuit, where there are only five judges in the Court of Appeals, ten different panels are possible; and the First Circuit, with only three judges, is the only court of appeals with a fixed composition for the decision of all cases. The strategies of counsel, in contemplation of primary appeals, must be quite different in the First Circuit than elsewhere in the national judicial system.

The panel usually makes separate decisions on the questions of jurisdiction and of the merits of the issues at dispute; but sometimes the jurisdictional decision is "reserved pending consideration of the merits," which is a legalistic way of saying that judges occasionally choose to put the cart before the horse. Such action is not taken arbitrarily, at least in a psychological sense, since the judges usually have a strong identification with some policy issue in a case when they thus depart from the usual sequence of decision-making. Both jurisdictional decisions and those on the merits are based upon initiating petitions and the opposing motions of appellees, plus the printed record of the trial; they differ in that negative jurisdictional decisions usually preclude counsel from having an opportunity to attempt to influence the court through written and oral argumentation.

Unlike the decrees of trial courts, which characteristically take the form of orders from the judge directly to the parties, or indirectly to them through judicial agents (marshals, jailers, etc.), the orders of courts of appeals are directed to district courts. Appellate judges, in other words, make decisions in the form of orders to trial judges. Such orders have become quite stereotyped, and in most cases they consist of one or a combination of the following three words: affirmed, remanded, reversed. "Affirmed" means that the court of appeals accepts and approves—technically, to the extent that it was questioned— the trial court's decision; "remanded" means that the trial court is directed to reconsider its initial decision, usually in the light of somewhat ambiguous guidance which the court of appeals provides, either in the form of a statement of instructions or through the citation of particular legal sources; "reversed" means that the appellate court disagrees with the decision below. Some reversals have the effect of terminating the case, usually in favor of the appellant; but others result in reconsideration by the trial court, and a few require that the trial process be recycled and repeated from the initiation stage.

### IMPLEMENTATION AND RECONSIDERATION

In most instances, implementation of the decisions of courts of appeals occurs by the return of the case for further action by the district court (or, in cases that are appealed directly from the regulatory commissions, on the part of the administrative agency). Reconsideration by the courts of appeals takes place but rarely, on motion of counsel for the losing party; as in the trial courts, such motions are routinely filed and denied, in order to "perfect the record"—they have no chance of being granted, unless at least one of the judges on the panel is willing to change his mind. However, the very fact that panels are utilized results in a special procedure which, in a technical legal sense, is a form of reconsideration. This is the *en banc* procedure, previously mentioned in Chapter Two, under which, upon recommendation of a majority of the panel for the case or in response to a petition filed by counsel for the losing party, the entire court participates in what is in effect an appellate review of the panel's decision. The procedure for *en banc* decision-making varies among the circuits. In some, the entire membership of the court is assembled to hear reargument, both orally by counsel and through the submission of revised briefs; in others, the membership simply is polled by the chief judge and a written ballot determines the outcome. Under either procedure, the judges who formed the decision-making panel for the case also participate in the decision *en banc*. The usual grounds for granting *en banc* consideration are that conflict exists between the decision of the present panel and that of another panel in some earlier but similar case.

In a small minority of cases, one or both of the parties chooses to continue the litigation by filing a petition with the Supreme Court, with the objective of recycling the process again by initiating proceedings there.

## SECONDARY APPEALS: SUPREME COURT PROCEDURE

### INITIATION

Most cases decided by the Supreme Court are appealed by use of the statutory writ of "certiorari." Under this procedure, the petitioner and (usually) his opposing respondent both file jurisdictional briefs, as described in Chapter Three, and either or both may subsequently file a brief on the substantive issues in dispute. In civil cases, and in criminal cases in which the petitioner can afford counsel and can meet such other substantial costs as the printing of the certiorari petition and brief and the record of the proceedings in the courts below, assignments are made to the Appellate Docket by the Clerk of the Supreme Court. The cases of indigent petitioners who file *in forma pauperis* are assigned to the Miscellaneous Docket. The difference is not insignificant: by no means all of them but *only* Appellate Docket cases are scheduled for oral argument, providing (usually) that they survive the jurisdictional screening. Over 95 per cent of the Miscellaneous Docket certioraris are dismissed; a few of them are decided summarily on the merits without any opportunity to influence the Court through oral argument; only the remainder are transferred to the Appellate Docket for the scheduling of oral argument. For a case to survive jurisdictional screening, at least four justices must vote to grant the petition (although with a minimal quorum of six or with only seven participating justices, three favorable votes suffice).

Apart from terminological differences, the procedures for processing statutory "appeals" are now substantially the same as those for certiorari cases. The "notation of probable jurisdiction" in an appeal has the same functional meaning as the Court's "grant" of the writ of certiorari, just as the "denial" of certiorari has the same significance as the "dismissal" of an appeal. The stereotyped reasons that the Court associates with dismissed appeals are no more informative than the silence with which certiorari is denied. The preceding chapter discussed the functional differences between the uses of—not the procedures for—certiorari and appeal; there are also historical differences between the writs,[21] but they are not relevant for present purposes.

Two other processes for initiating appellate review by the Supreme Court are used very infrequently. "Certification" is used when the judges of the court below are equally divided or when they wish to avoid making any decision upon what they consider to be an important question of (usually, constitutional) policy. Under such circumstances, a majority of the judges of the lower court can vote to pass the buck to the Supreme Court by suspending their own proceedings and by transmitting a copy of the record for the case, together with a "certificate" in which they ask the Supreme Court to respond to several questions that raise the policy issues about which the lower court declares itself to be "uncertain." Usually such questions are so dichotomously framed that they imply a "yes" or "no" response. Certifications are always (so far as we are aware) accepted in the modern practice of the Supreme Court, and they are placed on the Appellate Docket for oral argument and decision on the merits. The parties to the case, it should be noted, have no direct control over the use of this appellate process, and its infrequent use suggests that its invocation by the courts of appeals must be discouraged by informal norms operating within the system. Most certifications in recent decades appear to have come from the Court of Claims.[22]

The remaining means of invoking appellate review by the Supreme Court is through the use of the "extraordinary writs" of mandamus, prohibition, habeas corpus, and certiorari; requests for habeas corpus and for certiorari—which is not to be confused with the *statutory* writ discussed above—are extremely rare. The Court grants only one out of each several hundred requests for review by extraordinary writ, and usually less than half a dozen are granted over the course of a decade; the petitions are assigned to the Miscellaneous (i.e., the summary) Docket. Relics of the eighteenth-century jurisdiction of the court of King's Bench in England (to which, by some transcendental process, the United States Supreme Court is postulated to be the constitutional heir), the vestigial jurisdiction associated with these writs has degenerated in function to a point almost akin to that of the vermiform appendix in the human body. Their principal present use is to permit the Supreme Court to intervene directly in the decision-making process of trial courts; the requested writs take the form of orders to lower court judges, directing that they either do (mandamus) or refrain from doing (prohibition) specified acts which, presumably, are required or forbidden by their roles as defined by law.

ACCOMMODATION

Direct accommodation of disputes by negotiation between the parties occurs most frequently in the trial process and least often in cases that have been appealed to the Supreme Court. It seems evident that various factors, which have the effect of reinforcing the social distance between the parties to a case, would tend to have their greatest impact in cases that reach the stage of secondary appeals. For one thing, these are all cases that failed to be accommodated during earlier decision-making cycles. The investment of both parties in the outcome now is greater than at preceding stages, since the costs of extended litigations are decidedly cumulative. At the conclusion of each earlier cycle, the number of surviving issues (i.e., those upon which it is possible, under the rules, to base an appeal) diminishes; as a consequence, the policy issues presented in appeals to the Supreme Court are very small subsets of the issues raised at the pre-trial conference. Moreover, in granting certiorari or in noting probable jurisdiction in appeals, the Supreme Court very frequently limits the grant of jurisdiction to only one (or a few) of the larger number of issues about which the parties seek a decision.

Occasionally the facts so change that the original conflict of interest between the parties no longer obtains by the time the Supreme Court is ready to decide the case. Such cases usually are dismissed, on motion by counsel for one of the parties, as "moot": no matter what decision the Court might make (according to the legal theory), it could have no effect upon the resolution of the conflict in interests presented by the case. About a decade ago, for example, Communist spy Gerhard Eisler skipped his bail bond and fled the United States to reappear in Eastern Germany, after the Supreme Court had accepted jurisdiction in his appeal from a conviction for contempt of Congress. Since the United States no longer had, nor seemed likely to acquire, jurisdiction over Eisler's person, the case was dismissed (on motion of the Solicitor General) as moot, although over the protest of Justice Jackson, who argued in dissent that since the case had been fully argued and already decided, it provided an appropriate instrument for getting at the policy issue of the authority of congressional committees to compel testimony from witnesses. One infers that the unannounced policy decision must have been pleasing to Jackson, who proclaimed that he did "not think that [the Supreme Court] can run away from the case just because Eisler has."[23]

The other and more usual means of accommodation is for one of the parties to "confess error"—to concede, that is, that a decision below in his favor should be reversed. So far as we know, counsel for private parties may withdraw petitions or they may fail to contest those filed by opposing counsel, but they do not confess error; that action appears to be taken exclusively by the Solicitor General, as a function of his administrative responsibility for the work, in lower courts, of the United States attorneys and of the attorneys employed in other divisions of the Department of Justice. If the Solicitor General decides, after a case has been docketed by the Supreme Court and as a consequence of the more complete knowledge about the case that his staff necessarily acquires in the process of preparing a brief and for oral argument, that he disagrees in some important respect with action previously taken by those who represented the government in the case, he indicates by "confessing error" his unwillingness to assume further responsibility for defending the case before the Supreme Court, which usually responds by summarily reversing the decision below in the case.

## PERSUASION

The Supreme Court functions as a decision-making group for about nine months out of each twelve, beginning about the first week of October and continuing through the third or fourth week of the following June. During the early fall, the Court devotes relatively more time to jurisdictional decision-making, since a considerable backlog of docketed cases accumulates during the summer vacation; during the late spring, more decisions on the merits are announced. From late November through early May, the usual routine is keyed to a two-week cycle, although this is sometimes interrupted by an intervening week or two of recess during the winter. On the first four days of alternate weeks, the Court hears oral argument, with a conference on the following Friday for group discussion of the cases argued (among others); the other Mondays are devoted to the ritual of announcing outcomes and reading opinions in cases that have been decided, and the remaining days of that week are reserved for research and writing.

On days when oral argument is scheduled, it is held for two hours before and two hours after a brief (half-hour) recess for lunch. In most cases, counsel for each party is allocated one hour, although in some cases it is less; and in a few cases that the Court has earmarked for major policy pronouncements, several days may be reserved for this purpose. In the same type of "landmark" case—of which there will be only two or three in a decade—the Court may invite certain groups to participate in the oral argument as *amici curiae* ("friends of the court"); such invitations were extended to the states attorneys general, for example, in the School Segregation Cases and in the Tidelands Oil Cases. When the Court does this, it is expanding the focus of the points of view bearing upon the pending decision, in order better to inform itself of the probable consequences of the various decisional alternatives. Such a tactic is quite in accord with the specifications of the "realist" theory of decision-making.[24] Oral argument also may be presented by volunteer *amici* counsel, provided that both parties agree, or with the consent of one party and that of the Court. Under these circumstances, an *amicus* counsel must share the time assigned to counsel for the party whose position he supports, in contrast to the extra time the Court makes available to invited *amici* counsel.

Oral argument before the Supreme Court is, in considerable measure, direct interchange between the counsel and the justices. It

is not quite group discussion since the communication links are bilateral, in the form of questions and comments directed by individual
justices to the advocate, the advocate's replies, and the reading of his
prepared statement. Some justices do not hesitate to "correct" counsel
with whom they disagree; others feel free to offer advice and verbal
support to counsel with whom they agree. Consequently, the persuasion
that takes place is by no means a simple matter of judicial sponges
soaking up the words of advocacy that drip from the brimming prose
of advocates; the justices of the Supreme Court are the most influential
participants in the controversies argued before them.[25] They refuse
to play the role of dispassionate auditor in which they are cast by the
traditional view. The lack of more widespread awareness of the extent
to which oral argument—in reality, "with" rather than "before" the
Supreme Court—is a highly political process of social interaction is
due, probably, to the lack of any systematic procedure for publishing
the transcripts of oral argument,[26] and research based upon direct
observation of the proceedings rarely has been reported.

DECISION

The justices meet in Friday conferences with no one else present;
the proceedings are confidential, and no record is kept of the discussion, although the Chief Justice does maintain a handwritten record
of the outcome and voting division for each case. There are about ten
times as many jurisdictional decisions as there are decisions on the
merits; with a case load of about two thousand, it takes but simple
arithmetic to determine how brief must be the time available for discussion of the average case. Assuming twenty conferences for the
term—actually, there are usually less—the Court has a hundred
cases to discuss and to vote upon at each conference. What happens
is that a few cases receive a great deal of discussion, but most receive
none at all. By the use of consent lists, prepared by the Chief Justice with the assistance of his clerks, jurisdiction is denied unless at
least four justices vote in favor of granting it. In short, unless several
members of the group really want to get at an issue through the
instrumentality of a particular case, the case has no chance of being
"appealed" to the Supreme Court.

When the Chief Justice calls a case for discussion, he states his
own views first, and then the associate justices speak in the order of
their seniority. During the 1963 term, for example, the first three to
argue any case were Warren, Black, and Douglas—the three most
liberal members of the group. Small-group theory tells us that this
in itself gave an advantage to the liberals, since they could define the
issues and exercise a dominant influence in setting the focus of the

discussion. These first three also probably preëmpted at least half, rather than their "fair share" of a third, of the time available for discussion—or so, at least, do people tend to behave in other discussion groups of similar size about which we have direct observational knowledge. When the time for voting arrives, however, the sequence of participation is reversed; the most recently appointed "freshman" ⟨ associate justice votes first, and the Chief Justice votes last. Again, this gives an advantage to the most senior members; for with a group this small, a bloc of three (and Warren and Black and Douglas *do* vote as a bloc most of the time) are in a position to wield the "balance of power" on the Court. From the point of view of game theory, that is, the last three to vote can determine the outcome *either way*, provided they vote together and the remaining justices are divided. Of course, there will have been antecedent bilateral communication among the members of the group, so that probable votes are known more or less to all before the conference meets; and we do not intend, by the above remarks about the formal power advantages inherent in the discussion and voting sequences, to contradict what we shall state in Chapter Six concerning the primary importance of ideological differences as determinants of voting behavior. It is precisely because Warren, Black, and Douglas are highly and positively correlated in their belief systems that it is usually possible for them to vote as a bloc, and there are some issues on which it may be more important to decide cases with a show of unanimity than to win them with one-vote margins. The purpose of the conference is for the justices to attempt to persuade each other, and it is not to be presumed that their attitudes are so dogmatically entertained that none of them ever changes his mind about how he is going to vote in a case as the result of his having participated in the group discussion. Consequently, we might well infer that the formal discussion and voting sequences are not very important to the outcome of most cases, but that it is precisely in the making of the most marginal decisions on the most controversial issues (regarding which moderate justices are apt to be swayed one way or another) that the order of participation, for discussion and for voting, is likely to be most significant.

As the chairman of the conference, the Chief Justice also controls the agenda—that is, the sequence in which cases will be discussed. (There is probably a positive, but certainly a low, correlation among the sequence of numbers for cases on the Appellate Docket, their calendar position, and the order of their discussion in conference.) It is also the Chief Justice who is primarily responsible for the content of the Court's opinions in the cases for which the decisions are reported in per curiam form, and it is he who assigns the writing of the "Opinion of the Court" except when he is on the losing side of the issue, in which event the senior associate voting with the majority makes the assignment. Majority opinions are instruments for the articulation of the rationale for the decision that is acceptable to all members of the majority; hence, the larger the majority, the less the opinion of the Court can function as a vehicle for the expression of the unadulterated personal views of the individual "author" of that opinion. Justices who accept the majority decision but who reject, in whole or in part, the "official" rationale proffered in behalf of the majority can write separate (or joint, if two or more of them agree) concurring opinions; and one or more justices who disagree with the decision may (but will not necessarily)[27] dissent, with or without opinion, and if with opinion, either individually or collectively. Since it is customary to report only the name of the author of the opinion of the Court, plus those who concur and dissent, one identifies the other members of the majority by simple inference.

On the alternate Mondays that function as "Opinion Day," the Court assembles for the ritual of publishing its decisions (i.e., those on the merits) by means of the ancient device of oral delivery. It is the custom of the Court for justices to read their written opinions, but occasional nonconformists (such as Frankfurter) have preferred to give somewhat briefer—and frequently more colorful—oral, and to some extent extemporaneous, summaries of their prepared speeches (viz., written opinions). At the same time, printed copies of the written opinions are made available to the press and to anyone else who is present and interested.

IMPLEMENTATION

As we found to be true for the courts of appeals, the decisions of the Supreme Court are in the form of orders to lower courts. In substantial degree, the question of the ultimate enforcement of Supreme Court decisions is the same as that of the enforcement of trial court decisions. It differs primarily to the extent that trial court judges may be more strongly motivated to enforce their own decisions (with which, presumably, they are more or less in continuing agreement, most of the time) than they are to enforce Supreme Court decisions, the frequent effect of which is to order the trial judge to do the *opposite* of what *he* initially had decided. Further, the Supreme Court tends to get more "faithful execution of the laws," as it has decreed "the laws," from federal than from state judges.[28] Similarly, the extent to which the Court can depend upon the Presidency and the Congress to assist in the enforcement of the Court's policies depends upon the degree of communality between the value preferences of the majority of the Court, of the key minorities of the Congress, and of the President and whatever advisors he listens to on the issue.

The Supreme Court rarely grants a motion for rehearing and then changes an announced decision, although occasionally it does so in a spectacular way.[29] In order for this to happen, at least one justice must change his mind, as Robert Jackson once explained.[30] A much more common form of reconsideration (of the issue rather than of the case) occurs when a minority bloc in a particular decision solicits business by asking in effect that some counsel bring the same issue up again in a new case, by which time (because of anticipated personnel changes in the group) the minority may have become the majority.[31] Even more common is the complicated case, relating frequently to governmental regulation of economic relationships, for which decision-making by the administrative agency and the trial court does not lead up to a single event (which can be appealed only once) but instead consists of a set of decisions over an extended period of time. This sort of reconsideration, both of cases and of issues, is particularly likely to occur when the policy position of the administrative agency conflicts with that of a Supreme Court majority, as illustrated by the tension between the New Deal and the Hughes Court over governmental regulation of stockyard markets. The statutory policy had been established twenty years earlier, and it was not until F.D.R. succeeded in "packing the Court" that it was possible for the Department of Agriculture effectively to carry out this part of the congressional policy and program. But the Supreme Court finally yielded. The Court had, in effect, forced a reconsideration of the underlying issue of public policy more than a dozen times. Thus the national judicial system was able to delay the change for a generation but could not prevent it from taking place.

### CHAPTER FIVE

# Policy-Making Analysis

    The preceding chapter examined the processes of judicial decision-making through a description of the sequences of major actions. The discussion was almost entirely at the empirical level of observable events: who does what to whom and with what effects? In this chapter we shall employ an analytical rather than an empirical approach and shall undertake to interpret the process of judicial policy-making in terms of an explicit theoretical model. Our focus, in other words, now shifts from the manifest to the latent aspects of decision-making.

    "Decision-making" and "policy-making" are by no means synonymous. Individual decisions of different courts have differing policy implications—even in the same case—and for any given court, individual decisions may reflect a wide range of values in their policy significance. Indeed, judicial policy-making does not necessarily utilize case decisions as an instrument for articulation; the Supreme Court's notorious admission of corporations to the constitutional status of "persons" under the Fourteenth Amendment (which protected them from public control through state regulation)—a policy-making act of considerable importance—took the form of an oral "concession" by the Chief Justice to a railroad lawyer that the point need not be argued further since the whole Court was willing to "admit" it.[1] Most of the time, however, judges make policies through their decisions in regard to issues raised in cases.

### A SYSTEMIC MODEL OF JUDICIAL POLICY-MAKING

Figure 1 presents a model of judicial policy-making processes. The model is "systemic" because it portrays certain functional inter-relationships among stipulated structures; the relationships are ordered and are assumed to be relatively stable. The three structural components of the model are denoted as INPUT, CONVERSION, and OUTPUT units. We shall describe all three of these structural components in considerably more detail in the remaining sections of this chapter. The structures are linked by three sets of inter-action processes. The INPUT and OUTPUT structures interact with the CONVERSION structure through *input* and *output* processes, respectively; the OUTPUT structure interacts with the INPUT structure through *feedback* processes. These interaction processes correspond to the six stages of decision-making examined in the preceding chapter. Initiation and accommodation are *input* processes; persuasion and decision are *output* processes; and implementation and reconsideration are *feedback* processes.

This model is very general. Certainly it is applicable to the American national and state judicial systems with which we are concerned here. It probably also can be used to analyze the judicial systems of other countries. Of course, with such a degree of abstraction this model cannot distinguish the differences among even seemingly quite different systems, but the model can be used to guide empirical observations on the basis of which further distinctions can be made. Here we shall use the model to help analyze empirical data relating to the Supreme Court, although it could be used just as well to analyze the policy-making process of any other court in the national judicial system for which adequate empirical data were available.

There are pairs of interaction processes that correspond to pairs of structural components. The elements of the latter pairs, which Figure 1 depicts as independent from each other, are separated only in order to clarify the analytical relationships in the model. Empirically, "supportive" and "demanding" acts of input behavior may refer to the same actions. For example, the general counsel for the National Association for the Advancement of Colored People, at oral argument before the Supreme Court, and in the same sentence, may state that his organization agrees with the Court's recent inter-

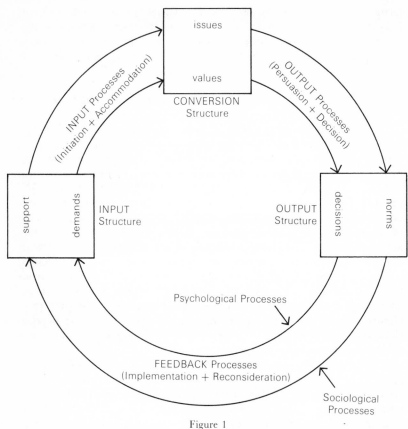

Figure 1
A Systemic Model of Judicial Policy-Making

pretation of the equal protection clause, which logically requires that the Court also approve (in the instant case) "lie-downs" in used-car lots to force the employment of more Negroes as salesmen.

Similarly, we can distinguish for conceptual purposes between "issues" and "values." Issues denominate the questions of policy to which the judge purports to respond in his decision, while values are the internalized beliefs of the judge. The judge, however, can take cognizance of issues in a case only through the intermediation of his own beliefs and expectations concerning the empirical events to which issues of public policy relate; that is, issues can be perceived by a judge only through his own personal system of values.

Hence, the issue is the manifest policy question to be decided; the values of the judge are the latent parameters that determine how he will define and respond to the issue.

In the OUTPUT structure, there is a close relationship between "norms" and "decisions." Decisions, as we know, are the orders of judges that provide directions for other actors in a particular case. Norms are probability statements about how judges can be expected to behave in making future decisions. Thus decisions are, from this point of view, descriptions of particular sets of empirical events, while norms are inferences—based upon such descriptions— about the likelihood that future judicial action will be consistent with past judicial action.

According to what we shall describe in Chapter Seven as "traditional theory," consistency is to be sought in logical interrelationships among norms; the theory that we shall there describe as "conventional" looks for consistency in the observable patterns of interaction between judges and other actors; "behavioral" theory focuses upon consistency in the *patterning* of individual sets of values, consistency *between* individual sets of values, and consistency among an individual's inputs and his values and his outputs. Both traditional and conventional theory denigrate the significance of the CONVERSION structure; traditional theory ignores the INPUT structure as well, while conventional theory postulates a deterministic cause-and-effect relationship between inputs and outputs: judges are viewed as a kind of output, as though the inputs define a tree from which a block of judicial wood is cut (as one kind of output) and the other outputs—such as policy decisions—are just chips off the old block. Quite to the contrary, behavioral theory generally, and our model in particular, assumes that the CONVERSION structure (which consists of judges and other persons who comprise the personnel of courts) is a critical and independent variable in the judicial policy-making process. To summarize, we can distinguish among the three theoretical approaches in the following way: traditional theory deals with univariate (OUTPUT) relationships, conventional theory with bivariate (INPUT–OUTPUT) relationships, and behavioral theory with multivariate (INPUT–CONVERSION–OUTPUT) relationships.

We can distinguish at the psychological level of analysis the demands that other actors make upon the values of individual judicial decision-makers. These demands may be thought of as stimuli which, after having been perceived by the judge, induce from him responses in the form of decisional acts (such as voting, writing an opinion, etc.). This results either in direct feedback to the parties, in the form of satisfying or rejecting demands, or it leads to a new demand upon another (usually a "higher") court, as the process recycles. At the sociological level of analysis, we can conceptualize support (which may be either affirmative, absent, or negative) as a patterning of individual acts of demand. Support tends to reinforce or to contravene particular degrees of acceptance or rejection of public policy issues, and public policy issues are collective value-perceptions—in the sense of intercorrelated individuals rather than of simple aggregations. Norms (which we have defined as predictions concerning the positions that one or a group of judges will take in regard to a given issue) are transmitted as feedback through channels of social communication and thereby condition the scope, direction, and intensity of supportive acts. Figure 1 postulates an outer, or sociological, limit and an inner, or psychological, limit for the processes of interaction that constitute policy-making in the model; but the core of interaction, between these limits, is sociopsychological—interaction among individuals in small groups and in face-to-face relationships. The postulated processes, far from being independent, are (like the corresponding components in the three structures) highly interdependent.

**POLICY INPUTS**

We can readily distinguish several major classes of inputs for the Supreme Court. In the most direct and literal sense, demands emanate from litigants, although such demands usually are translated into the legal idiom before being presented to the Court by counsel who are specialists in translating lay interests (and empirical events) into legal language (and other forms of legal behavior). Some litigants—many large corporations, for example—hire such specialists as part of their staff; for such litigants, supporting issues in and making demands upon the Supreme Court is a part of (as well as a part of the cost of) doing business. We may properly speak of "litigation management" as constituting one method of accommodation by means of which such an organization can conduct its relationships with the government, other organizations, its clientele, etc. The NAACP is an example of a litigant organization that has specialized, with extraordinary success during the past two decades, in making demands upon and providing support for the Supreme Court.[2] Indeed, the NAACP was so successful that Thurgood Marshall, the lawyer who personally had presented, in oral argument of cases, most of its demands upon the Court, himself was appointed to the United States Court of Appeals for the Second Circuit early in the Kennedy administration. The time was out of joint, or, rather, not yet sufficiently "in joint," for President Kennedy to have been willing to pay the political costs that might have been entailed by acceding to the NAACP's suggestion—whether made directly or through other groups—that Marshall be appointed to a Supreme

Court vacancy. Kennedy did accede to what was doubtless a similar suggestion from the AFL-CIO in appointing its General Counsel, Arthur Goldberg, to such a vacancy, with a delay en route as Secretary of Labor. Only thirty years ago, it was just as "impossible" to appoint a union lawyer to the Supreme Court as it remains today to appoint a Negro—or a female, irrespective of her race, religion, or previous occupation.

The explicit assumption of our model is that the Supreme Court perceives demands not as "objective content" but as functions of the litigants who make them. Let us assume that the NAM and the AFL-CIO each is party to a different case, in which they make equivalent demands upon the Court in regard to the extension of the jurisdiction of the National Labor Relations Board. Even if the demands were "objectively" the same, the Court would evaluate them as different because of the difference in the Court's expectations concerning the orientation towards policy issue of the employer's organization and the labor organization.

The status and competence of the counsel (who present demands to the Court) also are differentially perceived. We already have discussed the situational bias in favor of the Solicitor General, which we construed to be a function of his more frequent, more intensive, and more extensive interaction with the justices, in comparison with other counsel. Similarly (but to a lesser extent), lawyers of great reputation (such as Thurman Arnold, the late John William Davis, Edward Bennett Williams, or Frederick Bernays Wiener) can communicate with the Court much more effectively than can a lawyer from South Dakota who has been specially admitted to the Supreme Court bar to make his first appearance before the Court.[3] This is not to say that all of the justices will respond more favorably to arguments because they have been presented by renowned advocates; to the contrary, the *direction* of judicial responses to "leading counsel" will vary with both the justice and the lawyer. But whatever the direction of judicial response, it is likely to be more intense when the stimulus or the argument *qua* issue has been reinforced by the advocacy of a recognized personality who is experienced in interacting with the justices.

Lower courts are by no means equally prestigious in the eyes of Supreme Court justices. Of course, a few courts have the reputation of being outstanding, while a few others have the opposite reputation.[4] Not all justices would rank the lower courts in the same order, even when perception is consensual, and some justices tend more than others to weight as important the prestige of a particular lower court. Moreover, a lower court's prestige may vary with the issue. For example, the Court of Appeals for the Fifth Circuit has been imputed to entertain a pronounced antilabor bias,[5] while the Court of Appeals for the Second Circuit has (like the New York State Court of Appeals) received (especially from connoisseur Frankfurter) what frequently amounts almost to adulation as the Yankees of the American judicial league. Sometimes the Supreme Court has been able to take distinct advantage of lower-court prestige, as did Chief Justice Vinson in a politically conservative opinion supporting a decision approving the conspiracy convictions in a trial before Judge Medina (discussed in Chapter Four) of the leaders of the American Communist party.[6] Vinson attempted to advertise the position of the majority of the Court (for whom he spoke) as being really not illiberal, since the Supreme Court (as he pointed out) merely was approving the decision and supporting rationale that had been adopted in this very case by the Court of Appeals for the Second Circuit. That court had spoken, in turn, through no less august a personage than the great Learned Hand, author of *The Bill of Rights* and (both off and on the bench) of other reputedly liberal writings, and a federal judge whom most lawyers considered to be of much greater ability than all but a handful of the justices who have sat on the Supreme Court during the twentieth century.

We have spoken so far of the human actors whose roles in proceedings before the Supreme Court are such that they function as inputs. A second general source of inputs is the record of the case itself and the briefs and oral argument presented to the Court. As Chapter Four pointed out, lawyers tend to distinguish between "facts" and "law" in analyzing cases. Facts, in turn, can be divided into those *in* the case and those *of* the case. The former consist of descriptive statements about empirical events that relate to the conflict of interest between the parties. The Supreme Court is several steps removed from those events. One output of the trial is a particular version of the pre-trial events, reflecting a multiplicity of decisions of the trial judge or of the trial judge and the petit jury. Circuit judges may or may not agree with the trial court's determinations of the facts in the case, but usually the court of appeals can change only a few of the many that were decided by the trial court; under the applicable procedural norms, most factual determinations of the trial are foreclosed from effective *post hoc* review.

Not only are there these authoritative suppositions about what happened before the trial began, but from the point of view of the Supreme Court, the events that transpired in the decision-making processes of the trial court and of the court of appeals also constitute a set of facts: these are the facts *of* the case. Both of these two kinds of facts are in effect hypotheses, for which the associated levels of probability are unspecified, about the likelihood that a particular version of past human actions is valid. Such versions necessarily have highly differentiable validity; they are images of reality.

They function for the Supreme Court as stimuli that interrelate with issues.

The issues in a case are the perceptions of judges of what lawyers call "questions of law" and what many political scientists consider to be "questions of policy." Legal questions relate to normative propositions—assertions that persons ought to act in one way or another. In traditional theory, the task of judicial decision-makers is to examine the degree of correspondence between facts (statements about how people actually have behaved) and laws (statements about how people should behave). An alternative conceptualization of the relationship between factual and legal inputs will be described below as the policy conversion process in Figure 1.

There is a third general source of inputs, the critics of the Court. Law schools provide the most important forum for professional criticism of all the national courts, including the Supreme Court. Justices frequently speak at major law schools, and such affairs provide an occasion for informal intermingling of the justice with the faculty and students of a law school. Most of the justices select their administrative assistants from favored law schools; for over forty years, Justice Felix Frankfurter, who was appointed to the Court directly from the Harvard law faculty, served as either sender or recipient of such assistants. During the 1920's and 1930's, Frankfurter dispatched from Harvard to Washington a succession of young men (whom some called the "happy hot dogs") to work as law clerks for various justices, but for Holmes and Brandeis in particular; during the 1940's and 1950's, his faculty friends at Harvard continued the custom, sending him two of the honor graduates from each year's class.

The pervasive effect of the "old school tie" is very well illustrated by Jack W. Peltason, who offers many examples of the extent to which members of the Harvard law faculty have supported Frankfurter but attacked Justice William O. Douglas, a former professor on the Yale law faculty, while the Yale law faculty has reciprocated.[7] But although one's initial tendency is to smile at such academic antics and to discount any influence as arising from the traditional rivalry between the two universities, supporting behavior by the respective colleagues of Frankfurter and of Douglas can be understood at the psychological as well as at the sociological level. The reinforcing effects—and affects—due to the affiliation of the two justices with distinctive friendship groups are obvious enough, but a more fundamental explanation for the dichotomization of the supporting groups for the two justices may be found in the difference in the value orientation of both the justices and their supporters. Douglas has been the most liberal member of the Court during the past generation, and Frankfurter has been one of the most conservative (at least on economic issues). Both Douglas and Frankfurter have spoken and written vociferously, both on and off the Court, so there could be little doubt concerning their respective ideological positions and differences. Their faculty acolytes could not support the justices without also supporting the values with which they were identified; and since law professors generally are sophisticated men, they doubtless were well aware that a Harvard "vote" for Frankfurter was a vote for economic conservatism, just as a Yale "vote" for Douglas was a vote for liberalism on the Supreme Court.

The law schools also publish law reviews, which are edited by students and written partly by them and partly by law professors and lawyers. Members of the Supreme Court rely upon the law reviews to provide them with supporting arguments and rationales which they then can and do cite in their opinions in support of their decisions. The rationale for the Court's recent major decision on state legislative reapportionment, in *Baker* v. *Carr*, was taken directly from the brief submitted by Solicitor General Cox, which in turn relied heavily upon a then-recent article in the *Harvard Law Review*[8] written by the newspaperman who covers the Supreme Court for *The New York Times*.[9] The articles and case-commentary in the reviews also function as a nation-wide set of "listening posts" that aid the justices in gauging audience reaction to their own performance.

The influence of the law reviews upon judicial decision-making has not escaped congressional notice. Representative Wright Patman of Texas, for example, some years ago delivered a speech entitled "Effect of Lobbyists' Propaganda upon Our Supreme Court"; the congressman was particularly disturbed about several articles in the *Harvard Law Review* on national antitrust policy.[10] The law reviews certainly do take sides, but within certain limits of concern for objectivity and with at least seeming dispassion, and collectively they articulate arguments both pro and con most public policy issues. Popular periodicals and newspapers are less subject to such restraint; in such major issues as legislative reapportionment and public school prayers, both so-called news coverage of the Court's decisions and what ostensibly was editorial commentary spanned a spectrum of behaviors ranging from strong support to hysterical opposition. News coverage necessarily was biased by the fact that far more public speakers have attacked than have defended the Warren Court. The overwhelming majority of editorial commentators did favor the reapportionment decision, but an even more lopsided majority opposed the public school prayer decision. Generally, according to Professor Newland, wire service reporting of the Court's activities "reveals two serious faults. . . : choosing sensational material over more significant cases for reports and blowing up of stories to sensational dimensions."[11] By and large, the Supreme Court has had a "bad press" during the past decade, reflecting also, no doubt, the extent to which the relatively liberal national policies of the Court's majorities have been repugnant to most American newspaper publishers.

## POLICY CONVERSION

According to our model (Figure 1), the conversion structure is central in the judicial policy-making process. Conversion is the subprocess by means of which issues are recognized and decided as a result of group interaction and the integration of the values of the individual justices. The conversion structure consists of the values of the individual justices and the issues—their shared perceptions about the policy and factual questions raised by cases before them for a decision. In a formal sense, conversion as a process occurs when individual justices cast their votes on the disposition of a case at the group conference; and strictly speaking, the subsequent announcement both of the voting division of the Court, and of the opinions of the Court and of individual justices, are among the *outputs* of the conversion process. Conversion consists, therefore, of both psychological and social processes. When each justice decides how he will vote, that is a psychological process; but when he announces his vote, in a fixed order of articulation, as a contributor to a group decision that depends upon an integration of the preferences of the individual participants, that is a social process. Analysis of the interrelation between individual decisions and the group decision in a case involves us in sociopsychological study.

The very use of the words *conversion structure* seems to imply—and quite falsely—that values and issues are static entities which function strictly as catalysts (i.e., they hasten change but are not themselves changed) in the process that converts inputs into outputs. Actually, both values and issues are dynamic rather than static. Although not formally classified in the input category (which subsumes factors external to the judges themselves), values are from a functional point of view a major source of inputs for the decision; even more paradoxically, both issues and values become in part transformed into the outputs of the policy-making process. However, a justice's values are relatively stable in comparison to the external sources of inputs discussed in the preceding section; they change but slowly, while the support-and-demand inputs fluctuate widely from case to case, over a range of several thousand cases each year. Moreover, the support-and-demand inputs are more or less shared by all of the justices.

Although the values and issues are also shared, the means by which each justice acquires his values is a very individual matter. An individual's values are a product of socialization, and his socialization experience results from a combination of chance considerations operating within the political culture in which he has been reared. Supreme Court justices acquire their values in part as a consequence of having been born into a particular family at a particular place and time; nationality, race, family, and early as well as later education all have some influence in building the political character of each justice, as do marriage, law school training, and subsequent professional experience. Table IV presents a summary of three classes of judicial attributes (experience, appointing President, and partisan affiliation) and two classes of judicial values. Of course, it is not to be assumed that a mature man can be completely described by a handful of labels designated as "attribute" or "attitudinal" variables. His values, like his attributes, have been molded by a lifetime of experience. Nevertheless, it is quite possible that when we ask why he votes as he does in a particular case or series of cases (raising, for him, the same policy issue), a small number of variables may approximate *what is most relevant about him* closely enough to be useful in analyzing decision-making. If such a focusing of attention, for analytical purposes, were not possible, then we could say nothing of scientific value about the causes of the behavior of judges (or of any other complex living organisms, for that matter).

A tabulation such as that of Table IV illustrates some of the kinds of relationships that are investigated in studies of the effect of socialization upon judicial policy-making. This table implies a set of hypotheses about the relationship among the attribute variables (i.e., appointing President and partisan affiliation), or between an attribute variable and one or both of the attitudinal variables. The sample of data presented in this table, which relates only to the justices incumbent during the 1963 term, is too small for any statistically significant relationships to be apparent; but studies of larger samples of judges indicate that there are meaningful and important correlations among these (and similar) attribute variables and these (and other) attitudinal variables.[12]

ATTRIBUTES

Supreme Court justices invariably have been white males, whose average age (at the time of appointment) has ranged from forty-seven to fifty-seven years of age. Nine out of ten (86 per cent) have been of British ethnic origin, and of the others only two (Cardozo, Iberian; Goldberg, Slavic) were not descended from emigrants from northwestern Europe; no Asians, Africans, or even Italians ever have been appointed to the Supreme Court. Nine out of ten (88 per cent) have been Protestant; during the first century of the Court's existence, only one Catholic (Taney) was appointed out of a total of fifty justices, and although one Jew was offered a nomination to the Court, none

TABLE IV

Status, Selected Attributes, and Attitudinal
Orientations of Supreme Court Justices (1963 Term)

| Seniority status: | Name: | Major legal and/or political experience: | Appointed by: | Political party affiliation: | Attitudinal orientation | |
|---|---|---|---|---|---|---|
| | | | | | Political | Economic |
| 1 | Warren | SA (governor; state attorney general) | Eisenhower | Rep. | Liberal | Liberal |
| 2 | Black | SJ, NL municipal judge; U.S. senator) | Roosevelt | Dem. | Liberal | Liberal |
| 3 | Douglas | P, NA (law professor, chairman of S.E.C.) | Roosevelt | Dem. | Liberal | Liberal |
| 4 | Clark | NA (U.S. Attorney General) | Truman | Dem. | Conservative | Moderate |
| 5 | Harlan | P, NJ (corporation lawyer; U.S. circuit judge for 1 year) | Eisenhower | Rep. | Conservative | Conservative |
| 6 | Brennan | SJ (state judge) | Eisenhower | Dem. | Liberal | Liberal |
| 7 | Stewart | P, NJ (corporation lawyer; U.S. circuit judge for 2 years) | Eisenhower | Rep. | Moderate | Conservative |
| 8 | White | NA (U.S. Deputy Attorney General) | Kennedy | Dem. | Conservative | Moderate |
| 9 | Goldberg | P, NA (union lawyer; U.S. Secretary of Labor) | Kennedy | Dem. | Liberal | Moderate |

* Key to abbreviations for experience categories:

P = private    N = national    S = state    A = administrative    J = judicial    L = legislative was appointed prior to 1916; among the forty-four appointees since 1890 there have been five more Catholics and four Jews. Among the eighty-three Protestants, about nine out of ten (86 per cent) were affiliated with high social-status denominations (Episcopalian, Presbyterian, Unitarian, Congregational). During the first few decades after the establishment of the Court, most justices were born into the landed aristocracy; since then, they have been drawn primarily from the professional upper middle classes. As a group, they have been exceptionally well educated (in relation to the standards of the period in which they served), even in terms of non-legal education; five sixths of them either attended a law school of high standing or studied as an apprentice under a prominent lawyer or judge. Moreover, they were born into politically active families, as a consequence of which the justices, as young men, were both encouraged and aided in their own quests for political careers.[13]

Almost all of the justices had experience—frequently, quite extensive experience—in other public offices prior to their selection for the Supreme Court. Although the Republican Eisenhower preferred corporation lawyers, three of the most recent Democratic Presidents (Roosevelt, Truman, and Kennedy) tended to "promote" men from their own cabinets; a plurality (four) of the incumbent justices were appointed to the Court from positions in national administration. The same number also had had some prior judicial experience, but only Brennan's had been extensive; Black had begun his political career with a brief period as a municipal judge in Birmingham, Alabama, and Eisenhower had given both Harlan and Stewart a year or two of "seasoning" as federal circuit judges before he promoted them. Most of the incumbent justices have had little or no prior judicial experience, and this has been true of the Court throughout its history. It has been assumed by many who have speculated on the subject that judges with prior judicial experience would tend to "follow precedent" more than those without such experience, but the only scholarly analysis of empirical data has failed to confirm that hypothesis. To the contrary, there has been a slight (though not statistically significant) tendency for justices with prior judicial experience to vote to overrule precedents to a greater extent than do justices without such experience.[14] The same study reported that the relatively few justices (nine) who came from families in the lower socioeconomic classes dissented much more often than did the much larger group of justices (sixty-two) who came from aristocratic or upper-middle-class families. The former group were always a small minority on the Court; if there were important differences between their values and those of the upper-class majority of the Court, we should expect them to signify such differences by dissenting.

Table IV shows that only one of the incumbent justices (Brennan) was affiliated with a political party different from that of the President who appointed him. One out of nine is about the usual proportion of "nonpartisan" appointees; there have been eleven other instances, and during the half century spanned by the Taft and Eisenhower administrations, every President (with the solitary exception of Coolidge) crossed party lines in at least one of his appointments to the Court. But the usual practice has recognized that Supreme Court positions are among the most important sources of patronage available to an administration. Presidents expect to advance preferred policy goals in making such appointments, and a record of political party or administrative (and, as Schmidhauser has argued, of prior judicial[15]) service provides what are assumed to be important clues to the ideological orientation of appointees. Nagel has demonstrated that, in general, Republican justices have supported the use of judicial review of national statutes when the effect has been to advance economic conservatism, while Democratic justices have supported judicial review when the effect has been to further political liberalism.[16] Moreover, many of the justices have remained so intensely involved in the liberal-conservative ideological struggle that they have not hesitated to attempt to influence Presidents who were in the process of selecting new colleagues for them; indeed, for a justice to behave otherwise is politically irrational.[17]

During the Court's first century, geographical considerations were much more important than they are today. At a time when Supreme Court justices still rode circuit and participated in the decision-making of the circuit courts, there was a stronger functional reason why men should be picked from among the various subcultural regions of the country. Presumably such men would be more familiar with the variations in public policy that were preferred within their regions, more sympathetic to the cultural peculiarities of their regions, and hence more acceptable to the politically active denizens. Moreover, at a time when national politics were regionally organized, the ability of a justice to function as a regional political representative was important. Today, however, regional "balance" in the Court seems to be no more important a consideration than it is in the selection of a presidential cabinet. Hoover's appointment of Cardozo in 1932, for example, made three New Yorkers plus one justice each from Pennsylvania (Philadelphia) and Massachusetts (Boston), a clear majority of the Court, from a fairly short strip of the Atlantic seacoast. It is also quite possible to have a Court that (although selected for other reasons) appears to be regionally well balanced. The geographic distribution of the home residences of the incumbent justices listed in Table IV is as follows: two from the Northeast; two from the Middle West; two from the South; two from the far West;

and one from the Rocky Mountain region. Thus the Supreme Court inherited by Lyndon Johnson showed such a high degree of regional balance that it even included another Texan.

INTERACTION AND LEADERSHIP

There is consensus among many scholars using different methods of analysis that the justices of the Supreme Court, at least during the past four decades (upon which research thus far has tended to focus), have been divided consistently into subsets of relatively liberal more extreme groups of ideological partisans.[18] During the middle 1930's, for example, there was a liberal subgroup consisting of Bran-justices and of relatively conservative justices, with one or more moderate justices who have given consistent support to neither of the deis, Cardozo, and Stone; a conservative subgroup consisting of But-ler, McReynolds, Sutherland, and Van Devanter; and two justices, Hughes and Roberts, who gave somewhat greater support to the conservative bloc *before*, and to the liberal bloc *after*, President Roosevelt's attack on the Court in February 1937. During the 1940's, the liberal bloc consisted of Black, Douglas, Murphy, and Rutledge; the conservatives included Vinson, Burton, and Reed; while the other two justices, Frankfurter and Jackson, were even more conservative than the Vinson group on economic issues but more liberal than the Vinson group on issues of civil liberty. As Table IV indicates, the 1963 Court again contained a bloc of four liberals; but the retirement (at the end of 1961) of Frankfurter and Whittaker left only one consistent conservative, Harlan. Of the other four incumbent justices, Stewart was a moderate on civil liberty issues but a conservative on economic issues; Goldberg was a liberal on civil liberty issues but a moderate on economic issues; and Clark and White were conservative on civil liberty issues but moderate on economic issues.

A study of the Taney Court (1837–1860)[19] indicates that it, too, was divided between liberal and conservative justices and in regard to political and economic and social issues. The issues examined were state regulation of slavery, corporations, and interstate commerce—at the time, of course, there was little or no national governmental regulation of any of these subjects. In terms of equivalent contemporary policy issues, the politically liberal (pro-civil liberty) position was to favor the abolition of slavery, and the economically liberal position was to uphold state control over business corporations. Somewhat surprisingly, the important cleavage was not between Northerners and Southerners. Instead, it was between Jacksonian Democrats (on these issues, political conservatives and economic liberals) and Whigs (political liberals and economic conservatives).

As previously suggested, certain aspects of the role of the Chief Justice thrust him into a position of formal leadership.[20] Among the most important of his formal functions that facilitate his leadership of the group is his assignment of the opinion of the Court. (The Chief Justice makes this assignment when he votes with the majority; if he dissents, then the senior associate justice voting with the majority determines who will write the opinion.) The assignment to speak for the Court can be used to stake out a relatively extreme policy position, as when Warren has Douglas or Black write in a pro-civil liberty decision; but when such a decision is five to four, the opinion is likely to be assigned to the moderate judge who is the marginal member of the majority, because to do otherwise might result in losing the majority and hence control over the decision.

Recent research indicates that it is useful to distinguish between two kinds of group leadership: "task" and "social."[21] In leading the justices through the decision-making of the weekly conference, for example, one essential function is to get decisions made, so that the Court will not fall so far behind in its docket that criticism from outside will be attracted. To get decisions made, group discussion must be focused and to some extent limited, and this requires task leadership. But the discussion involves nine men—a relatively large "small group"—all of whom are quite independent of each other in their life tenure and among whom there are complex patterns of relationships of ideological affinity and conflict, depending upon the issue under discussion. Their attitudes toward public policy issues tend to be reinforced by their attitudes toward each other: some are close personal friends, and others are involved in what at times have been notorious "feuds." In other words, social leadership is necessary to control the level of emotional relationships in the discussions if decision-making is to proceed in an efficient manner.

Some Chief Justices, such as Hughes, have been outstanding in both leadership roles. Others have done well in one role and poorly in the other. Taft, for example, was a good social leader, but he depended upon Van Devanter to function as the effective foreman in constructing the Court's majorities for decision-making. Stone, on the other hand, was so much a democrat that he was not an effective task leader, and he was so much an ideological partisan that he was also ineffective in the social leadership role. An analysis of the level of consensus in the Court's decision-making under all seven of the Chief Justices between 1888–1958 has demonstrated that the justices were more deeply and variously divided in their voting under Stone than at any other time during the seven decades.[22] Efficiency in getting decisions made, however, is not the only relevant standard of effective leadership, nor is it necessarily the best criterion. It has been argued that in comparison with Hughes' autocratic management, Stone encouraged full and open discussion of the issues. If a major aspect of the Supreme Court's role is to educate its audience, then open articulation of value and policy disagreements among the justices is preferable to their being smothered under a spurious mantle of togetherness and contrived consensus.[23]

ATTITUDES

Sociometric analysis of interagreement in voting behavior, which focused upon a pool of all of the votes of all of the justices, in cases decided on the merits during a stipulated period, showed (as reported above) that the Court characteristically divided into a liberal bloc and a conservative bloc. But bloc analysis also showed that there were usually some justices who did not seem to affiliate with either bloc, and there seemed to be a considerable amount of inconsistent voting, even among the bloc members—inconsistent, that is, in the sense that in some decisions one or more justices would vote with members of the "opposing" bloc rather than with members of their own bloc. The latter findings were perplexing, and it was not until the introduction of more powerful research tools that they were understood. At first through linear cumulative scaling and subsequently through factor analysis and multidimensional scaling, studies of the voting behavior of Supreme Court justices have shown that there are three major attitudinal components of judicial liberalism and conservatism. In order better to distinguish among them, we shall henceforth refer to the three components as "attitudes," and we shall designate as "ideologies" the more general concepts of liberalism and conservatism.

The three major attitudes are (1) *political* liberalism and conservatism; (2) *economic* liberalism and conservatism; and (3) *social* liberalism and conservatism.[24] We shall exemplify and define in greater detail each of these attitudes in the concluding section of this chapter. Here it is sufficient to say that political liberalism is the belief in and the support of civil rights and liberties; political conservatism is the upholding of law and order and the defense of the status quo—no matter what may be the pattern of accepted values that the status quo happens to represent. Economic liberalism is the belief in and the support of a more equal distribution of wealth, goods, and services; the economic conservative defends private enterprise, vested interests, and broad differentials in wealth and income between the owners of property and laborers. A social liberal is a person who is liberal in both of the other two attitudes and who therefore upholds individual personal rights (political liberalism) but collective property rights (economic liberalism); a social conservative upholds collective personal rights but individual property rights. The social liberal favors change—disequilibrium—in regard to both personal and property rights; the social conservative favors the status quo—homeostasis—in regard to both. It is easy to see, however, that it is quite possible for a judge to feel that he is being consistent in his ideology if he favors political liberalism and economic conservatism, for this combination of attitudes means to uphold both the personal and the property rights of the individual. Similarly, a justice who consistently upholds the necessarily collectivized interests represented by the government will be politically conservative and economically liberal in his attitudes.

Let us assume that the attitude of social liberalism defines a position that is the core of a broader range of attitudes extending from political liberalism through economic liberalism, which together span the range of the liberal ideology (see Figure 2, below). Similarly, we can define an opposing conservative ideology. The range from economic conservatism to political liberalism defines the ideology of individualism; the opposite range defines collectivism.

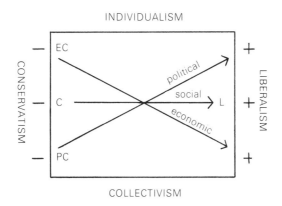

Figure 2
A Paradigm of the Relationship between Judicial Types and Output Norms

We find Supreme Court justices in all four categories of ideological type: some are liberals, some are conservatives, some are individualists, some are collectivists. Among the incumbents, we can see from Table IV that there are four liberals (Douglas, Black, Warren, and Brennan), one conservative (Harlan), two individualists (Goldberg and Stewart), and two collectivists (Clark and White). None of the last four justices fits the ideological types perfectly—Goldberg, Clark, and White because of their economic moderation, and Stewart because of his political moderation.

The attitudinal issues to which the justices respond are not necessarily manifest in either their opinions or the records of the cases. *Prima facie*, for example, no question of law is raised for decision by the Court when it reviews the decisions of lower courts (state or national) in Federal Employers' Liability Act evidentiary cases. The statutory law, presumably, is clear, or at least, to the extent that it is not, it was clarified long ago by interpretative decisions of the Supreme Court. The question at issue always is whether, given the unique set of facts that have been "found" by the trial court in the particular case, the evidence of employer negligence was sufficient to support a jury verdict of damages in favor of the injured railroad worker.

Conservative critics have castigated the Court throughout the past decade for its perverse persistence in wasting its time in hearing such appeals; the precious time of the Court, the critics insist, should be reserved for the decision of more important policy issues. (As Frankfurter again and again reminded his colleagues, it is not their role to play God; they cannot note the fall of every sparrow and attempt to correct all the mistakes of judgment of lower courts— if, indeed, they be mistakes.) But the issue is not exclusively "what really happened when the employee was injured"; the latent policy issue is: who should bear the economic costs of industrial accidents, when the system for allocation consists of a right to a lawsuit instead of a workmen's compensation schedule? Should the economic as well as the physical injury be borne exclusively by the worker (or his widowed family), or should at least the economic cost be collectively shared? Of course, the Supreme Court has no "legal right" to decide any such question, since the Congress presumably answered it (primarily in the negative) when it enacted the statute more than half a century ago. Consequently, the opinions of the justices tend to be confined to ostensibly legal questions of "contributory negligence" and the "weight of the evidence." Nevertheless, the latent question, which taps the justices' attitudes and to which they respond in their voting, is: where do your basic sympathies lie—with economic underdogs or with their employers? In case after case, no matter what the variation in the "facts," economic liberals vote to uphold the claims of workers, and economic conservatives vote against them.[25]

PREDICTION

In analyzing the prediction of judicial decision-making, it is possible to work with various classes of variables. The broadest and most diffuse class consists of the kinds of cultural factors discussed in Chapter One as "The Political Environment." The cultural variables define the range of variation for attribute variables, which include the kinds of personal background factors discussed above. Attributes, in turn, affect attitudes, which determine decisions. We expect, therefore, that prediction will be most likely to succeed between adjacent classes of variables: between cultural and attribute variables; between attribute and either cultural or attitudinal variables; between attitudinal and either attribute or decisional variables; and between decisional and attitudinal variables. This implies that the prediction of judicial decision-making behavior will be most successful if it is based upon the observation and measurement of judicial attitudes.

In their search for rationality in decision-making, lawyers have sought to find it in the patterns of policy norms, in the decisions and opinions that are the outputs of the conversion process.[26] One of the problems that they have encountered is that the norms appear to be continuously in flux, no doubt reflecting changes both in the composition of the Court and in the socioeconomic bases of the issues presented to it. There is a high degree of rationality in judicial decision-making, but it consists primarily of the *psychological* rationality of consistency in the structuring of attitudes in the minds of individual judges, rather than of the *logical* rationality of consistency in the structuring of the rationalizations for outcomes found in their written opinions. If judges did decide present cases in particular ways *because* their predecessors have so decided "similar" cases, then the principle of *stare decisis* would explain the conversion process. We should not then need to be concerned about judges' personal beliefs and individual attitudes, which would, in any event, be irrelevant to the outcomes of decisions and therefore to the outputs of courts. If this were true, *stare decisis* ought to operate, of course, only in phase with a "natural" chronology—that is, judges ought to decide present cases on the basis of past precedents; we should not expect to find them deciding cases, at some time in the past, on the basis of future "precedent" decisions that have not yet been established! Nevertheless, the recent work of a scholar who was seeking to validate— to prove that judges really do follow—the principle of *stare decisis* shows that in several different policy areas and with different courts, it was possible for him to predict the outcomes of decisions just as well (and in some instances, better) working *backwards* rather than *forwards* through time.[27] In short, the "legal precedents" could be predicted just as well from the "future decisions" as the latter from the former. What this suggests, of course, is that the underlying consistency was very high but that this consistency was in the attitudes of the judicial decision-makers toward the policy issues, not in cause-and-effect relationships among either the decisions or the output norms that the decisions are presumed to imply.

Attempts to improve the accuracy with which outcomes can be predicted have constituted an important research activity in recent years. Naturally, this is a question of considerable interest to, and with important practical consequences for, practicing lawyers. The usual approach to prediction of outcomes, which is highly quali- tative and intensely personal and subjective, is well illustrated by the success with which a Yale law professor predicted the outcome in the Supreme Court's first major reapportionment decision, *Baker* v. *Carr*.[28] With this should be compared, however, the equally successful pre- diction, by a practicing lawyer who made his forecast using Boolean algebra and a computer,[29] of a recent major civil rights decision of the Court.[30] The important difference between these two types of prediction is that the latter represents a technique that is communi- cable and transferable to other researchers and that can be replicated by them; the former does not. In the same research, the computer analyst found it necessary to distinguish among what he designated as three different types of *stare decisis*: traditional, local, and personal. By traditional *stare decisis* he meant the obligation of a lower court to follow the policy norms output by a higher court, or the obligation of the Supreme Court to follow its own precedents; by local *stare decisis* he meant the obligation of one panel of a court of appeals to follow the precedents established by other panels of the same court; and by personal *stare decisis* he meant the consistency of the individual justices with their own earlier voting behavior on similar issues. Evidently, in his analysis of personal *stare decisis* he was meas- uring the consistency of the attitudes of individual justices toward the defined sub-issue of political liberalism. His attempt to predict the Supreme Court's decision in *Gideon* v. *Wainwright* (discussed be- low) on the basis of traditional *stare decisis* was unsuccessful; but when he programmed his computer in terms of the personal atti- tudes of the then incumbent justices of the Supreme Court, he did very well indeed.

The research on outcomes focuses upon the particular decisions in individual cases; a different but at least as important recent emphasis has been upon statistical prediction—that is, upon sets of aggregate outcomes, which characterize the Court's decision-making behavior in grosser but more comprehensive terms than does the prediction of individual case outcomes. One such study has analyzed the Supreme Court's jurisdictional decision-making in order to specify the attributes of cases that the Court is most likely to accept for decision-making on the merits.[31] Another recent venture attempted, with only partial success, to extrapolate from various quantitative indices of the Court's output in several recent terms to the equivalent indices for the term that was then getting under way.[32] The most fruitful and probably the most fundamental work done to date, however, has been the prediction of pattern relationships in voting behavior on the basis of the assumption of stability in individual attitudes. The rank-order relationships of the justices, on scales of political and economic liberalism, are highly stable from term to term.[33] As techniques for the analysis of the content of issue inputs become more refined, it may be possible to predict both the outcomes and other aspects of the decision-making behavior of the Supreme Court (and of other courts as well) on a systematic basis and with considerable accuracy. Prediction would thus serve to validate the construction of theory about judicial behavior, which in turn might have important implications for understanding the behavior of persons other than judges.

## POLICY OUTPUTS

One way to conceptualize the Supreme Court's output is in terms of the policy norms that are associated with the decisions in cases. According to our theory, such policy norms are isomorphic with the major attitudinal components in terms of which we measure ideological differences among the justices. Inferences about the attitudes of individual justices and about the policy norms associated with decisions are both based upon scaling (rank-order) measurement of sets of judicial votes. We shall discuss below the major subcomponents of the Court's outputs as functions of the attitudinal variables considered above.

There are three important sets of subcomponent norms: political, social, and economic. The political norms are the output counterpart of the political liberalism attitudinal component; similarly, the economic norms are equivalent to positions on the economic attitudinal variable. The social norms correspond to an attitudinal position midway between political and economic liberalism. In other words, the social norms correspond to a continuum representing the attitudinal position (see Figure 2) of justices who are consistently either liberal or conservative on both political and economic issues; stated otherwise, the social policy norms constitute the heart of the ideological differences that separate liberals and conservatives.[34] Social norms define the policy area in which the Court's decisions have had the greatest impact upon the American polity during the past two decades. Political norms have been of secondary importance, while economic norms have been relegated to last place. It is worth noting that only three decades ago it would have been necessary to reverse the order of importance; at that time, the Court's economic norms were its most important output, then political norms, and last social norms. No doubt, this reversal is both an index and a result of the shift in the ideological control over the Court that has occurred during the past thirty years. The Hughes Court of the middle 1930's was dominated by conservatives; the Warren Court of the middle 1960's is dominated by liberals. The defense of the status quo in the 1930's did not require the "Nine Old Men" of the New Deal era to consider directly the issues involved in social norms, but the Supreme Court's most conspicuous effect upon the federal polity during the past decade has been to force the consideration of social issues by other decision-makers.

SOCIAL NORMS

There can be little question that the Supreme Court's most important decisions since the end of World War II have been in regard to the issues traditionally denominated as "civil rights": racial equality, representational equality, and citizenship equality, all of which constitute varying facets of the norm of equal rights of American citizenship. Typical of the Court's extension of its policy of racial equality are several recent decisions upholding integrationists in their recourse to direct economic and political pressure[35] and protecting, from harassment in state courts and by state legislatures, organizations which work for integrationist goals.[36] The Court has followed up *Baker* v. *Carr* with several more recent decisions that have extended the policy requiring representational equality in state legislatures.[37] The changes that have occurred as a result of the Court's racial integration and legislative apportionment decisions are so conspicuous that we all are familiar with them. Somewhat less well publicized have been the Court's decisions in regard to equal citizenship status and rights for Americans abroad—or seeking to go abroad.[38] In fact, this is the only policy basis upon which the Supreme Court has declared acts of Congress to be unconstitutional during the past decade, and there have been no less than eleven such decisions.[39] (It has been unnecessary for the Court to declare acts of *Congress* unconstitutional[40] in order to establish its policies regarding racial equality and legislative reapportionment, because in these latter areas it has been almost exclusively state legislation at issue. The Court has not hesitated to declare such state statutes unconstitutional, generally on the rationale that they are in conflict with the equal protection clause of the Fourteenth Amendment.) Judging from the outputs, civic equality is the value that ranks highest in the beliefs of a majority of the justices of the Supreme Court at the present time.

There are four major subcomponents of political policy norms. All four are concerned with what traditionally have been called "civil liberties": personal privacy, fair procedure, religious freedom, and political freedom. Some justices apparently have perceived the issues of personal privacy and religious freedom to be sufficiently different, both from each other and from fair procedure and political freedom, that it is questionable whether these four ought to be associated together in a common category.[41] Since the end of World War II, however, there has been consensual agreement among the justices that fair procedure is attitudinally isomorphic with political freedom, and a majority at least would associate the other two issues as well. By "attitudinally isomorphic" we mean that when the justices differ in their voting behavior in the decision of cases raising the issues of either fair procedure or political freedom, they do so in the same rank order. This does not mean that the direction of the policy outputs has been the same for these two issues. In recent years, the Court's policies have been most liberal in regard to personal privacy and fair procedure; they have been (relatively) most conservative in regard to political freedom; and they have been generally (but not consistently) liberal in regard to religious freedom.

*Personal Privacy.* The legal questions subsumed in this issue are those of searches and seizures (in relation to the Fourth and Fourteenth Amendments) and involuntary confessions (in relation to the Fifth and Fourteenth Amendments); from a behavioral point of view, questions of both physiological and psychological privacy are relevant.[42] In the 1960 term, the Court overruled the conservative precedent that had been established in 1949, when the Court was dominated by Truman appointees, and established the policy that evidence obtained as the result of police invasions of personal privacy would not be admitted in either a state or a national court.[43] The trial courts of the nation were directed by the Court, in short, to punish illegal police behaviors by ignoring what often would be the most relevant "facts" necessary to convict criminals. Two years later, however, the Court took a step backwards, in a five-to-four decision which posited the norm that the admission of evidence seized incident to an arrest without a warrant is permissible if the police have information which would support a reasonable belief on their part that the suspect was committing a continuing offense.[44] The latter outcome would have been quite different were it not for the fact that Justice Black, who voted with the majority, has been throughout his quarter century on the Court much more conservative in his attitude toward the issue of personal privacy than toward the issues of fair procedure and political freedom. A different aspect of the issue was presented recently by a case which challenged a Connecticut statute that proscribed birth control clinics; this is a question that is complicated by religious and ethnic interest divisions, but a majority of the justices voted to invalidate the statute as an invasion of the right to marital privacy.[45]

*Fair Procedure.* This issue concerns the rights of accused defendants to a fair hearing and/or trial in proceedings before national or state courts, administrative agencies, and legislative committees. Term in and term out, the Supreme Court has in recent years decided more cases relating to this issue than to any other; generally, the decisions have been increasingly liberal. Typical are several decisions of the 1962 term. In *Gideon* v. *Wainwright*[46] the justices unanimously postulated the new policy norm that indigent criminal defendants in state trial courts must be provided lawyers at public expense; this had been the Court's requirement for the national courts since 1938. The Court thus overruled a twenty-year-old precedent that had established the policy only for defendants charged with capital offenses—viz., the same policy that had applied in the national courts from 1790 until 1938. (But *Betts* v. *Brady* [1942] had been a relatively liberal policy pronouncement for its day, because previously there had been *no* national policy regarding the right to counsel in state courts.) This right of the indigent to counsel in the trial courts was then buttressed by a series of decisions that established the new policy that, state law to the contrary notwithstanding, the majority of impecunious as well as the minority of affluent criminal defendants must be permitted to appeal their convictions to appellate state courts.[47]

*Religious Freedom.* Lawyers distinguish between questions of "freedom of religion" and "the separation of church and state" because of the grammatical disjunction in the language of the First Amendment (which employs, incidentally, neither of the quoted phrases); but the justices themselves do not appear to make such a distinction in their attitudes and voting behavior, so neither shall we. In recent years, the Court has been quite active in this area; the result has been to engender more public controversy and discussion than has been provoked over any other of the issues that we discuss except racial equality and legislative reapportionment. A majority of the Court's conservative critics have attacked the generally libertarian policies of religious freedom supported by a majority of the justices as being "atheistic" and "Communist inspired," as when the justices unanimously declared unconstitutional as a test oath a Maryland state constitutional provision that required notaries public to declare their belief in God.[48] In the Sunday Closing Cases, however, preponderant majorities of the justices upheld the right of Christian popular majorities to compel Jews (and other Sabbatarians), in their entrepreneurial and employment practices, to observe the Christian Sabbath; to the extent that this resulted in economic hardship for Jews (who, unlike Christians, thus were compelled by a combination of conscience and the Christian law to close their shops two days a week), they could be comforted by Chief Justice Warren's implication that this was a small sacrifice for a Jewish minority to make so that Christians could enjoy the peace and quiet of family picnics and other leisure activities "customary" on the day of rest. Clearly, this was not a very liberal policy. However, whatever good will the Court might have attracted from the Christian majority by its conservative policy on Sunday closing was dissipated by its decisions in the next two terms, to the effect that there should be no recitation of the Lord's Prayer or reading from the Bible in public schools.[49]

*Political Freedom.* Throughout the 1950's, the two major questions of political freedom with which the Supreme Court dealt were: (1) the suppression of the Communist party and its satellite organizations; and (2) the censorship of books, magazines, and motion pictures. In short, the issues were the extent to which there should be communication of relatively extremist ideas in matters of politics and sex. The Court vacillated on the Communist issue throughout the 1950's, and in a series of decisions in the 1960 term, a majority of the justices in effect upheld the authority of both national and state legislating investigative committees to punish witnesses who had engaged in earlier public criticism of the committees[50] and also upheld what some libertarians thought amounted (in the language of the eighteenth century) to "bills of attainder" against the Communist party[51] and its members.[52] (In this same term, a five-to-four majority upheld a lower court decision, the effect of which seemed to be that a person who took seriously the Declaration of Independence could not become a lawyer in Illinois.[53]) It seems clear that the Court in recent terms has approved a relatively conservative policy permitting suppression of political dissent. At the same time, the Court has been quite liberal in its policy-making in regard to the censorship of artistic expression.[54] In sharp contrast even to the years of World War II, during the past decade there has occurred a somewhat wholesale loosening of the puritanical ties by which the mass media had been confined. As a direct consequence of the libertarian policies of the Supreme Court, for example, what might be called the proletarian response to the Court's liberalism has taken the form of the proliferation of much bad art accompanying the more open communication of ideas about sex (viz., nudist movies in color and the endless array of girlie magazines in drugstore racks).

Our analysis of the workload of the lower national courts indicated that most cases raised questions of conflicting property interests rather than of civil rights or liberties. Although there is variance from term to term, in the period since World War II the Supreme Court has decided on the merits almost precisely the same number of cases raising economic issues as it has cases raising social or political issues. With the single exception of the claims of injured workers under the Federal Employers' Liability Act and related statutes[55] (discussed on p. 122, above), the Court generally has not taken a policy position in conflict with that of Congress, the administration, or most state legislatures. To the contrary, the Supreme Court has played a supporting role, adjusting legislative policies (through statutory interpretation) but not opposing them as the Hughes Court did so conspicuously thirty years ago. Generally, therefore, the economic policies supported by the majority of the justices have been relatively liberal. The Court has tended to be pro-union, pro-governmental regulation of business, antimonopoly, and supportive of state taxation (against business claims that it violates various provisions of the national Constitution). The liberal majority, however, has construed economic liberalism to require the upholding of unions, even though doing so has had the effect of forcing individual members to support (through union dues) a political party or candidates other than those preferred by such members,[56] and even when unions discriminated against their own members.[57] Characteristic of the Court's decisions upholding governmental regulation of business is *United States* v. *Parke Davis*, an antitrust case in which the majority upheld action by the Department of Justice to stop a major drug producer from rigging retail prices at artificially high levels. An example of the Court's typical response today to claims that state taxation is unconstitutionally in conflict with the commerce or equal protection clauses of the national Constitution is *Alaska* v. *Arctic Maid*,[58] in which an eight-man majority upheld a 4 per cent tax on salmon freezer ships; only Harlan was sufficiently conservative in his economic attitude to dissent in favor of the freedom of "interstate commerce" (viz., business enterprise) from state regulation.

# Ideology and
# Judicial Review

The Constitution of the United States was a by-product of a physical revolution that took the form of a successful civil war; it was also the product of a revolutionary ideological movement—an uprising of aristocrats and men of property in the face of what they perceived to be a crisis created by the democratic excesses of the war and postwar periods (roughly, 1775–1788). The liberal democratic ideology of the Declaration of Independence, which had served its purpose as a call to arms for the masses, was displaced in a counterrevolution of the right, which found its fruition in the conservative framework for policy-making that became the Constitution. The Bill of Rights, it will be recalled, was not a part of the proposal put forth by the Philadelphia Convention but was engrafted to it as the concession that the right had to make to the left to make ratification possible. By 1790 the conservative counterrevolution had resulted in similar changes in almost all of the state constitutions, with the establishment of such conservative checks and balances— to displace the dangerous radicalism of unicameral legislatures responsible to popular majorities—as bicameralism and independent chief executives and state judiciaries. But for the next dozen years, the notion that judges had authority to make interpretations of the Constitution binding on the executive and the legislature was a minority view, even among Federalists. It is true that "At the apex of the governmental system which Hamilton and his associates aimed to permanently entrench in the American way of life was an independent and for most important practical purposes a supreme Judiciary."[1] But most conservatives thought of judicial review as a veto over possible legislative attempts to dominate the judiciary. Somewhat ironically, many liberals also favored a limited power of judicial review, once an independent executive had been restored in lieu of the king, but for the quite different reason that they hoped the judges would uphold civil liberties against the arbitrary and zealous acts of administrative officials. After Jefferson's first administration, however, the question was put in the broader terms that Hamilton had urged; since then, it has always been a matter of the extent to which, and with regard to what areas of policy, the Supreme Court can make decisions that must be accepted—at least in the short run—by Congress, the President, and the states and their subcomponents, as well as by private individuals and groups.

The basic ambivalence of political attitudes toward judicial review has persisted from the time of the Philadelphia Convention until today. Conservatives have looked upon the courts as a bulwark to safeguard property rights generally and privilege and preferred status in all forms, while liberals have expected courts to protect individual liberty and civil rights. By and large, in fact, the strongly conservative orientation of the legal profession has resulted in the courts' functioning much more in accord with the conservative than with the liberal ideal.

The reasons for the conservatism of the legal profession have often been adduced. The common-law tradition looks backward to the problems of the past and to the accommodations for those problems that were contrived by judges of an earlier day. With very few exceptions, commentators upon and teachers of law have looked upon it as a great stabilizing force, the purpose of which is to improve the predictability of future outcomes of present human decisions, rather than as an instrument for helping to bring about social, economic, and political change. In practice, lawyers typically associate with—and find their own economic interests to be aligned with—the business sector of the community; throughout American history, the lawyer who has risen to a position of national preeminence has generally done so on the basis of his demonstrated ability to defend and represent with exceptional ability and unusual success the interests of whatever form of wealth was dominant at the time. Thus the great lawyers have utilized their skills to bring the law into congruence with the demands for special advantage of the land companies, plantation owners, railroad magnates, cattle barons, and lumber kings of the nineteenth century; of the great industrial combinations (née trusts) of the twentieth century, including big oil, coal, steel, shipping, automobiles, air transport, and hydroelectric power, or of big labor. In the near future, we can expect to find great lawyers identifying their careers with the complex of industries that has emerged in relation to the development of atomic power and space exploration. As the most distinguished elite group of the legal profession, judges have tended to include predominantly those lawyers who, because of their background and experience, were in the most conservative wing of the profession. Thus it is not surprising that most judges have, in their decisions, identified with conservative rather than liberal ideals.

## STRUCTURAL THEORIES OF JUDICIAL REVIEW

### THE SEPARATION OF POWERS

The relative influence of conservative and liberal ideas in the decision-making of the United States Supreme Court can be traced by examining the major trends in the Court's use of judicial review and the patterns of constitutional norms that the Court has preferred. Usually, judicial review is defined in normative terms as a function of judicial activism and restraint, concepts which are themselves derived from the structural constitutional principles of the separation of powers and of federalism. (We shall discuss at a later point in this chapter a functional theory of judicial activism and restraint.) Thus it is argued that the separation of powers demands that the Court ought (or ought not) to exercise restraint by deferring to the decision-making of Congress and/or the President, who are directly elected by the people and hence are politically responsible while the justices themselves are said to be politically irresponsible. Thus liberalism frequently is equated with judicial restraint and conservatism with judicial activism. As examples of constitutional interpretation based upon such an approach, we might consider Marshall's decision in *Marbury* v. *Madison,* which often is cited as both the initial and a most extreme instance of an activist attempt by the justices to extend their power over legislative and executive policy-making; a more recent instance is *Panama Refining Co.* v. *Ryan,* in which the Hughes Court declared unconstitutional part of the National Industrial Recovery Act of the New Deal era. It happens, of course, that in both of these instances there had been a recent major shift in party control over the Presidency and the Congress; hold-over justices, who had been appointed by the conservative (Federalist and Republican) administrations that recently had been repudiated at the polls, used judicial review to attempt to check political changes initiated by the newly installed liberal (Democratic-Republican and Democratic) administrations of Thomas Jefferson and Franklin Roosevelt. Therefore, in both examples, the orthodox conception of judicial review (as an institutional instrument for defending conservative values) is compatible with the outcomes of the Court's decisions; the consensus is that, in terms of the substantive content of the public policy issues at stake in these cases, the Court upheld the conservative position. But the concept no longer is compatible with the impact of the Court's decisions once judicial review is used to check conservative policies of Congress and the President. Suppose that Marshall's Court had struck down the Alien and Sedition Acts, or, similarly, suppose the Chase Court had declared unconstitutional the Reconstruction Acts. It is only in the contemporary period that we find a majority of the Supreme Court taking a more liberal position on public policy issues than Congress and the President, but it is now clear that judicial review is by no means restricted to serving as a conservative check on liberal policies. Therefore the structural theory of judicial review, which presumes that judicial review necessarily is a conservative weapon, is false.

FEDERALISM

A second structural theory of judicial review is based upon the constitutional principle of federalism. According to this theory, the Court ought (or ought not) to defer to state policy-making—to uphold "states' rights" (in legal terminology). Liberalism generally has been identified with judicial restraint in the review of state action, while conservatism has been equated with activist judicial decisions that declare state action to be unconstitutional. Hamilton and Jefferson were in diametric opposition on the desirability of expanding the authority of the new national government, and the Marshall Court did implement the Federalist point of view in many decisions, such as in *McCulloch* v. *Maryland* and *Gibbons* v. *Ogden*. But who would characterize the states' rights decision of the Taney Court in *Dred Scott* v. *Sanford* as a liberal decision? Obviously, the tenability of the association of judicial activism with conservatism depended upon the validity of the assumption that state governments were "closer to the people" and more responsive to their electorates than was the national government. Certainly, such an assumption is most dubious today. The recent focusing of attention upon reapportionment has demonstrated conclusively that there is no more distortion of representation in the national House of Representatives than in many of the states; and the Senate, though constitutionally malapportioned (under the "one man, one vote" principle), is chosen from such relatively large constituencies that on most contemporary issues it takes a more liberal position than does the House. The Holmes-Brandeis notion of the states functioning as "laboratories for social and economic experiments," however meritorious it may have been fifty years ago, no longer fits the most patent facts of political life. As a rough generalization, it is true that the states tended to be both more politically responsive and more liberal in their policy-making than the national government during the nineteenth century and the first three decades of the twentieth; but the nation and the states have reversed roles since the advent of the Great Depression and the New Deal. Consequently, continued judicial deference to state policy-making no longer has the general effect of upholding liberal values.

The difficulty with both of the structural theories of judicial review is that they were developed to explain a set of relationships that no longer obtain in regard to congressional-presidential policy-making, vis-à-vis either the Court or the states. In normative terms, the values relied upon to justify judicial review in the earlier period function instead to justify judicial restraint in the contemporary period. In short, the judicial liberal no longer can have his cake and eat it too. This explains the dilemma that has troubled many of those who seek to resolve today's problems on the basis of the judicial "philosophies" of Holmes and Brandeis, for whom it was possible to advocate judicial restraint toward the review of state legislation establishing, for instance, a minimum wage law for female laborers, with the effect of upholding both principles—state experimentation in social policy and the furtherance of liberal social policies. But when a state today enacts an anti-union statute, a purported disciple of Holmes and Brandeis (such as the late Justice Frankfurter) must choose between liberalism defined as legislative deference and liberalism defined as support for organized labor. The former congruence between institutional and substantive values has been displaced by what is today often a conflict between them.

### TRENDS IN SUPREME COURT POLICY-MAKING

A more satisfactory explanation of the role of ideology in Supreme Court decision-making than that offered by the two structural theories can be based upon an examination of the substantive values that the Court has tended to prefer at different periods of time. If we further distinguish between the Court's policies in regard to civil liberties and economic issues, four basic periods can be denoted. Table V shows that the Court has favored civil liberties only during the contemporary period, while it has alternated between long periods of economic conservatism and of economic liberalism.

TABLE V

Supreme Court Policies
toward Political and Economic Liberalism, 1790–1965

| Period | Dates | Political Liberalism | Economic Liberalism |
|---|---|---|---|
| 1. Federalist/Marshall | 1790–1835 | − | − |
| 2. Taney/Miller | 1836–1890 | − | + |
| 3. Modern Conservatism | 1890–1937 | − | − |
| 4. Modern Liberalism | 1937–1965 | + | + |

TABLE VI

Attitudes of Supreme Court Justices
toward Civil Liberties and Economic Policy, 1790–1965

| Period | Dates | Political | | Economic | |
|---|---|---|---|---|---|
| | | Liberalism | Conservatism | Liberalism | Conservatism |
| 1. Federalist/ Marshall | 1790– 1835 | | | Iredell Johnson | Jay Marshall Story |
| 2. Taney/Miller | 1836– 1890 | Harlan (Sr.) | | Daniel Campbell Miller Waite | Story Field |
| 3. Modern Conservatism | 1890– 1937 | Harlan (Sr.) Holmes Brandeis | Brown Moody Taft Sanford | Holmes Brandeis | Fuller Peckham Van Devanter McReynolds Taft |
| 4. Modern Liberalism | 1937– 1965 | Murphy Rutledge Black Douglas Warren Brennan | Reed Minton Vinson Clark | Black Douglas Murphy Rutledge Warren Brennan | Frankfurter Jackson Harlan (Jr.) |

TABLE VII

Dominant Constitutional Norms Invoked in
Supreme Court Decision-Making, 1790–1965

| Norms | Period | | | |
|---|---|---|---|---|
| | Federalist/ Marshall 1790-1835 | Taney/ Miller 1836-1890 | Modern Conservatism 1890-1937 | Modern Liberalism 1937-1965 |
| Vested (natural) rights | ● | | | |
| Contract clause | ● | ● | ● | |
| Commerce clause | ● | ● | ● | |
| Diversity clause | | ● | ● | |
| 10th Amendment | | | ● | |
| 14th Amendment (due process and equal protection) | | | ● | ● |
| 5th Amendment | | | ● | ● |
| 1st Amendment | | | ● | ● |
| 6th Amendment | | | | ● |
| 4th Amendment | | | | ● |
| 8th Amendment | | | | ● |

In Table VI, the justices are classified according to the major periods and in terms of those who have been most extreme in their support of economic and political liberalism and conservatism. There were relatively few civil liberties decisions made by the Court before the Civil War; during the period 1837–1860, for example, there were only five non-unanimous decisions in which slavery was the major issue.[2] The data, or at least the studies that have been made thus far, are not adequate to support a valid and reliable classification of the attitudes of the justices toward civil liberties during the antebellum era. Otherwise, the justices listed are notable for the typicality of their representation, in both their voting and opinion behavior, of the liberal and conservative points of view in regard to the characteristic forms in which issues of economic and political policy arose at different times in the history of the Court. In the discussion that follows, we shall supplement both Tables V and VI with references to the dominant legal norms which the Court invoked to support its decisions (as summarized in Table VII) and also to some of the decisions typical of the three earlier periods.

THE FEDERALIST/MARSHALL ERA

As Table VII shows, the primary legal norms with which the Court worked during the Federalist/Marshall period were the contract and commerce clauses and an extraconstitutional "higher-law" theory of vested rights.[3] During the first decade of the Court's existence, few questions of constitutional interpretation were decided, although the political conservatism of the justices was amply demonstrated by their efforts to establish federal crimes on a "common-law" (in lieu of a statutory) basis and by their active participation on circuit in the prosecution (under the Sedition Act) of the supporters of Jefferson.[4] The most important decision politically of the pre-Marshall Court was *Chisholm* v. *Georgia,* which would have had the effect of extending considerably the scope of judicial review in the federal courts over state action; but this decision was overruled explicitly in less than two years by the adoption of the Eleventh Amendment to the Constitution. Under Marshall the Court wrote its natural-law theory of vested rights into the contract clause in such decisions as *Fletcher* v. *Peck,* upholding the Yazoo Land fraud and denying to the states the power to control the disposition of public lands, and *Dartmouth College* v. *Woodward,* upholding the right of a former king of England to give a private American corporation rights in perpetuity and denying to the states the authority to substitute public control over higher education for such closed corporations. State authority to regulate business enterprise was denied by the Marshall Court, now in the name of the commerce clause, in decisions such as *Gibbons* v. *Ogden* and *Brown* v. *Maryland.* There were no important decisions upholding claims of civil liberty during this period, and criminal trials in the federal courts—except for political crimes, during the Adams and Jefferson administrations—were relatively rare. The Marshall Court did decide *Barron* v. *Baltimore,* a case involving a claim of *property* right under the eminent domain clause of the Fifth Amendment and holding that the states were not bound by the Bill of Rights; the effect of this decision was clearly anti-civil libertarian.

THE TANEY/MILLER ERA

During the second period, the Court continued to rely upon the contract and commerce clauses as the primary constitutional norms to buttress the rationalization of decisions, but these were now redefined to support quite different outcomes than had been their function in the hands of Marshall. State authority to encourage economic development was upheld by the Taney Court, in preference to a monopolistic claim of vested right, in *Charles River Bridge* v. *Warren Bridge;* and in *Cooley* v. *Board of Wardens of Port of Philadelphia* the Taney Court upheld state authority to regulate selective aspects of foreign and interstate commerce, subject to the approval of the Court itself. The Court also undertook to encourage an expansion of the diversity jurisdiction of the federal courts, with the ostensible objective of aiding economic development through the establishment of a uniform system of judge-made commercial law. In *Swift* v. *Tyson* the Court ruled that a section of the Judiciary Act of 1789, requiring that the federal courts follow state law in diversity cases, applied only to state statutory law—not to judge-made or common law. Of course, *Swift* v. *Tyson* is an exception that contradicts our general characterization of this period as one of economic liberalism, for the enlargement of the authority of federal courts to make policy independent of both Congress and the state legislatures was good Federalist doctrine.

Nor was the Taney Court any less conservative than the Marshall Court in questions of civil liberties. *Luther* v. *Borden* involved what we might call today a reapportionment controversy: the Dorr Rebellion attempted to extend the suffrage beyond the extremely narrow and aristocratic base authorized by the pre-Revolutionary colonial charter that still functioned as Rhode Island's state constitution in 1841. The Taney Court denied a judicial remedy to Luther, who had supported Dorr, and thus in effect upheld the status quo and the conservative state government with the minority-rule electoral base that supported it. In the *Dred Scott* case, the Taney Court not only upheld the constitutionality of slavery but went out of its way to declare that the national government had no authority to prevent the extension of slavery to the national territories; Negroes were declared to be incapable of enjoying the status of citizenship under the Constitution of the United States because they were inferior beings who had no rights that the white man was bound to respect. Negroes had no civil rights or liberties under the Constitution, although the "dominant race" who owned them could, of course, claim constitutional rights to property in slaves.

Chief Justice Taney died during the Civil War; we have selected Associate Justice Samuel F. Miller to symbolize the latter half of the second period because he was the outstanding member of the Court at that time. The Court continued to rely upon the same constitutional norms (the contract, commerce, and diversity clauses), although the Fourteenth Amendment—which was adopted soon after the Civil War—became the principal repository for the higher-law theories of natural law and natural rights, particularly near the end of the period. What distinguishes the Miller Court from the succeeding period of Modern Conservatism is that it resisted the widespread and continuing attempts of the legal-business community to induce it to convert the new amendment into a check upon state regulatory power over the rapidly developing industrial system. Typical decisions were those in the Slaughterhouse Cases, in which the Court upheld the authority of a state to regulate butchering and the movement and storage of animals within a large city, and the Granger Cases, in which the Court sided with farmers by upholding state authority to regulate the rates to be charged by grain elevators and by railroads. Both of these decisions thus were economically liberal. The Miller Court's civil liberties decisions, however, were just as conservative as had been those of earlier periods of the Supreme Court.

The Court had explained in great detail, in Justice Miller's opinion in the Slaughterhouse Cases, that the Thirteenth, Fourteenth, and Fifteenth Amendments all had been adopted—in effect, as the terms of the victors upon the vanquished—for the sole and exclusive purpose of safeguarding the civil rights and liberties of the recently emancipated Negro slaves; therefore, such new constitutional norms as the privileges and immunities, equal protection, and due process clauses of the Fourteenth Amendment had no bearing upon the property rights of businessmen and their claims to be constitutionally exempt from governmental regulation. That was in 1873, during the middle of the Reconstruction period. Ten years later, however, six of the nine justices were different men, and the Court announced in the Civil Rights Cases that discrimination against Negroes by hotels, theaters, and railroads was not prohibited by the amendment and that, therefore, the congressional legislation which *did* prohibit such discrimination was unconstitutional; only public discrimination by the state itself would be illegal. But the Miller Court already had ruled in *Hall* v. *DeCuir* that a Louisiana statute *prohibiting* racial segregation on common carriers within the state was an unconstitutional burden upon interstate commerce; thus the upshot seemed to be that, in the view of the Supreme Court, neither the national nor the state governments could prevent segregation and discrimination against Negroes. The Miller Court also decided that the Fourteenth Amendment had not changed the policy announced by the Taney Court in *Barron* v. *Baltimore*: the Bill of Rights applied only to the national government. The criminal defendant in *Hurtado* v. *California* had no right to a due process of law that included indictment by a grand jury; only Mr. Justice Harlan (Sr.), the former slave-owner from Kentucky who had also dissented alone in the Civil Rights Cases, agreed with Hurtado. Patently, the above decisions were anti-civil libertarian in effect. The general consequence of the policies adopted by the Miller Court was that, some twenty years after its adoption and at the close of the second period, the Court had refused to use the Fourteenth Amendment to restrain the states in regulating either business or Negroes or the conduct of criminal trials.

## THE ERA OF MODERN CONSERVATISM

The third period begins at the end of the first century of the Supreme Court's existence. It is characterized by a complete reversal of the Court's policies in regard to economic issues, with both state and national authority to regulate the economy restrained by a bewildering array of constitutional norms that now commended themselves to the Court's majorities. In addition to the commerce and diversity clauses—and the contract clause, which was increasingly displaced by the due process clause of the Fourteenth Amendment—the Court invoked and manipulated the First, Fifth, and Tenth Amendments, and both the due process and equal protection clauses of the Fourteenth. Prior to 1890 the Court had had little occasion to concern itself with national regulation of business enterprise, because there was very little statutory or administrative basis for such regulation by the national government until the impact of Populism in the late 1880's resulted in the establishment of the Interstate Commerce Commission (1887) and the adoption of the Sherman Antitrust Act (1890). But the legislative and executive systems of the national government began for the first time to define a continuing general set of liberal socioeconomic programs, and there was a vast increase in counterpart activity by the states, at about the same time that the transition was completed from an essentially agricultural to an essentially industrial economy. Of course, the new legislative and executive policies of both the national and state systems were direct responses to the changed social and economic conditions brought about by industrialization; and the conservative interests that had lost control over the legislative and executive systems shifted their major attention—successfully—to the control of the judiciary in general and of the United States Supreme Court in particular. As explained by Arnold M. Paul, a leading scholar of the process of the change in the Court's policies at this time:

[B]y the 1890's it was a root principle of American conservatism that in time of social crisis, when rampant populism might threaten the established order, the Supreme Court must act as counterweight to the election returns, as defender of minority rights against majority rule. From the conservative point of view, this meant primarily the protection of property rights. . . . The great danger to be guarded against in America, so the conservative tradition ran, was a thrust from below, an upsurge of *the democracy* resentful at the growth of concentrated wealth and determined to use its majority power to effect redistribution. . . . The right-wing Federalists, . . . led by Hamilton and later by Marshall, had early regarded the judiciary as potentially the key bulwark of conservative defense. Certainly, in the Jeffersonian and Jacksonian periods the federal judiciary became the principal exponent of the conservative interest, the development of the contract clause and the vested-rights doctrine representing to conservatives just the kind of additional counterbalances deemed imperative to protect property rights and creditor claims in an era of advancing democracy and aggressive equalitarianism. . . . The line of conservative thought . . . emerging [in the late 1880's and early 1890's] may well be termed a form of neo-Federalism, a recrudescence of a traditional conservatism fearful of restless majorities upsetting the social order and the rights of property. . . . [T]he neo-Federalism of the 1890's opened the door to what was to prove in succeeding decades a full proliferation of judicial obstructionism. The Supreme Court of the United States became . . . an impediment to constitutional democracy[, e]xaggerating its powers beyond proportion in the period 1890–1937.[5]

The turning point had come in the Minnesota Rate Case (*Chicago, Milwaukee & St. Paul Ry.* v. *Minnesota*), in which the Court announced that state administrative regulation of railroad rates was unconstitutional unless subject to judicial approval. Thus railroad lawyers would no longer be directed, as in the Granger Cases, to take their cases to the electorate if they considered states rates to be too low; under the Minnesota Rate Case, they were now invited to take their cases to the courts, which would decide (under the due process rubric) what during the preceding decade had been a political question, meet only for the determination of the voters and their legislative representatives. By 1895 the floodgates were opened, and in that year the Supreme Court announced a whole series of pro-business decisions. The following are the better-known harbingers of the new conservatism on the Court: The Sugar Trust Case (*United States* v. *E. C. Knight Co.*), emasculating the Sherman Antitrust Act by removing (albeit temporarily) manufacturing from its scope; *In re Debs*, affirming the criminal conviction of a union leader for the offense of leading what had been a peaceful strike, against the Pullman Company in Chicago, until President Cleveland ordered the regular army into action against the workers and against the wishes of the Governor of Illinois, who protested the need for and the use of troops in order to maintain order; and *Pollock* v. *Farmers' Loan and Trust Co.*, in which the first peacetime national income tax was declared unconstitutional. There was a constant output of similar decisions during the next forty years.

The Court's policies remained conservative, so that the pattern of conservatism in both civil liberties and economic issues was indeed the same as that for the Federalist/Marshall period, thus supporting Paul's characterization of the Modern Conservative period as one of "neo-Federalism." Typical of the Court's civil liberties decisions during this period were *Plessy* v. *Ferguson*, upholding a Louisiana statute *requiring* segregation on common carriers within the state (cf. *Hall* v. *DeCuir*, above) against constitutional claims based on the Thirteenth and Fourteenth Amendments and establishing for the next half century the doctrine of "separate but equal rights" for Negroes; *Schenck* v. *United States*, denying the constitutional right of freedom of the press to a socialist protestant against universal military suffrage; and *Gitlow* v. *New York*, approving the criminal conviction by a state court of a leading communist writer for having published a communist "Manifesto." There was, however, one significant difference between the civil liberties decisions during the third and the earlier two periods. It was not a qualitative difference in the direction of the outcome of such decisions but was rather a quantitative difference: the sheer volume of cases raising claims of civil liberty, against both national and state action, was much greater and was accelerating as the period drew to a close. There was also a difference in that Harlan (Sr.) alone dissented in behalf of civil liberties claims during the second period, while both Holmes and Brandeis (and during the last few terms of the period, Stone, and Cardozo [*vice* Holmes]) frequently argued the civil libertarian cause during the third period. In this sense, the half century of dissents by Harlan (Sr.), Holmes, and Brandeis were one factor that helped to pave the way for the Court's conversion to a policy of civil libertarianism, just as Field had dissented for a quarter of a century in behalf of free enterprise, initially alone but subsequently in the company of Bradley and others, and thus had helped to make possible the Court's reversion to a policy of economic conservatism during the third period.

The fourth period marks a reversion to the policy of judicial restraint with regard to economic issues that the Court had followed throughout the middle decades of the nineteenth century. But even more importantly, perhaps, it denotes the first time in our constitutional history that the Supreme Court has followed a policy of judicial activism in support of civil rights and liberties. The contract clause was forgotten, and the policy upon which federal diversity jurisdiction had been based for a hundred years was sharply reversed —the decision in *Swift* v. *Tyson* was labeled by the Court itself as "unconstitutional" in *Erie Railroad Co.* v. *Tompkins*. The commerce clause was reconsidered and found to contain the major basis of constitutional support for a vast increase in national regulatory programs; at the same time, the commerce clause was also capable of accommodating many of the programs of state regulation of business that would have been declared burdens upon interstate commerce at any time during the four decades prior to 1937.

But the most impressive changes occurred in the content of the Fourteenth Amendment. During the third period, the due process and equal protection clauses of this amendment had only one function: to protect private property against "meddlesome" and "arbitrary" public interference. These same constitutional clauses were emptied of their economic content by overruling decisions of the Roosevelt Court during the decade subsequent to 1937,[6] and they became instead the repositories for many of the civil liberties enumerated in the Bill of Rights. Due process initially came to mean the First Amendment rights—freedom of speech, press, assembly, and religion; later, it subsumed the right to a fair criminal trial (with cognate clauses in the Fifth, Sixth, and Eighth Amendments); and recently it has been extended to include the right to privacy analogized to the Fourteenth Amendment. Similarly, the equal protection clause of the Fourteenth Amendment (which is prima facie applicable only to the states and not to the national government) has been found to contain guarantees to racial equality and fair electoral representation that have been fed back into the due process clause of the Fifth Amendment, so that the process of federalization of civil liberties has developed on a broad front, with the states and national government alike bound by constitutional clauses that heretofore had been thought to apply only to the one or to the other, but not to both. We shall not undertake at this point, as we have done for earlier periods, to suggest decisions typical of the fourth period, because in Chapter Five we already have exemplified in considerable detail the policy content of the Supreme Court's contemporary output.

## A FUNCTIONAL THEORY OF SUPREME COURT POLICY-MAKING

An understanding of the reason for the Court's infrequent but dramatic reversals on both major policy issues requires an examination of the relationship of political lag to the Court's decision-making. We may begin with the Dooley dictum that "no matther whether th' constitution follows th' flag or not, th' supreme coort follows th' iliction returns."[7] It is inevitable that in the *long* run the Supreme Court will follow the election returns: but it takes a very special set of circumstances for this to take place in the *short* run. This is because (as we explored in detail in Chapter Five) a major input for the Court's decision-making consists of the belief systems of the justices themselves, and the content of judicial values is largely determined by the choices that Presidents make in their appointments to the Court. A major swing in public opinion (such as that which resulted in the elections of Jackson and Franklin Roosevelt, and the absence of which resulted in the defeat of William Jennings Bryan) produces Presidents who are sufficiently extreme (in position on the liberalism-conservatism continuum) that they seek to place on the Court justices who also represent the values of the new majority. If the new political majority can hang together for at least a decade, it is virtually certain that the value orientation of a majority of the justices of the Supreme Court will be transformed. But there may also be a lag of several years before the normal attrition in Court membership (through death and retirement) creates enough vacancies for a reversal in the control of the Court to take place. Thus President Jackson appointed five Democratic associate justices, in addition to Taney, during his eight years in office; and with the exception of one Whig, only Democrats were appointed to the Court during the next quarter of a century. Conversely, beginning with Lincoln's appointments in 1862, and with the exception of Field (a "Peace Democrat" whom Lincoln appointed in 1863), only Republicans were appointed to the Court during the next quarter of a century. It was not until the 1880's, however, that the issues of slavery, the war (and its advent and aftermath), and territorial expansion were displaced by a rising concern for the economic and social problems brought about by the Industrial Revolution.

Students born in the middle of the twentieth century, accustomed to perceiving the Democratic party as a generally more liberal party than the Republican, may need to be reminded that Populism was a revolt against both major parties and that Grover Cleveland, although he was the only Democrat to be elected to the Presidency during the fifty-two years spanned by the Lincoln and Wilson inaugurations, was no liberal. Cleveland appointed four Democrats to the Court during his two separated terms of office. These included

Chief Justice Fuller, a corporation lawyer from Chicago who displaced Field as the leader of the Court's conservatives; L. Q. C. Lamar and White, both conservative Southerners; and Peckham, an upstate New Yorker who wrote the majority opinion in *Lochner* v. *New York*—the case that frequently is considered to symbolize the extreme of the Court's economic conservatism. President Harrison's four appointments, during the Cleveland interregnum (1889–1893), were just as conservative as Cleveland's, as exemplified by his choice of David Brewer, a Republican from Kansas who happened to be Field's nephew. These men, plus Field himself, comprised a majority of the Court during the critical years 1888–1896; it was they (and the Cleveland-Harrison administrations that put them in office) who were responsible for the Court's conversion from a general policy of economic liberalism to one of economic conservatism during the early 1890's. Indeed, it was in part in reaction to the decisions of 1895 that William Jennings Bryan emerged as the Democratic-Populist presidential candidate in 1896, and it was Bryan's defeat by McKinley that assured the continuation of the Court's newly embraced economic policies: "The judicial triumph of conservatism in the spring of 1895 had been confirmed by the political triumph of 1896."[8]

In the transition from the second to the third periods, the Supreme Court changed first and anticipated the election returns that signified the defeat of Populism, because the two major parties had closed ranks during the middle 1880's and for the next dozen years offered the electorate a choice between conservative candidates only. The inevitable result was that the Court itself was packed with conservatives. As a regional party, the Populists were strong enough to force the enactment of liberal legislation, but they did so at the cost of pushing the Supreme Court to a much more conservative position, because of the failure of the People's party to control the Presidency—and therefore the Supreme Court.

Woodrow Wilson was the only Democratic President, other than the conservative Cleveland, to serve between Lincoln and Franklin Roosevelt. One might ask why Wilson's election did not foreclose the third period and change the Court. There are several reasons why it did not. First, he did *not* come to office as the result of a major change in public opinion, such as supported Jackson and Franklin Roosevelt. Wilson was a minority President whose first term was made possible only because of the third-party candidacy of Theodore Roosevelt; the progressive legislative reforms to which he was committed were limited to his initial two years, in part because of the advent of the First World War. Second, Wilson made too few appointments to effect a major change in the Court; his predecessor, Taft, had taken great care to pack the Court with men who shared his own conservative views, and Taft had made six appointments during the three years preceding Wilson's inauguration. During his eight years in the Presidency, Wilson himself had only three vacancies to fill, one of which materialized only because Associate Justice Charles Evans Hughes resigned in 1916 to become the Republican presidential candidate in opposition to Wilson. Moreover, Wilson's selections were not such as to maximize his influence upon the Court: the first, McReynolds, was an arch-conservative who was paired for the next two decades in opposition to the liberal Brandeis, who was second, while his third selection, Clarke, was so liberal that he resigned from the Court after half a dozen years in order to campaign more actively for world peace. Thus the net impact of Woodrow Wilson's appointments was by no means great enough to change the direction of the Court's policy-making.

## POLITICAL LAG AND COURT-PACKING

A century before the New Deal, Andrew Jackson had packed the Court as a matter of course, appointing a majority of five justices as vacancies materialized and then inducing Congress to expand the size of the Court (during his closing months in office) from seven to nine in order "to insure a majority in that tribunal favorable to State Banks and negro slavery."[9] The "gold Democrat" Cleveland, in his first term, and Harrison (a "gold Republican") had between them appointed a new majority to the Court before the second Cleveland inaugural and the Panic of 1893, with which it coincided. In the first of these instances, there was no lag between the electoral and judicial changes; in the second, the judicial change actually preceded its electoral ratification—a case of the election returns following the Supreme Court! But with Franklin Roosevelt and the transition from the third to the fourth period, it was different. Here the question of lag was critical; it was the *failure* of the Supreme Court to follow the election returns that resulted in the constitutional revolution of 1937.

Although Roosevelt had won decisively in 1932 and had been reëlected in 1936 by what was then the most overwhelming plurality in history, a majority of the Supreme Court pursued a recklessly activist policy in declaring unconstitutional several of the key statutory provisions of the New Deal program. Three months after his reelection to a second term, not a single vacancy had occurred in the Court's membership, and the four justices of the core conservative bloc (two Republicans and two Democrats) had served for an average tenure of over nineteen years. It appeared to Roosevelt that all of them were following the example of the late Chief Justice Taft, who had written to his brother the year before his own death: "I am older and slower and less acute and more confused. However, as long as things continue as they are, and I am able to answer in my place, I must stay on the court in order to prevent the Bolsheviki from getting control."[10] (The letter was written in 1929, and the apparent reference is to justices who might be appointed by Hoover, whom Taft considered to be a dangerous radical.) With a number of cases further challenging the New Deal already docketed for decision during the next five months, Roosevelt chose to launch a public attack upon the Court, in a message to the Congress on February 5, 1937, accompanying his proposal to reform the Court.

The President made two tactical errors: (1) he chose to be devious and attacked the justices for being old and inefficient instead of for the real reason, which was that they were too conservative; (2) consequently, he did not distinguish among them but attacked the whole Court, thus including Chief Justice Hughes and such liberal justices as Brandeis and Cardozo. Roosevelt's request for authority to appoint a bevy of "assistant justices" to help the "Nine Old Men" with their work was turned down by Congress, as public opinion rallied to the defense of the Court as an institution and as the justices themselves lobbied very effectively with the congressional opposition, to the administration, in both parties.[11] Hughes and Roberts, during the preceding six years—and also up to this point in the then-current term—had voted consistently with the conservative bloc of four; but the threat was now sufficiently great that, weeks before the Congress had reached a decision on the President's "court-packing" proposals, "Hughberts" began, on March 1, 1937, to form a new majority with the liberal bloc of three, voting to sustain the constitutionality of the New Deal legislation at issue.[12] One effect of this stratagem was to help defeat Roosevelt's plan by demonstrating that no external reform of the Supreme Court was necessary—because the Court already had reformed itself. The same new majority of the Court hung together (over the vociferous protests of the now dissenting conservatives) until the end of the term in June, when the senior conservative justice— Van Devanter, who had been appointed to the Court by Taft in 1911—resigned. Before the end of his second term, Roosevelt had appointed a new majority to the Court.

A second and probably a more important effect of the Hughes-Roberts "switch in time that saved nine" is that there proved to be no turning, either back or away, from a complete reversal in the Court's policies toward both economic issues and civil liberties. The Supreme Court had indeed followed the election returns, but only under extreme duress; yet it was only another twenty years until the Court was again anticipating election returns, this time by formulating more liberal policies than either the Presidency or the Congress were prepared to support, except in part and then with reluctance.

The reasons for this, the dilemma of the Warren Court, will now be discussed.

Although it is by no means a function unique to judicial policy-making, procrastination is both a characteristic and an indispensable aspect of the decision-making process in the national judicial system. From the point of view from which lawyers typically discuss what Hamlet referred to as "the Law's delay," judicial procrastination is an undesirable and dysfunctional characteristic of judicial systems. This is thought to be so because procrastination is evidence of inefficiency, laziness, incompetence, or (more likely) of all three in combination; in terms of the interests of litigants, one of the best-known maxims of Anglo-American culture is that "justice delayed is justice denied." There are, however, other relevant perspectives than efficiency and individual justice that ought to be considered in discussing judicial procrastination.

Some theorists of the American political party system have emphasized that the essential task of the politician is not to *raise* issues but, rather, to reduce the level of political tensions by *sublimating* issues as much as possible. This is, of course, a conservative point of view, and throughout the third period of Modern Conservatism the national courts in general and the Supreme Court in particular were very successful in keeping sublimated both of the major issues of equalitarianism—racial integration and legislative apportionment—that are of central importance in the Court's policy-making today. But just as soon as the Roosevelt Court had a marginal liberal majority, the Court began to champion a series of equalitarian causes, none of which had any substantial support either elsewhere in the national political system or in the state political systems. First came a series of decisions, which were to extend throughout the decade of the 1940's, upholding the right to proselytize of the radical right-wing religious movement known as Jehovah's Witnesses,[13] whose closest counterpart among indigenous American political movements appears to have been the "Know-Nothing" party of a century earlier. Half a dozen years later, during the middle of World War II, came the first of the liberal "white primary" decisions[14] that were of particular importance to subsequent policy development in regard to both racial integration and fair representation. Also during the 1940's, there were several decisions invalidating racial discrimination in commercial accommodations for interstate and international travel, in restrictive racial covenants, and in the graduate admission policies of state universities. And at the close of World War II, in June 1946, the Court came within one vote of announcing the policy on reapportionment which, lacking that single vote, became delayed for sixteen years.[15]

The reasons for the sixteen-year delay may be briefly summarized as follows: Rutledge (one of the four liberal justices) wrote an opinion in which he stated his agreement with the other three liberals, who dissented in favor of reapportionment; but Rutledge nevertheless voted with the three conservatives to form a four-to-three majority in favor of the status quo. Both Rutledge and Murphy died two years later, but in any event it would have taken five favorable votes to have established a pro-reapportionment policy, with a full Court of nine justices participating; *Colegrove* v. *Green* was decided under quite exceptional circumstances, with only seven justices participating due to a vacancy in the Chief Justiceship, which occurred more than six weeks *after* the case was argued and about seven weeks before the decision was announced, and due to the absence of Jackson, who had been prosecuting Nazi war criminals in Nuremburg throughout the 1945 term of the Court. (Incidentally, Jackson's notorious public statement, in which he protested to an international audience against what he alleged to have been Black's lobbying with President Truman, in order to prevent Jackson from succeeding Stone as Chief Justice, was released to the press on the same day—June 10, 1946—on which his colleagues announced their decision in the *Colegrove* case.) It was not until Brennan's appointment in 1956 that the critical majority necessary to the decision of *Baker* v. *Carr* was available, and by then the Court was too preoccupied with the enforcement and expansion of its racial integration policies for the time to be ripe for the opening of a second front in what we might call its war with the "Old Deal"—the reactionary and antidemocratic forces that still remained dominant, at the close of World War II, in so many sectors of American political life.

It is precisely here, in the timing of the relationship between the Court's racial integration and fair representation policies, that judicial procrastination appears to have had instrumental value for the realization of greater social justice. The School Segregation Cases were initially argued in December 1952, immediately after Eisenhower's election; they were re-argued again a year later, and the basic decision on the merits came in May 1954. But the Court withheld its mandate and restored the cases to the docket for additional argument, which was to be focused upon the question of how the Court's substantive policy decision was to be enforced. A year later, in May 1955, the Supreme Court announced its "mandate" decision: the United States district courts were told, in effect, that it was up to them to try to figure out how to persuade or to force local communities to desegregate their public schools, and they were told to proceed with this task "with all deliberate speed." The Supreme

Court itself proceeded to avoid reviewing any of the "enforcing" decisions of the lower courts[16] during the next three years, until the events of 1957 in Little Rock had raised the question of enforcement as a policy issue upon which the attention of the entire nation was focused. When the showdown came in September 1957, it was visiting United States District Judge Ronald N. Davies from North Dakota who acted to enforce the 1954 policy of the School Segregation Cases; and it was not until a year later that the Supreme Court finally intervened in an enforcement question[17] by backing up the Court of Appeals for the Eighth Circuit, which had reversed the anti-integration slowdown authorized by John E. Miller, the regular district judge for the western Arkansas district. Even then, almost six years after the issue initially was argued before the Court, there were no integrated schools in two of the school districts (in Virginia and in South Carolina) that had been formal parties to the initial litigation; and even today, more than a decade after the "mandate" decision, there is one entire state (Mississippi) and many counties in other states in which all public schools remain segregated.[18] A literal reading of the record, as we have described it, suggests that the Supreme Court procrastinated in reaching a firm decision on the school segregation issue and that its mandate to the lower courts—to act "with all deliberate speed"—was an open invitation for them to procrastinate. However, the Supreme Court had no assurance that it would receive any support from the Eisenhower administration or from a Congress in which the coalition of conservative Republicans and Southern Democrats was relatively more powerful than it had been for over a quarter of a century; only minimal help could be expected from state judges in the very parts of the country where segregation was most entrenched; and the national district judges upon whom the Court was going to have to rely were themselves mostly Southern Democrats. We can assume that the justices who decided the School Segregation Cases were convinced that they had—or could obtain—the long-range support of a national majority; but there was no short-run way in which such a national majority could help the Court in getting public schools desegregated. Acting, as it did, under such limitations, a quick decision with a demand for rigid implementation would have forestalled the possibility of political support being mustered to back up the Supreme Court, so procrastination was perhaps the only way to make possible pragmatic solutions to the problem of means of implementation.

The issue of racially segregated schools, however, was as old as the nation. Why had it taken the Supreme Court almost a century to find out that "separate educational facilities are inherently unequal" and therefore unconstitutional? Why had it taken until 1964 for the Supreme Court to discover the nascent principle of fair representation—one person, one vote—in a clause of the Constitution that had lain dormant since the year before the establishment of the Supreme Court?[19] It was not until the Democratic party mobilized the Negro vote in the big cities of the Northeast and the Midwest, not until the demographic changes that accompanied and followed World War II (including the migration of millions of Negroes from the South to the big cities elsewhere in the country), not until the general educational upgrading of the populace that accompanied the affluence of the war and postwar periods, and not until many other basic changes had occurred in the structure of American political society (mainly within the past three decades) that there was anything like a national political majority in favor of racially integrated public schools.

Thus there are two reasons why the Court did not act sooner. First, the Supreme Court did begin to define a broad policy of racial integration, initially in areas less politically sensitive (because less fundamentally important) than the public schools, *just as soon as* Roosevelt had replaced a majority of the justices. Second, not only was it of some importance that the Court begin to build its general policy of racial integration first (as it had been doing) in less sensitive areas than public education, but it is also probably true that there was no supporting national majority prior to the early 1950's. If these assumptions are correct, then it was not so much the Supreme Court that procrastinated on the issue of public school integration; it was more the American people who procrastinated, awaiting a more enlightened day when the fruits of the public school educational system would be not merely an elite but a mass of citizens who did not believe in the intolerance, the bigotry, and the economic irrationality that underlay the structuring of two systems of public schools—the one generally educationally inferior to integrated public school systems, and the other much worse.[20]

With the incumbency of the Kennedy administration in 1961, the Supreme Court could count upon the support of the Department of Justice to aid and to augment the activities of the district courts in the enforcement of the Court's various (and still expanding) policies of racial integration. And the announcement, at about the same time, of the returns of the 1960 Census, in relation to the malapportionment of state legislatures and the districting of the national House of Representatives, resulted in a number of lawsuits throughout the country, several of which were pressed upon the Court. By 1961 it was politically feasible for the Court to consider raising another major issue of national policy; there was majority support among the justices to support a policy of fair representation, and such a policy was likely to attract the support of a national majority, since the object of the policy was to deëmphasize the political influence of minorities and to expand the influence of majorities.

Although we might say that the Supreme Court had procrastinated on the issue of fair representation throughout the first six decades of the twentieth century, a broader perspective would suggest that procrastination, with regard to most policy issues most of the time, is the normal posture of the Supreme Court, just as it is also the normal posture of the Presidency and of the Congress. From this point of view, entropy is to be assumed, unless and until special conditions arise to overcome it. Our analysis has suggested that three of the functional prerequisites to major policy innovation by the Supreme Court are (1) that the Court be "packed" with a majority of justices favorable to the proposed policy change; (2) that a national majority favor the change; and (3) that the general political context be such that the Court's making the policy would not seriously jeopardize the Court's capacity to assure the realization of other major policies to which it remains committed.

### JUDICIAL ACTIVISM AND RESTRAINT

We are now in a position to suggest a functional theory of judicial activism and restraint. The Court's basic policies remain stable over long periods of time, and changes that do occur reflect very fundamental changes in the general political system, of which the Court is a component part. The justices themselves are goal oriented, and their basic goals are the same as those that motivate other political actors. Majority rule among the justices determines the policy goals that the Court supports, and it is the underlying stability in the general political system that accounts for the continuity in the Court's policy-making, by assuring that the judicial majority will reflect the dominant majority in the larger political system. If Supreme Court justices were appointed for four-year terms in phase with the presidential electoral cycle, then it could be anticipated that there would be considerably less stability in the Court's policy-making, because Court majorities would be more responsive to the short-run waves than to the long-run currents of political change. Under our constitutional system, it is precisely at the times of major realignment in the political party system that the Supreme Court is most likely to become involved in conspicuous and dramatic conflict with the Presidency and the Congress, because the majority of the justices then represent the minority in the new political realignment.

One possible definition of judicial activism is that it consists of any attempts of justices to change the policies of the Court. When a majority of the justices agree upon the direction of change that they deem desirable in regard to a particular policy, the position of the Court is activist. If the effect of such changes is to bring the Court's policies into correspondence with preceding changes in congressional and presidential policies, the Court is not usually *perceived* as being activist, since observers of the Court's action tend to focus upon conflict between the Court and either the President and Congress or spokesmen for the states. Therefore, the Court is perceived as being most activist when it changes its policies so as to conflict with the policies established by other major decision-makers of the national or the state governments. Conversely, a majority of justices who agree with previously established Court policies can be considered to have exercised judicial restraint; that is, when other major decision-makers change their policies and the Court does not change, conflict occurs because the justices refuse to accept the policy change, which constitutes judicial restraint. This concept of judicial activism, therefore, though perfectly consistent and logical, must be rejected because it results in a definition of judicial restraint that contradicts common sense, ordinary usage of the words, and the usual understanding.

An alternative functional theory of judicial activism and restraint defines activism in terms of disharmony, and restraint in terms of harmony, between the policy of the Court and that of other decision-makers. We define "other decision-makers" quite broadly, to include (1) Congress, the President and administrative agencies, and lower national courts, and (2) the analogous officials of state governments. Table VIII specifies the types of possible relationships:

TABLE VIII

Activism and Restraint in Supreme Court Policy-Making

|  |  | Other Decision-Makers | |
|  |  | Static | Dynamic |
|---|---|---|---|
| Supreme Court | Static | (1) Restraint | (2) Activism |
| | Dynamic | (3) Activism | (4) Restraint or Activism |

According to this theory, the Court is activist whenever its policies are in *conflict* with those of other major decision-makers. If we consider the first cell of Table VIII, it is clear that when there is no change in the policy of either the Court or another decision-maker, there will be no conflict between them,[21] and we have defined restraint to mean the absence of conflict. In the second cell, the Court adheres to an established policy (i.e., it "follows *stare decisis*") in spite of the fact that another decision-maker has made a policy change, while in the third cell, the Court changes its policy but the other decision-maker does not; in either situation, the Court has taken an activist position because its policy is in conflict with that of another major decision-maker. In the fourth cell, the Court's position may be one of either activism or restraint, depending upon whether the *direction* and *rate* of the change in the Court's policy are different from or the same as those of the other decision-maker: when the policy changes are in opposite directions or unequal in rate, the Court is activist, and when the policy changes coincide, the Court exercises restraint. It should be clear both that this analysis applies irrespective of the substantive content of the policy at issue and that it applies equally to instances in which the Court's position is liberal and those in which it is conservative.

The most typical example of the restraint that results from static agreement is found in the Court's many decisions denying jurisdiction to review the decisions of lower courts, when the lower court has followed the Supreme Court's policy and that policy is in agreement with that of, say, the Congress. In such an instance there is rarely any reason for the Supreme Court to make a decision on the merits, unless the Court wishes to publicize the fact that it has *not* changed its position on the issue. An example of such a decision on the merits is *United States* v. *Midwest Oil Co.,* in which the Court followed the unbroken judicial and presidential and congressional precedents of a century in upholding the authority of the President to make temporary withdrawals of public lands.

The second type of situation, in which the Court remains static in the face of an outside policy change, is one that typically occurs because of the frequent lag between change in the Court's personnel and the more rapid change that occurs in other political decision-making systems. The conflict between the Hughes Court and the New Deal provides an obvious example, as exemplified by the Sick Chicken Case (*Schechter Poultry Corp.* v. *United States*). The administration had established a national program for price-fixing in retail sales, labor regulation, and production control (*inter alia*) that went far beyond anything similar that had been attempted in peacetime; and the Court stuck to its more recent commerce clause precedents, declaring the statute to be unconstitutional.

The third situation, and the second type of activism, is that in which the Court becomes the protagonist in policy-making, while other political decision-makers stand pat. The School Segregation

Case (*Brown* v. *Board of Education*) is one of many recent examples. In that decision, the Court announced a national policy of public school integration which neither the President nor the Congress was immediately prepared to support, let alone to make; the fact that this policy was to a greater or lesser extent in conflict with the practices of every state in the Union requires no demonstration.

Of the two possibilities that can arise in the fourth situation, dynamic agreement between the Court and other policy-makers is the more common. For example, the Court exercised restraint in *National Labor Relations Board* v. *Jones & Laughlin Steel Corp.*, one of the first major decisions to follow the Court's policy reversal after Roosevelt's assault, by agreeing to the same kind of expanded interpretation of the commerce clause that it had refused to accept less than two years earlier in the Sick Chicken Case. The other possibility is for the Court to change in the opposite direction from a policy change by another decision-maker, as exemplified by the decision in *Pollock* v. *Farmers' Loan and Trust Co.*, the case in which the first peacetime national income tax was declared unconstitutional. In 1881, the Court had upheld a temporary national income tax that had been adopted during the Civil War. But the statute enacted in 1894 was generally (and correctly) recognized as constituting a major policy change in the direction of economic liberalism; the Court's decision, under the circumstances, was an equally major policy change in the direction of economic conservatism.

Judicial review, in the narrow sense of declarations by the Court that national or state legislation is unconstitutional, is simply one of the technical forms that judicial activism can assume when the Court finds itself in conflict with legislative policy-makers. When the Court majority takes one of the positions that we have classified as constituting restraint, it is possible, of course, for an individual justice or a minority of justices to behave as activists, in which event he or they will dissent from the decision of the majority. It follows that when a majority of the Court is activist, dissenters will argue in their opinions the virtues of judicial restraint, just as a majority will preach restraint to activist dissenters. Both of these types of behavior are readily observable in the opinions of the justices throughout the history of the Court. As a relatively liberal justice, in regard to both civil liberties and economic issues, on an activist conservative Court, Holmes' frequently employed strategy of arguing judicial restraint (rather than the substantive merits of the issue) was quite rational and probably impaired the position of his more conservative colleagues much more effectively than a direct attack might have done. Holmes' famous dissent in *Lochner* v. *New York*, for example, did not quarrel (as Harlan did) with the majority on the question of whether a ten-hour day would be more healthful for employees in bakery sweatshops than a sixteen-hour day; Holmes argued instead the proposition that, right or wrong, the state legislature rather than the United States Supreme Court had the constitutional right to establish policy on the question. On the other hand, a justice who utilizes the same argument in behalf of judicial restraint, at a time when the Court frequently is dominated by a majority of activist liberals, has no alternative but to dissent consistently in what functionally is a defense of conservative values. This is precisely the posture that was assumed during his last two decades as a Supreme Court justice by Frankfurter, an avowed proponent of both civil liberties and economic liberalism *before* he joined the Court but also an acknowledged student and avowed disciple of Holmes.

To summarize, from a functional point of view, the Court is activist when its decisions conflict with those of other political policy-makers, and the Court exercises restraint when it accepts the policies of other decision-makers.

### CHAPTER SEVEN

# The Study of Judicial Policy-Making

## APPROACHES TO RESEARCH

For an understanding of research in judicial decision-making, three theoretical approaches are important: traditional, conventional, and behavioral. Lawyers and philosophers use the term "jurisprudence" to refer, in general, to the theory of the ways in which judges decide cases, and they define traditional theory narrowly. In contemporary jurisprudence, traditional theory is "analytical positivism" (or "Austinism") and modern theory is either "sociological" or "realist." However, all of these jurisprudential approaches are considered to be part of the traditional theory of judicial decision-making in the following discussion.

In presenting these three approaches to the study of judicial decision-making, we wish to underscore that, in practice, it is not a matter of the traditional having been displaced by the conventional nor the latter by the behavioral. They are by no means mutually exclusive alternatives, and all three approaches coexist today in research, writing, and teaching related to the American judiciary. In many areas of the general field of study, the only knowledge we have is that which has been accumulated by scholars following the traditional or conventional approaches, and both of these continue to attract the interest and support of many more students of the judiciary than does the behavioral approach. Moreover, judicial behavioralists also investigate both "law" and "groups"—law as a set of normative propositions that give preference to particular patterns of values, and groups as the collectivities of individuals who are associated together for decision-making purposes. It is probably accurate to say that the conventional approach tends to dominate political science teaching about the judiciary, while the behavioral approach characterizes the bulk of the research in the subject being done by political scientists. Our approach in this book is a mixture of the conventional (since we discuss primarily the activities of judges from the point of view of their membership in institutional groups) and the behavioral (since our theory of decision-making and the conversion process uses sociopsychological conceptualism, and since much of the substantive data we have reported, together with our interpretation of these data, have relied upon behavioral research).

## TRADITIONAL

The fundamental postulates of the analytical theory of law proposed by the nineteenth-century Englishman, John Austin, are that positive law is what *is*, not what ought to be; that positive (or written) law represents the will of the sovereign; and that therefore positive law is the sovereign's command which must be enforced by executive officials and judges. American legal writers found it easy to substitute a "popular sovereign" for the king of England and notions of the "public will" for the command of the sovereign. The relevant policy-making model is the simplistic one to which we have made earlier reference: the people elect legislators who make laws that it is the duty of judges to enforce in their decisions. In the words of Wolfgang Friedmann:

> The analytical lawyer . . . is not concerned with ideals; he takes the law as a given matter created by the State, whose authority he does not question. On this material he works, by means of a system of rules of legal logic, apparently complete and self-contained. In order to be able to work on this assumption, he must attempt to prove to his own satisfaction that thinking about the law can be excluded from the lawyer's province. Therefore, the legal system is made watertight against all ideological intrusions, and all legal problems are couched in terms of legal logic.[1]

The proponents of sociological jurisprudence turned their attention to the source of the norms that provided the policy content of the decisions of appellate courts, but none of them ever attempted to operationalize the question of the relationship between the needs and demands of "society" and the choice of the individual judge. Roscoe Pound and others proposed that the ultimate source of such norms must be the ideals of natural law; Hans Kelsen avoided the problem by leaving the selection of norms up to the "free discretion" of each judge. The legal realists, or proponents of "experimental jurisprudence," attempted to shift attention away from appellate courts to the decision-making of trial courts. Their preoccupation was with a forthright empiricism that rarely was guided by any systematic theoretical formulations; they conceived their job to be to "get at the facts" of what judges did in decision-making. As a consequence, they produced many studies reporting the facts (as they perceived them) about what courts were doing, and this was no doubt a needed supplement to the logic-chopping of the analytical positivists and the norm-study of the sociological jurists. But the realists did not produce a systematic theory of judicial decision-making roles.

At the present time, these three influences coexist like a crazy quilt in most writing and discussion by lawyers, although the analytical predominates among the practicing bar, the sociological among judges, and the realist among law professors. In most contemporary texts and casebooks that discuss American constitutional law, the gross structure and arrangement of materials assumes the analytical approach, while the content of the materials presumes that interest will focus upon the relationships among the norms discussed in the judicial opinions that are either summarized in the texts or reproduced in the casebooks. The facts dug up by the legal realists are not usually considered to be very relevant to the study of constitutional law. To these considerations should be added the mystique in which lawyers typically attempt to enshroud the subject of judicial decision-making whenever they discuss it for the benefit of laymen (i.e., non-lawyers).

The other major component of the traditional theory of judicial decision-making is the historical approach. The assumption underlying this approach is that by examining the ways in which previous occupants have acted in roles similar to those of incumbents, we shall better understand the behavior of judges today. Empirical research employing the historical approach has assumed generally one of two forms. The most common form has consisted of the life histories of judges, written either by the judges themselves, their relatives, journalists, or scholars. The quality of these studies varies greatly. Those written by judges or their relatives generally suffer from selective perception in their use of the available evidence and tend to eulogize their subjects. Those written by scholars usually attempt a more objective appraisal, but they tend to focus upon such data as the family of a deceased judge may have been willing to make available from among those private papers of a judge that were not destroyed or lost prior to his death. In the case of some Supreme Court justices, for instance, the private papers of a justice have not been released for research purposes until after the demise of other living persons to whom reference was made in the papers; the effect of such delay is, of course, to render much more difficult the task of validation of various "facts" asserted in the justice's papers. Nevertheless, the best of such biographies (such as Mason's *Stone*, Fairman's *Miller*, Swisher's *Taney*, and Beveridge's *Marshall*)[2] have provided very useful sources of data for students of other more general questions of judicial behavior. In recent years there have appeared several studies based upon the same types of sources as the judicial biographies, but with the objective of analyzing directly such more general questions as the suppression of dissent as a function of political compromises among the justices[3] and the influence of incumbent justices upon the appointment of new judges and justices.[4]

Another emphasis of historical research has been the writing of general analyses of the role of the Supreme Court as an institution, usually in combination with a consideration of the decisional output of the Court and the accompanying majority opinions. A few authors have attempted to discuss the entire period of the Court's existence up to the time when they wrote, while others have focused upon particular subperiods. There do no appear to have been similar historical studies of other federal courts or their judges.

CONVENTIONAL

Until the end of World War II, the traditional approach completely dominated studies of the judiciary by political scientists, and it still is the dominant approach in the law schools. Among most political scientists, however, the traditional approach has now largely been superseded as the central focus of inquiry by what is essentially a political sociology of the judicial process. This new orthodoxy is usually called the "political process" approach, and it clearly has become a conventional approach, the one most widely accepted by most political scientists.

One political scientist, Martin Shapiro, recently attempted to explain the political process approach to an audience of lawyers. In order to cast his subject within the framework of legal conceptualism, he called it "political jurisprudence," which he defined as follows:

> This new movement is essentially an extension of certain elements of sociological jurisprudence and judicial realism,

combined with the substantive knowledge and methodology of political science. Its foundation is the sociological jurist's premise that law must be understood not as an independent organism but as an integral part of the social system. . . . Moreover, the new jurisprudence shares with all modern American thinking about law the premise that judges make rather than simply discover law. Without this premise there could be no political jurisprudence, for one of the central concerns of politics is power and power implies choice. If the judge had no choice between alternatives, if he simply applied the rule supplied him by the tablets and reached the conclusion commanded by an inexorable legal logic, he would be of no more interest politically than the IBM machine that we could soon design to replace him. "Political" can only be linked with "jurisprudence" when it is realized that choice inheres in those phases of human endeavor that have traditionally been the object of jurisprudential study. . . . Political jurisprudence is, among other things, an extension of the findings of other areas of political science into the realm of law and courts, an attempt to rationalize the presence of public law as a field of study within the discipline, and an effort to round-out political science by somehow integrating legal and judicial facets into the total picture of political life.[5]

The basic assumption of the political process ("political jurisprudence") approach is that judges are policy-makers, just like Presidents and congressmen and many administrators. Therefore, the appropriate subject to be studied in investigating the decision-making of courts is not law but the politics of the judiciary. Law, of course, is not ignored; but it is regarded as the policy output of constitutional conventions, legislatures, Presidents, courts, and administrative agencies rather than as some mystical essence. This concept contrasts sharply with that of traditional theory, which characteristically defines law as a "seamless web," a body of logically interrelated norms that somehow is greater than the sum of its component parts. Moreover, the traditional theory denies that judges make law; instead, they "find" or "discover" it, through an expertise that is a product of their legal training and official status. Political process theory assumes that judges do make law but that their function in so doing is primarily a catalytic one.

The fundamental unit upon which political process theory builds is the social group, and politics can be completely described in terms of interaction among groups. Individuals are associated with a bewildering multiplicity of different groups, many of which are distinguished by a formal organization and many of which are much more informal—so much so, in fact, that they are spoken of as being "unorganized" or even as "potential" groups. Groups all have "interests," whether the members of the groups are aware of such interests or not; a group's interest consists of the goals common to, or typical of, the group's members. But the relationship of any group to its interest is tautological: an interest is what a group has, and groups do what they do because they are pursuing their interests. Thus the normative problem of what groups ought to do is avoided by assuming that groups do in fact what they ought (rationally) to do.

It is easy to construct large organizations, which typically consist of various organized component groups. In addition, there often are "unorganized" groups within organizations. Component organization groups compete with each other and with a host of outside groups as well. The judges who comprise the membership of an appellate court, such as the United States Supreme Court, are a group. The group of nine may also consist of several unorganized subgroups of the justices, of course. Each justice also is a member of an organized subgroup consisting of his law clerks and secretaries. The offices of the Clerk of the Court, the Librarian, the Marshall, and so forth, also define organized subgroups. And so on.

Groups compete with each other while pursuing their interests, and they attempt to maximize their influence upon decision-makers who can make or maintain policies that will favor the groups. Consequently, there is an interplay of what usually are called "pressures" but sometimes are denominated as "forces." It should be clear that given this Newtonian model, the result must be that decisions of public officials are vectors which are the direct product of the combination of forces brought to bear upon the decision-maker. The result, therefore, is a conception of judicial decision-making that is just as mechanical as John Austin's hierarchies of sovereign power, but the political process theorists require much more elaborate engines to do their work. The residual category of traditional theory, *the law*, has been replaced by the residual category of the process theory, *the group*. Both tend to ignore the psychological characteristics of judges as being essentially irrelevant to what is assumed to be significant in their official behavior.

However much the political process approach may lead to a theoretical dead end, its influence upon empirical research during the past generation has been important. At least, the process theorists induced political scientists to attempt to describe judicial action as a form of political action and to describe judges as decision-makers whose choices frequently entail important political consequences.

BEHAVIORAL

Beginning about the middle of the 1950's, a third approach came to assume increasing importance in the study of judicial decision-making. The behavioral approach focuses upon the discrete human beings who act as judicial decision-makers. In particular, the behavioral approach investigates the sociopsychological dimensions of judicial decisions: How do the attitudes and belief systems of the judge as an individual affect his choices, and how do his personal relationships with other individuals affect his choices? Consequently, the family background, educational training and vocational experience, and political and religious affiliations of judges become relevant data for observation and analysis. Similarly, the social context of judicial choice must be explored: Who are the colleagues of an appellate court judge? How and to what extent is he influenced by them? How and why do the personal values of the judge enter into his official choices, emerging in the form of the "intent of the Constitutional fathers," of the legislature, or of a higher court?

Behavioralists assume that the study of "law" and "courts" should be undertaken as an aspect of modern social science. The cognate academic disciplines from which judicial behavior has borrowed most extensively, for theoretical and methodological guidance, have been psychology (for the analysis of individual judicial attitudes), sociology (for small-group analysis), and economics (for the analysis of rationality in decision-making). Behavioralists do not attempt to explain everything they observe in terms of a single concept, and they investigate questions that either would not or could not be studied systematically under either the traditional or the conventional approach. Perhaps the most important difference, however, is found in the insistence of the behavioralists upon employing explicit theoretical models, from which operationalized hypotheses can be inferred, to guide their empirical research. Statistical methods are used as the basis both for testing the significance of findings and for predicting future relationships on the basis of present knowledge about those that have obtained in the past. The ultimate test of the power of any science lies, of course, in its capacity to increase man's ability to anticipate future events and their probable consequences. In addition to explaining the past (as in the traditional approach) and describing the present (as in the conventional approach), the behavioral approach is concerned with predicting future developments in judicial behavior.

As practitioners of a science that is only a decade old, judicial behavioralists might well bemoan "the petty done, the undone vast." The specific accomplishments during the first decade related primarily to systematic examinations of judicial voting records, correlating such voting data with variables representing the political and economic attitudes of individual judges; their ethnic, socioeconomic, and political background characteristics; the differentiation of subsets of judges (in appellate courts) into cohesive blocs; and leadership, influence, and bargaining processes in courts conceptualized as small groups.[6] Thus, for example, the analysis of the policy-making process in Chapter Five is based predominantly upon the theories, methods, and substantive findings of behavioral research. Indeed, this book in its entirety could not have been written without the work, however incomplete and unfinished, that has been done thus far in judicial behavior. Yet it is also true that we have relied to an even greater extent upon the much larger volume of research that has been undertaken by proponents of the conventional and traditional approaches.

#### CRITIQUE

It is not surprising that academic spokesmen for the two older research approaches have voiced increasing concern about the many inadequacies they discern in the behavioral approach. In part, such concern often reflects the perhaps understandable exaggeration with which claims frequently are stated by pioneers of new techniques in attempts to command the attention of a disinterested—if not inhospitable—professional audience. There is also a not very scientific but altogether human tendency on the part of those persons who constitute the academic establishment, for the time being, to view any new approach as something quite difficult to understand (as it literally is for them, since they have been trained in other workways) as well as a foolish if not dangerous movement (that threatens to shake the very foundations of the work upon which their own careers have been built). The point is well illustrated by events in the development of American jurisprudence that took place a few decades ago.

Among law professors, two of the most eminent spokesmen for new directions in legal research have been Roscoe Pound, the late Dean Emeritus of the Harvard Law School, and the late Professor Karl N. Llewellyn of the Columbia Law School. At the turn of the century, Pound (who had been trained in biology) led the attack upon Austinism,[7] as he became the spokesman for the new sociological jurisprudence that was based upon a political metaphor derived from Darwinism (as the major contribution of nineteenth-century science).[8] But in middle life, during the 1920's, Pound led the attack upon the pretensions of the upstart young law professors who were advocates for the then-new movement called "legal realism."[9] Llewellyn, as a leading spokesman for legal realism, defended the new research approach against what he considered to be the ridiculous and uncomprehending charges that Pound had ventured;[10] but a generation later, in his own valedictory to the legal profession, Llewellyn felt impelled to record his grave misgivings about the utility and implications of the new behavioral research in law.[11]

Similar misunderstandings have existed in traditionalist perceptions of much of the newer work, irrespective of whether its orientation has been conventional or behavioral. It is charged, for example, that legal institutions and processes are *unique* and that it is fruitless to attempt to study courts and judges as one might, more appropriately, study politicians or officials of the two "political" branches of the government. A law school graduate, Theodore Becker, has articulated the legal point of view:

> [Judicial behavioralists are guilty of] an attempt to handle some of the delicate problems inherent in transplanting methodology initially shaped for the study of very different social environments . . . [and by] and large, judicial behavioralism generally has not begun to consider the [Supreme] Court as a court. Few of its practitioners have viewed the judicial decision-making process in its uniqueness. Most have treated it no differently from any other decision-making process, e.g., from the street corner gang to the Congress. This failure to see the courts as unique is partially demonstrated by the hasty application of techniques and theories which were devised for other purposes. . . . [T]he mysteries of the judicial process, as a distinctive process, remain almost totally inviolate despite some significant advances. . . . [H]e who attempts to study and formulate attitude universe [*sic*] of the Justices of the Supreme Court from their case opinions, in order to predict future opinions, has a near impossible task because of the nature of that institution. Particularly in important policy decisions, the justices select the next factual stimulus (case) *specifically on the basis that it is somewhat unique* as well as important. They choose to hear a particular case precisely because it has a *distinctly different factual essence that is somewhat beyond all the specifics which already comprise the analytic attitude universe which the analyst has conceptually imposed retrospectively on the judges.* Then how can this new boundary delineation help predict the next situation which will once again be beyond the established boundary? . . . The peculiar facets of the judicial process would seem to further heighten this problem and make the development of so-called judicial attitude universes from case votes and/or case opinion verbiage doomed to the same

degree of predictive failure that plagues even the most well informed and legally intuitive constitutional lawyers when they are faced with a crucial policy case.[12]

Becker challenges not merely the judicial process approach (implicitly) and the judicial behavior approach (explicitly); his remarks, taken at face value, deny the possibility of modern social science. If all institutions are unique—and there is no particular reason, other than professional ethnocentrism, which might lead one to assume that legal institutions are more unprecedented than legislatures, churches, or marriages—then any attempts to develop a systematic body of verified knowledge about human behavior in general, and political behavior in particular, are foredoomed (as Becker says) to failure. Fortunately for social science, the key to the weakness of his argument is provided by the very words that he has chosen to emphasize. The long sentence which is largely italicized (by Becker) in the above quotation is an explicit avowal of Austinian (analytical positivistic) dogma, ingenuously stated as though such "first principles" (for him) are indeed empirical facts in a scientific sense. Another young legal writer, Martin Shapiro, who has read much the same literature that was sampled by Becker, has been induced (by his own very different value premises) to reach an opposite conclusion on the merits of quarantining the law from examination by the theory and methods of political science:

> Probably the principle complaint about political jurisprudence is that it obscures the uniqueness of law and legal institutions. In constantly repeating that courts are political agencies and judges political actors, and dealing with courts and judges as an integral part of government, political jurisprudence does tend to emphasize the similarities between courts and judges and other political institutions and politicians. But if all this seems to add up to the statement that judges are just a bunch of politicians, then the mistake is in the eye of the beholder and in the unfavorable connotation frequently attached to the words politics and politician. The study of things political is, to be sure, partially aimed at exposing similarities between various political actors and institutions, but surely it is also aimed at discovering their difference[s]. The State Department, the Cook County [D]emocratic machine, the Vatican, the ICC and the Supreme Court are all political agencies and share certain common features. But in saying this, I suppose no one believes that I am saying that the Secretary of State, Jake Arvey, the Pope, the chairman of the ICC and Chief Justice Warren are or should be

exactly the same kind of men, thinking the same kind of thoughts and doing exactly the same kinds of things. If I say that Al Capone and F.D.R. were both politicians, I am not saying that the President was just a gangster.[13]

A closely related matter is Becker's charge that behavioralists have not yet disproved that variation in the "legal reasoning ability" of judges really is the significant factor that accounts for differences in judicial votes, opinions, and decisions. "After all," he asks, "why is it any less feasible or logical to assume that substantial similarity in voting is strongly influenced by a substantial equality in legal reasoning ability? Perhaps legal competence is the key cohesion-inducing factor."[14] And perhaps (one is tempted to add) there really is a Santa Claus, Virginia. It is true that few behavioralists have undertaken to test explicitly the hypothesis that the analytical positivists are right,[15] although at least one has been working for over a decade, using behavioralist methods in an attempt to prove that the principle of *stare decisis* really is the *deus ex machina* in judicial decision-making; his efforts to date seem to prove the contrary.[16] The reason why more attention has not been paid to this matter is that most judicial behavioralists believe that scientific knowledge should be cumulative and that it is wasteful of resources for them to redo what is generally accepted as the best and soundest work of the legal realist and the judicial process approaches.[17] As Shapiro has remarked:

> The argument that there are neutral principles indwelling in the law itself and discoverable by a specifically judicial or lawyer-like mode of thought, is basically an attempt to return jurisprudence to the position of splendid isolation that it enjoyed in the heyday of analytical jurisprudence. This attempt has been largely inspired by and is a direct challenge to political jurisprudence. . . . The political jurist begins with what any fool could plainly see if his eyes were not beclouded by centuries of legal learning, that judges and courts are an integral part of government and politics, [and that they] would be meaningless and functionless outside of government and politics and are, therefore, first and foremost political actors and agencies.[18]

Indeed, behavioralist attempts to refute Becker's "slot-machine theory of jurisprudence"[19] have been explicitly criticized by leaders of the conventional approach as constituting the pointless whipping of a dead horse: "[The behavioralists'] contribution is not . . . to demonstrate that the personal values of the jurists are significant in determining their decisions, for this is a truism that few [today] find of much interest even to discuss."[20]

If the most common complaint of traditionalists is that behavioralists fail to comprehend how idiosyncratic law and judges are, their next best charge is that when behavioralists occasionally do arrive at correct conclusions they merely prove in an unnecessarily complicated way what any intelligent scholar (or, in the alternative, any ordinary person with common sense) knows anyway. For example, Wallace Mendelson (like Becker, a lawyer-political scientist hybrid), in criticizing an early report of judicial behavior research, stated that the author's "point apparently is that what others may know 'intuitively,' he knows 'objectively.' . . . Surely . . . we must feel disappointment when a selected example of perfection [a perfect cumulative scale, or Guttman scalogram] yields such commonplace results."[21] A closely related charge is that behavioral findings, even when valid, typically are useless. Thus Walter Berns, a student of the conservative political philosopher Leo Strauss, asks:

> Even if we were to concede that the methodological obstacles could be overcome, of what use is this quantitative analysis and to whom is it useful? Ulmer, in his article on the racial exclusion cases, says it will be of use to lawyers and to political scientists specializing in public law, although he does not explain why this should be so in the latter case. . . . [T]here is serious doubt that Ulmer's conclusions will add to what the lawyer already knows in general and, in those borderline cases where, conceivably, the lawyer might be assisted by Ulmer's conclusions, whether those conclusions will hold up. . . . Ulmer cannot be any more certain of the answer than the practicing attorney, who, incidentally, is likely to seek an appeal in all borderline cases with or without the benefit of Ulmer's numbers.[22]

Since Berns, like his mentor Strauss, is a great believer in "common sense," particularly in preference to what Berns has called "behavioral non-sense,"[23] Shapiro's comments on this point are particularly pertinent:

> [T]here has been some outcry that the results [of behavioral research, especially in judicial attitudes] have not been worth the effort, that statistical approaches have only tended to confirm what we knew already. This argument is really part of the general debate between behaviorists and non-be-

haviorists in which the behaviorists are accused of employing fancy methodologies to prove the commonplace. But it can hardly be possible that all our truisms and cliches are correct since many tend to contradict one another.[24] Systematic analysis designed to test traditional knowledge cannot, therefore, be wasted even when it tends only to confirm some of our previous impressionistic notions.[25]

### 3. IS LAW AN ESSENCE?

Traditionalists are disturbed about the personal values of behavioralist researchers—but not, as one might suppose, from the point of view that the research in judicial behavior may be biased by the beliefs of the scholars who design and carry out the work. To the contrary, concern is expressed that (1) behavioralists engage in the foolish if not downright immoral practice of attempting to distinguish, in their research, between what is and what ought to be; and (2) since such attempts are futile, it is particularly alarming that behavioralists do not believe in the right values. Thus comes lawyer Mendelson to tell us that behavioralists do not believe in law:

> The confessed error of the legal realists was their exaggeration of the law's discretionary element, at the expense of its rule element. Today, perhaps, the neo-behavioralists are in danger of making the same mistake. For them, too, apparently, law—regarded as a body of rules—is largely a myth. Indeed, it appears that a major burden of their studies of the judicial process is to demonstrate that law is not an important element in court decisions. . . . Having discovered the ancient truth that there is and must be pliability in the law, neo-behavioralists—like the early realists—discount the equally ancient truth that there is and must be law in the law. . . . The knight errantry of judicial activism has bred in the neo-behavioralists (among others) an iconoclasm toward law and the judicial process that goes beyond the bounds of reason. . . . I suggest that the judge's art, when greatly practiced, is far too subtle to be measured by any existing behavioral technique. The law, said Holmes, is the painting of a picture—not the doing of a sum.[26]

And only God can make a tree—but this maxim does not prove the impossibility of a science of botany. Lawyer Becker adds that behavioralists do not even believe in *stare decisis*:

> One is hard pressed to see how their work even tends toward any theory of *judicial* decision-making. Where in their

work do they build in the peculiar systemic factors, e.g., the existence of a large body of authoritative precedent; the deeply embedded notion of judicial role and *stare decisis*. . . ?[27]

And philosopher Berns complains that behavioralists refuse to make moral judgments about judicial policy-making:

> (There is no difference in principle between the role of Lawgiver, or framer of constitution, and legislator or judge; the latter two merely work within the framework of an already defined public good, one defined with greater or lesser specificity.) . . . Thus, consideration of the problems arising in political life point to the question of the best possible political order or the best possible laws: all political decisions, whether by the framers of constitutions, legislators, administrators, judges, or masters in chancery, are based, consciously or unconsciously, on a view of what is good for man. . . . Behavioral science denies the very possibility of knowledge of what is good for man and, necessarily therefore, denies the possibility of an objective common good. It therefore denies the very premise on which the old-fashioned political and legal science was built. . . . The new science eschews all interest in the best political order or in the best laws, and confines itself to acquiring information as to the way men behave. . . . Since the goodness of a law or a constitution cannot be verified empirically, which means that its goodness cannot be seen or touched by one of the senses, questions of the goodness of laws are of no concern to these new scientists as scientists. The social scientist "cannot be an advocate in his role as scientist."[28]

As Shapiro has noted, "many scholars view the reduction of values to psychological data, which then become part of the 'is,' as the final positivistic rape of moral philosophy. Similarly, the emphasis on purposive elements in law-making may be viewed as a false reduction of law to will and appetite ignoring elements of reason and justice."[29] Berns and Shapiro make it clear that the dispute here bears no special relationship to the study of courts and judges but rather is a part of the much broader issue (discussed below) of whether social science is either desirable or possible. In the specific form in which Mendelson and Becker have sought to cast the question, we can note that judicial behavioralists do indeed treat as hypotheses and seek to investigate the very propositions that Mendelson and Becker would define as a priori absolutes. The behavioralist's faith is that, although he may not succeed completely in keeping his personal values from biasing his research findings, he will at least minimize their effect by being as explicit as he can in developing procedures and techniques that make it difficult for his own beliefs to prejudice the result of his work.

The traditionalist, to the contrary, seeks to maximize the influence that his subjective preferences will have upon his judgments as a scholar, and his conclusions about his subject therefore are maximally biased by what he wants to find in whatever evidence he chooses to accept. The point is well exemplified by Mendelson's attachment to his own research subject, which largely has centered around a single judge, Felix Frankfurter.[30] Mendelson has defined Frankfurter's role on the Supreme Court as one of judicial *restraint*, which in turn is defined as faith in the constitutional principles of separation of powers and federalism: the good judge defers to the policy decisions of the people's representatives in Congress and in the state legislatures. Libertarian activists are bad judges who wilfully substitute their own judgment on policy issues for the decisions of chief executives and legislators, and this is undemocratic because judges are politically irresponsible. Such a rationalist model of democratic decision-making is also somewhat simplistic; the logical consequences of the model (together with Mendelson's unabashed identification of his own value position with that of his subject, Frankfurter) have led him to claim that the late Mr. Justice Frankfurter had no attitudes and that judicial behavioralists are therefore wrong in classifying him as a conservative:

> [A]mong his colleagues, such a judge must be the least prejudiced by liberal or anti-liberal bias; in this sense, then, the freest to consider each case on its own merits—our closest approximation of the non-partisan magistrate. The judge in question is Felix Frankfurter. . . . To put the same point differently: I think that neo-behavioralism has been overinfluenced by the judicial activists—who are, after all, essentially behavioralists. . . . I suggest, in short, that modern behavioralism is a by-product of libertarian activism, just as legal realism was a by-product of laissez-faire activism.[31]

Mendelson confuses the judicial behavior research approach with one form of judicial behavior as empirically observable activity. Chapter Six discussed various theories of judicial activism and restraint and showed that there is no necessary relationship between either activism or restraint, and liberalism or conservatism. The present chapter shows that none of the major research approaches that we consider—traditional, conventional, and behavioral—is clearly or consistently identified with any particular set of values, liberal or conservative. Traditional,[32] conventional,[33] and behavioral[34] researchers agree[35] that most judges do have attitudes toward the public policy issues that confront them for decision; that Frankfurter is an exception is at least dubious.[36] Most scholars also have attitudes toward the phenomena that they seek to understand. Mendelson exemplifies what can happen when a scholar gets his own values mixed up with those of the judge whom he purports to study. Judicial behavioralists believe that such an admixture burns with more heat than light.

#### 4. DO COUNTERS THINK?

An old slogan in the argument between behavioralists and their critics is the claim that "Thinkers don't count, and counters don't think." The vehemence with which the view is expressed by otherwise well-educated and intelligent men leads one to suspect that extremely poor teaching of grammar and high school mathematics must have been widespread a generation or so ago. The disdain for quantification often is most stridently articulated, for example, by humanists who have dedicated their lives to the teachings of the political philosophers of classical Greece—forgetting that the study of mathematics was central in the Greek mode of thought, including the Greek cosmology.[37] A leading political scientist, John Roche, has put it this way:

> It was formerly alleged that when a scholar came to a weak point in his argument, he threw in a Greek quotation; now it often appears to me that he breaks out into calculus. . . . I object to the spell of numerology which seems to have fallen over the study of politics, and my objections do not run against the techniques but against the basic assumptions of the new Establishment. . . . What I object to is not quantification, but bogus quantification, the assumption that one can create a measurable thing merely by assigning it a numerical symbol. No one in his senses doubts that we can tabulate Republican votes, but does it follow that we can count Oedipus complexes on the same easy basis? The first calculation involves counting heads; the second, measuring their content.[38]

In short, only political phenomena that come prepackaged in "natural" units as entities are appropriate for measurement. It is all right to count votes, but any attempt to measure the attitudes of voters is "bogus quantification"—"bogus," apparently, because more difficult both to undertake and to understand.

This anti-intellectual bias against mathematics stands independent of a person's general orientation toward either educational or political values. For example, earlier in the same essay from which the above quotation is taken, Roche—for no apparent reason—takes pains to deny that he is really (to use his own words) a "defender of the *ancien régime,* as the de Maistre of public law."[39] Roche's own research approach in public law, a subject on which he has written widely and well, is conventional rather than traditional; he is a former dean at a major university (Brandeis) whose educational orientation certainly is considered to be progressive, and he currently is the national chairman of Americans for Democratic Action (ADA), an organization reputed to constitute the avant-garde of American political liberalism. It may indeed be necessary to measure something akin to Oedipus complexes in order to explain why so many otherwise open-minded academics are dogmatic in their rejection of quantification as a research tool. As Shapiro has explained:

> First of all quantification or statistical analysis is not an independent approach to any body of subject matter. At its best it suggests neither what questions are significant, what data [are] relevant, nor what ought to be done with the answers. Quantification is simply a tool and in political jurisprudence it is usually a tool for expressing more clearly and systematically observations that have been or might be made by other methods. Quantification may be used without any particular intent to contribute to an essentially political analysis of courts as it is in the *Harvard Law Review*'s annual statistical description of the previous term's work of the Supreme Court. . . . Indeed, the attempt to lump all "counters" together is really a function of the basic distaste to be found among many students of law for any other than their own traditional language. It is rather as if English and American lawyers accustomed to writing in English, and impatient with irregular verbs, lumped all the legal studies of French writers under the category French jurisprudence. Once the lumping is done, it is much easier to make blanket statements about the absurdity of writing about law in French than it is to analyze in detail whether any of the French writers have had anything useful to say in their peculiar language. . . . We all count. Some of us use our fingers and some use statistics. Unless there is a special virtue in primitive or half-conscious methods of counting, I do not see the objection to statistics. As a matter of fact both simple counting and relatively sophisticated statistical analysis have been used by eminently respectable and lawyer-like figures. It is, therefore, probably not statistics alone but statistics used in conjunction with attitudinal and behavioral studies that are the main target.[40]

The argument here is the somewhat implausible one that judicial behavioralism is not and cannot be scientific. This is said to be due, in part, to the unique nature of the subject matter—a topic we already have considered. But particular concern is expressed also about the abuse of scientific method, when misguided attempts are made to apply it in the study of judges and courts. Roche tells us, for example, that:

> [T]he use of content analysis to set up a scale of mathematical determinants of judicial action is predicated on the assumption that judicial decision-making is at root a process that proceeds mathematically. Similarly, the use of game theory for analytical purposes takes for granted what in reality must be demonstrated: that judges are gamesmen.[41]

Readers who are familiar with the rules of traditional logic will recognize the scholastic tenor of Roche's syllogism. If modern physics had taken Roche's advice to heart, the age of space exploration would indeed remain in the realm of science fiction instead of being a present reality. Einstein's theory of relativity posits a mathematical model of our universe in a context of infinite space and time; Roche's argument is that Einstein was unscientific because his "theory for analytical purposes takes for granted what in reality must be demonstrated"—that (for example) the structure and physical characteristics of the atom are similar to those of the universe.

The capacity to predict uncertain events is certainly a requirement of any mature science, including social science. Seemingly, Becker asks the sixty-four-dollar question when he queries: "Could these judicial behavioralists, through their various methods, have predicted the way the Supreme Court would decide most important policy cases before the decision was made known?"[42] The question was intended to be rhetorical, but actually the answer was available in reports of research published prior to Becker's own essay.[43] Judicial behavior certainly is not yet a mature science, however, and present attempts at predicting judicial decisions may seem quite crude a generation hence.

Roche claims further that scientists never try to predict individual behavior and that, therefore, attempts to predict the behavior of individual judges are unscientific. Judicial behavioralists, he says,

> seem to have confused the scientist with the bookmaker. The scientist deals in prediction only in statistical terms, *i.e.*, on the basis of adequate samples, and never engages in the *hubris*

of trying to predict the behavior of individual units. . . . Thus
when [judicial behavioralists] invoke the authority of science
for predicting the actions of a few judges on the basis of
statistically trivial samples, they are in a tradition that owes
more to the racing form than to the work of Fermi, Heisen-
berg, or Einstein.[44]

Roche is simply not well informed, at least about prediction in
modern science. Much of astronomy, in its early stages, was concerned explicitly with predictions of the behavior of an individual
unit—earth. Sociology is concerned with predicting aggregate behavior, but psychology (educational psychology, for example) is concerned with predicting individual behavior. At any rate, Roche is
quite confused about how judges, as individuals, are related to attempts thus far to predict their behavior. In both of the examples
cited in footnote 43, for instance, judges are conceptualized (and
are treated for purposes of statistical measurement) neither as entities
nor as items but rather as *variables* that affect the outcomes (the
decisions of the Supreme Court) that are being predicted. A group
of nine judges is a small sample for measuring many kinds of statistical relationships, but there are many nonparametric statistical tests
that have been devised—by statisticians, not by judicial behavioralists—explicitly for work with small samples. Moreover, the votes
of nine justices in one hundred twenty cases—not an unusually
large number for the Supreme Court to decide non-unanimously
in a single term—yields a sample of over one thousand items (individual votes), which is quite large enough for most standard para-
metric statistical measures to apply.

Becker worries about a related problem. He thinks that the
"facts" presented to a court are not the same as the "facts" reported
in the opinion(s) of the judges in a case, and that neither judicial
opinions nor judicial votes can be used to validate each other, since
opinions and votes are the same. Hence, attempts to predict votes
from opinions, or vice versa, are circular. The interrelationships
among (1) events dehors the judicial system and judicial perceptions
thereof, (2) judicial opinions, (3) judicial votes, and (4) court decisions are discussed at such length in Chapter Five that further comment would seem unnecessary, were it not for the urgency with which
Becker pleads his cause:

> As we read it, [the judicial behavioralist], in Hullian
> fashion, establishes a Stimulus-Response bond with the "case"
> (that is, the facts as stated in the judicial opinion itself) as
> the stimulus (S) and the vote (the decision of the Court) as
> the response (R). The judges themselves, i.e., their attitudes,

are conceived of as being an intervening variable between the S and the R. Even if [our behavioralist] is using the voting pattern alone, he must, in order to classify that vote, rely upon the facts of the case as stated in the opinion itself. But are the facts as they are stated in the judicial opinion the same "facts" presented to the Court for decision? The case opinion itself was not that which confronted the perceiving organisms (the judges) at the argument. That set of facts (presented in the opinion) was not the same which filtered through, after perception, the attitude net (behavioral predisposition set) and triggered the response. The case opinion itself represents a distillation of the stimulus, which was the actual factual situation presented to the Court. Hasn't [the behavioralist] utilized the response itself as a stimulus? . . . After-the-fact facts are not the real thing. It is hardly surprising to obtain high correlations between such "facts" and the vote—since both the "facts," i.e., the opinion's facts, and the vote are responses which are closely interrelated and actually indistinguishable.[45]

The crux of Becker's argument is his assumption that there is some objective reality called "facts" that exists somewhere "out there" in the real world. Such a notion is just as metaphysical as the assumption that there is an objective "law" that exists independently of what men think and do.[46] After-the-fact facts are not the real thing because there is no real thing, and for purposes of predicting judicial decisions, it would be much more important to know how a group of judges would perceive the facts than it would be to know how other persons (including analysts of judicial behavior) perceive the record of a case. Assuming, however, that the temporal relationship between and the accessibility of judicial perceptions of facts and judicial decisions are such that these data are not available for prediction purposes, then analyst perceptions of case records doubtless afford an incomplete substitute for the judicial perceptions but the next best source of data to which an analyst might turn. Those judicial behavioralists who have worked in this field do not appear to have been (as Becker's comments imply) confused about the distinction between "facts" as the record of a case and "facts" as the authoritative version reported in a majority opinion.[47] Judicial behavioralists who have used cumulative scaling as a method for studying judicial attitudes certainly have been aware that they have treated the opinions and votes of a judge, in any given case, as alternative modes of response that are clearly distinguishable but closely linked. The falsity of Becker's claim that voting and opinion data are "actually indistinguishable" is perhaps best demonstrated by those research studies that have utilized exclusively either voting data[48] or opinion data[49]—and in the particular studies cited no attempt was made to observe or to measure directly the content, in terms of substantative values, of either the judicial votes or the judicial opinions. The capacity to make distinctions is a function of the humans who undertake to study judicial behavior; "distinguishability" is inherent in neither any particular form of data nor the events (in this instance, judicial decisions) which provide the basis for the observations that lead to the data.[50]

### 6. IS SOCIAL SCIENCE DESIRABLE?

Even if we can assume that a science of judicial behavior is feasible, there remains the question whether society ought to permit inquiry into the wellsprings of judicial decision-making. Walter Berns, for example, has warned that "there is no reason for law to imitate physics or engineering. On the contrary, a grasp of the fundamental problems might reveal that there is an irresolvable tension between science, in its old or its new sense, and politics, and that any attempt to resolve the tension is likely to have terrible consequences in the political world; that the political world must be ruled not by science but by prudence."[51] Becker explains why: judicial behavioralists are a threat to society because law is the opiate of the people; behavioral research might lead to popular rejection of the myth of judicial objectivity, and that in turn could lead to societal instability and dysequilibrium:

> [Is it] not possible that the United States' society needs a "bevy of Platonic guardians" to guard the ramparts from mob-rule-acting-as-and-through-legislature? Is it not possible that the "myth" of the "objectivity" of the Court and courts is quite functional for this or for any society? What if it is a *key* function for stability and/or equilibrium? . . . If . . . the real genius of American politics has be[e]n in the establishment of the legitimizing and checking functions of the Supreme Court, then such a scientific discovery [as the proof that judges make policy and act politically] made, verified, and popularized by political scientists could be positively disastrous.[52]

Lawyers frequently argue that *they* can be trusted to keep the secret that judges are policy-makers but that the common man must never know such intimacies of the judicial chamber. At root, the plea is simply another variation of the rationale for the Platonic white lie, and it rests upon a fundamental distrust of democracy. Lawyers may covet their mystique and seek to cloister it, but as Pritchett once remarked (paraphrasing Clemenceau), "law [i]s too important a matter to be left to the lawyers."[53] An open political society requires that we reject the idea of what Jerome Frank once called "*a government of lawyers, and not of men.*"[54] If a democratic society cannot survive the shock of assimilating the kind of information about courts and judges likely to be disseminated by judicial behavioralists—or, indeed, by political behavioralists, since the underlying issue is quite general[55]—then the chances for survival of the American political system are indeed small.

### 7. IS BEHAVIORALISM NONPOLITICAL?

Even traditionalists long have been fond of quoting from Holmes, who more than eighty years ago wrote:

> The very considerations which judges most rarely mention, and always with an apology, are the secret root from which the law draws all the juices of life. We mean, of course, considerations of what is expedient to the community concerned. Every important principle which is developed by litigation is in fact and at bottom the result of more or less definitely understood views of public policy; most generally, to be sure, under our practice and traditions, the unconscious result of instinctive preferences and inarticulate convictions, but none the less traceable to views of public policy in the last analysis.[56]

Most readers doubtless will understand what Holmes says to be a discussion of the political behavior of judges; it is therefore necessary to explain that, in the view of certain conventional theorists, "political behavior" is defined narrowly and rigidly to consist exclusively of interactional relationships among so-called interest groups. Thus Peltason recently has commented:

> It is difficult to understand the intensity of the attack upon [behavioralist] research by those who champion [traditional] scholarship, for there is not much difference between the basic assumptions and goals underlying the two approaches. Like traditional scholars, jurimetricians [*i.e.*, behavioralists] are concerned with explaining the decisional choices of particular judges. They have the same non-political orientation toward judicial decision-making, the same holding constant of all factors except those that are part of the formal processes. There are differences: jurimetricians do not think it is inappropriate to use the same techniques to study decisions of

men who are judges that are used to study decisions of men who are not judges; their variables are attitudes and facts rather than legal rules (or precedents) and facts; their dependent variables are decisions rather than opinions, and they clearly identify the criteria they use to classify decisions.[57]

Certainly, both traditionalists and behavioralists consider themselves each to have more in common with the conventional approach than they do with each other, and the conventional approach does mediate between the other two in terms of chronological development. Probably all that needs to be said about Peltason's comparison of the traditional and the behavioral approaches is that both traditionalists and behavioralists would agree that the conventional approach *is* political but (especially as defined by Bentleyans) much too confined to a particular (and outmoded) school of sociology. The Bentleyan approach is just as hostile to the "mind-stuff" of behavioralism as it is to the "rule-stuff" of traditionalism.[58] However, the conventional approach has had an important influence upon political analysis of the judiciary:

> Notwithstanding the limitations of the Bentleyan frame of reference for adequate understanding of individual human behavior—since it eschews all considerations of perception, cognition, and indeed both rational and irrational factors affecting human choice—the interest group (or political process) approach has made a very valuable contribution to the study of judicial decision-making, since it directed the attention of investigators to a different range of data. Instead of limiting description to the formal processes of courts, the interest group approach . . . pointed toward a focus upon the host of ancillary and informal activities that go on outside of the courtroom. It resulted in a shift of emphasis, among political science students of public law, from the legal aspects of politics to the political aspects of law-making by judges. It also led to research designs that took investigators out of the law library and into the field.[59]

A variation on the theme that behavioralism is merely traditionalism dressed in wolf's clothing is the argument that judicial behavioralists are engaged in a retrogressive trek back to the law library. Becker says that "analyzing the pattern of judicial votes and and the verbiage of judicial opinion in order to generalize about judicial motivation . . . has thus far been a simple backtracking to the law library and a total reliance upon the judicially-uttered syllable."[60] Peltason agrees that to explain why there has been a flurry of one particular type of what has come to be known as judicial behavior research— but which might be more accurately described as the application of statistical techniques to judicial decisions—is the same explanation of why there has always been so much of concentration of attention on the decisions and opinions of the Supreme Court: each year the Court produces hundreds of new decisions, these decisions are readily available and provide a constant flow of data that can be dealt with without having to leave one's office. . . . [T]here is a danger that those aspects of the judicial process that cannot be analyzed from the documents conveniently provided by the Government Printing Office will be ignored, and analysis of decisions will be continued to the point of diminished returns.[61]

If these claims were valid, the conclusion might follow that behavioralism does not differ significantly from the traditional approach. But it is not true that behavioralists place "a total reliance upon the judicially-uttered syllable"; to the contrary, they rely upon opinion language only as evidence of what judges are willing to say for public consumption. Whether such language may also be accepted as evidence concerning judicial beliefs is a hypothesis that must be investigated empirically. Traditionalists, behavioralists, practicing lawyers, and judges (and also, incidentally, conventionalists) all go to the law library for access to raw data, but they go for widely varying reasons. Neither is it true that, as Peltason states, judicial behavioral research "might be more accurately described as the application of statistical techniques to judicial decisions"; as discussed above, statistical techniques can be and are used to evaluate data relating to research that has been guided by any of the three approaches. It is true that the greater rigor of behavioralism has led it to place much more reliance upon statistical measurement than have the traditional and conventional approaches; but statistics itself is just as neutral toward the theories with which it may be associated as are law reports toward the ways in which their data may be processed.

Parsimony is a basic principle of social science research. Behavioralism had to start somewhere, and doubtless it seemed rational to begin experimental work by minimizing the costs of data collection (data gathered through field research is expensive in terms of both research time and money) in order to stay within the low levels of budgetary support available for work with untested theories and untried methods. Moreover, it was also sensible to take advantage of the cumulated knowledge that had been stockpiled by the traditional and conventional work—which was, of course, based primarily upon the law reports of appellate courts in general and the Supreme Court in particular.

There is undoubtably considerable merit in the argument that the time has come when political scientists ought to pay considerably more attention to courts other than the United States Supreme Court, to judges other than Supreme Court justices, and to relationships within judicial bureaucracies and between them and other bureaucracies. In recent years, this is precisely what has been happening, as the major focus of interest in judicial behavioral research gradually has shifted away from the Supreme Court. Certainly, admonitions that such a shift is desirable have been increasingly insistent. Shapiro has noted that "Political jurisprudence is also open to the criticism that it has focused almost entirely on the Supreme Court and constitutional law . . . [and] up to this point little has been done to relate the tools that administrative, organizational and communications theorists have developed for the study of other hierarchically organized bureaucracies to the study of courts. This kind of endeavor should become a core area of political jurisprudence in the future."[62] And two political scientists who have attempted, in their own research, to remedy in part the deficiencies that they denote supply a bill of specifications:

> Within the last two or three years a few scholars . . . have begun to pay attention to the state courts. Their efforts have, however, been limited in both scope and technique. . . . A second limitation of the recent studies of state courts is their conception of judicial politics solely in terms of supreme court judges, a bias in judicial scholars that Jerome Frank has called "the upper court myth." This bias has led to the neglect of the judicial process in its entirety. On the state level the functions of the prosecutor, the jury, and the entire output of the lower courts have not yet been included in the study of the judiciary. One suspects that those scholars who take the supreme courts as their definition of judicial politics simply echo the myopia of students of the national judiciary where the functions of the Attorney General's Office, the role of the United States Attorneys and the flow of claims through lower federal courts have been neglected for refined quantitative analysis of the Supreme Court.[63]

Finally, as Shapiro points out, "it is likely to be urged that [behavioral jurisprudence] considers courts and judges to the almost total exclusion of law."[64] As a professor of sociology has stated the point:

> We must avoid equating judicial decision-making and the legal process. Published judicial decisions constitute a minute and extremely biased sample of the universe of legal action. In fact the analysis of judicial decisions in abstraction from their organizational contexts and the larger universe of legally oriented action is the methodological device used to force the legal process into the categories of attitude psychology.[65]

But Shapiro thinks that political science research in judicial policy-making "will naturally expand from a political analysis of the judiciary to an analysis of the entire law-making process and its relation to traditional jurisprudential concerns."[66]

The preceding six chapters of this volume are intended to constitute a step in the direction of expanding the context of the subject matter deemed relevant for instruction in introductory work about American courts, judges, and constitutional law. To the extent that it fulfills that purpose, it may help to stimulate further inquiry into those aspects of judicial behavior that can be learned from studying neither the Supreme Court nor in the law library. Certainly, however, there is much need for further research both in libraries and in the field, in regard to all types of judges and their interrelationships with other actors in the American political system.

## STUDENT RESEARCH

There are many different kinds of research in judicial policy-making that students can undertake. Many of the arguments reviewed in the preceding section of this chapter can be treated as hypotheses, and their validity as descriptive generalizations then could be investigated by students; the appended bibliography should prove useful for beginning such investigations. Other research possibilities will vary for students in different colleges or universities, depending upon such variables as the size of the community, the facilities of the college library, and the research orientation of the instructor. However, there are some projects that can be carried out in any locale. We shall describe below four different kinds of possible student research projects, at least one corresponding to each of the three major research approaches discussed in this chapter. The first and third of the projects require good library facilities, but the other two are field projects for which little or no library research is required. These four projects are no more than suggestive of the range and diversity of the possibilities; we are confident that the ingenuity of imaginative students and instructors will produce many more.

*Legal Doctrinal Analysis.*  Examine the opinions written in all cases decided by the Supreme Court in either of the two series specified below. Show how the legal doctrine was modified by each successive decision in the series and how the Court, under the principle of *stare decisis*, was obliged logically to decide each case as it did, if the Court were to follow (as it presumably did) the relevant precedents. Describe the resulting doctrine as an evolutionary development in which the latest decision in the series is a logical extension of the principle of law established by the first decision.

    A. The right to counsel in state courts: from *Betts* v. *Brady* (1942) through *Gideon* v. *Wainwright* (1963).

    B. The admissibility in state courts of evidence procured as the result of an illegal search and/or seizure: from *Wolf* v. *Colorado* (1949) through *Mapp* v. *Ohio* (1961).

*Field Interviewing.*  Examine a sample of decisions (in regard to subjects such as zoning, urban redevelopment, racial integration, legislative reapportionment or redistricting) recently made by any court in or near your community. State a set of hypotheses about the probable effect of the decisions upon the groups whose interests are likely to have been affected by the decisions, and vice versa. Interview leaders and members of the relevant community group to ascertain the extent to which these persons consider themselves to have been involved in the decisions. Were they aware of the decisions? If so, do they agree or disagree with the decisions, and why? Did they attempt either directly or indirectly to influence the outcomes? In what way (if any) have the groups with which they are affiliated changed their policies, programs, or activities as a result of the court's decisions? What actions have they taken in order to influence other groups, councilmen, legislators, administrators, or political party officials to act to support, modify, or overrule the policy decreed by the court's decisions? In what way has the court reacted to such post-decisional group and individual activity?

*The Correlation of Attitudes and Attributes.*  Examine the voting behavior of the judges of either (1) a state appellate court or (2) a United States court of appeals. Include in your sample of data at least twenty decisions in which the court has divided; you may need considerably more decisions than this if you choose to work with the national court. Limit your selection of cases to those raising *either* economic *or* civil liberties issues for decision. Your instructor will show you how to construct a scalogram.[67] Classify the judges according to their political party (or factional) affiliation. To what extent do you find a correlation between judicial attitudes (liberal or conservative, as measured by the cumulative scaling analysis) and partisan affiliation? You readily can substitute other judicial attributes (e.g., ethnic background, religion, age) and test the corresponding hypotheses, depending upon what may seem to be reasonable for the court with which you choose to work. A closely related alternative project involves carrying out the scaling as suggested above for a national court of appeals (except in the First Circuit) and then examining the stability of the attitudes of individual judges in the context of differently composed panels. (Does a liberal judge vote differently when he is teamed up with two other liberals than when he is teamed up with two conservatives? or with one other liberal and one conservative?) The data also can be analyzed in terms of the transitivity of judicial voting behavior in the context of the different panels.[68]

*Field Observation.*   Make a continuing field investigation of one of the local courts in the community in which you reside. To do this reasonably well, you will need to devote several hours a week for at least a month. Check in advance with the clerk of the court to find out the calendar (what cases will be heard when). Your instructor can direct you to the relevant sociological literature on the techniques of direct observation. Try to observe a variety of different types of cases—civil as well as criminal, and without as well as with a jury. Perhaps you can join with others in a group observation project, if a variety of courts (appellate as well as trial, and national as well as state) are available in your community. Or you may wish to team up with other students to observe the same events: in a criminal trial, for example, one of you might focus upon the jury, another upon the prosecuting attorney, a third upon the judge, a fourth upon the defense counsel, etc. You may wish to do some reading in role theory or in interaction process analysis theory to guide your observational work and your interpretation of the data.

## FOOTNOTES

CHAPTER ONE

**1.** Gabriel A. Almond, "Comparative Political Systems," *Journal of Politics,* XVIII (1956), 393. Cf. William C. Mitchell, *The American Polity: A Social and Cultural Interpretation* (New York: The Free Press of Glencoe, 1962); Talcott Parsons, "The Law and Social Control," and Harry C. Bredemeier, "Law as an Integrative Mechanism," in William M. Evan (ed.), *Law and Sociology* (New York: The Free Press of Glencoe, 1962), pp. 56–90; David Easton, *A Framework for Political Analysis* (Englewood Cliffs, N.J.: Prentice-Hall, Inc., 1965); Don Martindale (ed.), *Functionalism in the Social Sciences* (Philadelphia: American Academy of Political and Social Science, 1965).

**2.** Martin Landau, "On the Use of Metaphor in Political Analysis," *Social Research,* XXVIII (1961), 331–353.

**3.** David Easton, "Limits of the Equilibrium Model in Social Research," *Chicago Behavioral Sciences Publications,* No. 1 (1953), pp. 26–40.

**4.** Jack W. Peltason, *Federal Courts in the Political Process* (New York: Random House, 1955), pp. 1–2.

**5.** Charles Grove Haines, *The Role of the Supreme Court in American Government and Politics, 1789–1835* (Berkeley: University of California Press, 1944), pp. 119–121.

**6.** See, generally, Glendon Schubert, *Constitutional Politics: The Political Behavior of Supreme Court Justices and the Constitutional Policies That They Make* (New York: Holt, Rinehart and Winston, Inc., 1960), pp. 240–251. For several case studies of statutory interpretation, see Glendon Schubert, "Policy Without Law: An Extension of the Certiorari Game," *Stanford Law Review,* XIV (1962), 284–327; Bernard D. Meltzer, "The Chicago & North Western Case: Judicial Workmanship and Collective Bargaining," and Charles L. B. Lowndes, "Federal Taxation and the Supreme Court," both in Philip B. Kurland (ed.), *The Supreme Court Review—1960* (Chicago: University of Chicago Press,

1960), pp. 113–157 and 222–257.

**7.** John R. Schmidhauser, "The Justices of the Supreme Court: A Collective Portrait," *Midwest Journal of Political Science,* III (1959), 43–44, 47.

**8.** Walter F. Murphy, "Chief Justice Taft and the Lower Court Bureaucracy: A Study in Judicial Administration," *Journal of Politics,* XXIV (1962), 453–476; Walter F. Murphy, "In His Own Image: Mr. Chief Justice Taft and Supreme Court Appointments," in Philip B. Kurland, *The Supreme Court Review—1961* (Chicago: University of Chicago Press, 1961), pp. 159–193; David J. Danelski, *A Supreme Court Justice Is Appointed* (New York: Random House, 1964).

**9.** E. Adamson Hoebel and Karl N. Llewellyn, *The Cheyenne Way: Conflict and Case Law in Primitive Jurisprudence* (Norman, Okla.: University of Oklahoma Press, 1941).

**10.** Max Gluckman, *The Judicial Process Among the Barotse of Northern Rhodesia* (Manchester, Eng.: University of Manchester Press, 1955).

**11.** Walton H. Hamilton, "The Path of Due Process of Law," in Conyers Read (ed.), *The Constitution Reconsidered* (New York: Columbia University Press, 1938); Wallace Mendelson, *Capitalism, Democracy, and the Supreme Court* (New York: Appleton-Century-Crofts, Inc., 1960), Chapter 4; Arnold M. Paul, *Conservative Crisis and the Rule of Law: Attitudes of Bar and Bench, 1887–1895* (Ithaca, N.Y.: Cornell University Press, 1960).

**12.** Benjamin Twiss, *Lawyers and the Constitution* (Princeton, N. J.: Princeton University Press, 1941).

**13.** John R. Schmidhauser, *The Supreme Court: Its Politics, Personalities, and Procedures* (New York: Holt, Rinehart and Winston, Inc., 1960), p. 19 and Chapters 2 and 4, *passim;* and Joel Grossman, *Lawyers and Judges* (New York: John Wiley & Sons, Inc., 1965).

**14.** Jerome Frank, "The Cult of the Robe," *Saturday Review,* XXVIII (October 13, 1945), 12–13, 80–81, and *Courts on Trial* (Princeton, N.J.: Princeton University Press, 1949), pp. 254–261.

**15.** See Stuart S. Nagel, "Off-the-Bench Judicial Attitudes," in Glendon Schubert (ed.), *Judicial Decision-Making* (New York: The Free Press of Glencoe, 1963), pp. 41–42.

**16.** William O. Douglas, "Stare Decisis," *Record of the Association of the Bar of the City of New York,* IV (May 1949), 152–179.

**17.** See particularly the distinction between "traditional" and "personal" *stare decisis* discussed in Reed C. Lawlor, "What Computers Can Do: Analysis and Prediction of Judicial Decisions," *American Bar Association Journal,* XLIX (April 1963), 337–344.

**CHAPTER TWO**

**1.** See Forrest Talbott, *Intergovernmental Relations and the Courts* (Minneapolis: University of Minnesota Press, 1950), especially Chapter 2 (on the Minnesota state judicial system), Chapter 3 (on justice courts), and Chapter 6 (on the removal of cases from state courts to national courts).

**2.** For an introduction to the literature on judicial reform, see generally Arthur T. Vanderbilt, *Minimum Standards of Judicial Administration* (New York: New York University, Institute of Judicial Administration, 1949); *Bad Housekeeping: The Administration of the New York Courts* (New York: The Association of the Bar of the City of New York, 1955); any issue of the *Journal of the American Judicature Society;* and a variety of pamphlets issued from time to time by the Council of State Governments of Chicago, Illinois, and by the National Institute of Municipal Law Officers of Washington, D.C.

**3.** *A Guide to Court Systems,* 2nd ed. (New York: New York University, Institute of Judicial Administration, 1960), pp. 26–31; *Bad Housekeeping* (ftn. 2 *supra*), pp. 21–32, 35–36.

**4.** See Jack W. Peltason, *The Missouri Plan for the Selection of Judges* (Columbia: University of Missouri Studies, Vol. 20, No. 2, 1945), and William J. Keefe, "Judges and Politics: The Pennsylvania Plan for Judge Selection," *University of Pittsburgh Law Review,* XX (1959), 621–631.

**5.** James Herndon, "Appointment as a Means of Initial Accession to Elective State Courts of Last Resort," *North Da-*

*kota Law Review,* XXXVIII (1962), 60–73; cf. Kenneth N. Vines, "The Selection of Judges in Louisiana," in Kenneth N. Vines and Herbert Jacob, *Studies in Judicial Politics* (New Orleans: Tulane University Studies in Political Science, 1962), VIII. Chapter 4, esp. p. 115.

**6.** The Chief Justice of the United States, *Annual Report of the Proceedings of the Judicial Conference of the United States, September 19–20, 1962* (Washington: The Director of the Administrative Office of the United States Courts, 1962), pp. 52–53.

**7.** Cf., however, the excellent earlier survey by Alfred Lepawsky, *The Judicial Systems of Metropolitan Chicago* (Chicago: University of Chicago Press, 1932), a portion of which is reprinted in John R. Schmidhauser, *Constitutional Law in the Political Process* (Chicago: Rand McNally & Company, 1963), pp. 113–122.

**8.** *State Court Systems: A Statistical Summary Prepared for the Conference of Chief Justices,* rev. ed. (Chicago: Council of State Governments, July 1962), a mimeographed pamphlet that is intermittently revised and republished and is summarized in the section on "State Judicial Systems" in *The Book of the States,* published by the council in even-numbered years.

**9.** Cf. Hans Zeisel, Harry Kalven, Jr., and Bernard Buchholz, *Delay in the Court* (Boston: Little, Brown & Co., 1959), and A. Leo Levin and Edward A. Woolley, *Dispatch and Delay: A Field Study of Judicial Administration in Pennsylvania* (Philadelphia: University of Pennsylvania, The Law School, Institute of Legal Research, Studies in Law and Administration, 1961).

**10.** For a more detailed description of the structure and functions of the system, see *A Guide to Court Systems* (ftn. 3, *supra*), pp. 32–39, and *Bad Housekeeping* (ftn. 2, *supra*), pp. 32–34, 37–121. For an excellent analysis of the political inputs and outputs of the system, see Wallace S. Sayre and Herbert Kaufman, *Governing New York City* (New York: Russell Sage Foundation, 1960), pp. 522–554.

**11.** Viz., in Manhattan.

**12.** This represented an overall increase of about 30 per cent in the size of the

national judiciary during the decade since 1954. The number of district judges increased by 39 per cent; circuit judges by 20 per cent; and there has been no change in the number of Supreme Court justices since 1837, except for half a dozen years (1863-1869) when the size of the Court was manipulated by Unionists during the Civil War and Reconstruction periods.
**13.** *Ex parte Bakelite Corp.*, 279 U.S. 438 (1929), and *Federal Radio Commission* v. *General Electric Co.*, 281 U.S. 464 (1930).
**14.** *Federal Radio Commission* v. *Nelson Bros.*, 289 U.S. 266 (1933), and *O'Donoghue* v. *United States*, 289 U.S. 516 (1933).
**15.** See the discussion, of these statutes and the related decisions of the Supreme Court, in Glendon Schubert, *Constitutional Politics* (New York: Holt, Rinehart, and Winston, Inc., 1960), pp. 284-303.
**16.** *Glidden Co.* v. *Zdanok* and *Lurk* v. *United States*, 370 U.S. 530 (1962).
**17.** Also in this category, of course, are the twenty-three judges who are members of the District of Columbia Tax Court, Juvenile Court, Court of General Sessions, and Court of Appeals. These judges, plus those of the United States District Court and the Court of Appeals for the District of Columbia—who review their decisions —comprise the municipal judicial system.
**18.** For example, the system is more flexible, and can better be accommodated to the shifting demands of changing workloads, if retired Supreme Court justices, and active judges of all of the other national courts located in the District of Columbia, can be pooled for temporary assignments where the need is greatest. This means that a judge from the Customs Court might preside over a murder trial in the District Court, or a circuit judge from the Court of Appeals might be assigned temporarily to the Court of Claims (or, in either instance, vice versa), or that a retired Supreme Court justice might be assigned to work in any (other than the strictly municipal) of these so-called "lower" national courts in the nation's capital city.
**19.** *American Insurance Co.* v. *Canter*, 1 Peters 511 (1828).
**20.** Her advanced age may explain the rating, since Bernard G. Segal, Chairman

of the American Bar Association's Committee on the Federal Judiciary, has stated that there are two principal reasons for rating a prospective judge as not qualified: (1) if he is over sixty-five years of age; or (2) if he lacks significant trial experience, either as a judge or as a practicing attorney.
**21.** In recent terms, the Supreme Court has considered on the merits an average of less than two cases per term from the Court of Claims, while denying or dismissing certiorari in 93 per cent of the petitions for review. During the period 1917-1945, the Supreme Court did accept jurisdiction in fourteen customs cases, but it has reviewed none since then and it has taken no patent cases on direct appeal since at least 1930; thus it has been about two decades since any decision of the Court of Customs and Patent Appeals has been reconsidered by the Supreme Court. The Supreme Court has not yet reviewed any decision of the Court of Military Appeals and apparently has not been asked to do so; cf. *Burns* v. *Wilson*, 346 U.S. 137 (1953).
**22.** *Lurk* v. *United States*, 370 U.S. 530, 589 (1962).
**23.** The bankruptcy rules and those governing criminal procedure after a verdict has been reached go into effect (like the Court's own rules) upon promulgation by the Supreme Court, instead of being reported to Congress, with a delay of three months before they become effective.
**24.** Joseph Tanenhaus, Marvin Schick, Matthew Muraskin, and Daniel Rosen, "The Supreme Court's Certiorari Jurisdiction: Cue Theory," Chapter 5 in Glendon Schubert (ed.), *Judicial Decision-Making* (New York: The Free Press of Glencoe, 1963).

**CHAPTER THREE**
**1.** Cf. *Dick* v. *New York Life Insurance Co.*, 359 U.S. 437 (1959).
**2.** *Erie Railroad Co.* v. *Tompkins*, 304 U.S. 64 (1938). During the preceding century, however, the national courts were supposed to develop a body of national policy independent from that of

the states or of any particular state. See *Swift* v. *Tyson*, 16 Peters 1 (1842). Before 1842, the presumption was similar to the one now obtaining.

**3.** *Thompson* v. *City of Louisville*, 362 U.S. 199 (1960), on certiorari to the Police Court of Louisville, Kentucky.

**4.** Glendon Schubert, *Quantitative Analysis of Judicial Behavior* (New York: The Free Press of Glencoe, 1959), pp. 49–55.

**5.** Jerome Frank, "Are Judges Human?" *University of Pennsylvania Law Review*, LXXX (1931), 17–53, 233–267.

**6.** Henry J. Abraham, *The Judicial Process* (New York: Oxford Press, 1962), p. 156.

**7.** See Glendon Schubert, "Civilian Control and Stare Decisis in the Warren Court," Chapter 3 in Schubert (ed.), *Judicial Decision-Making* (New York: The Free Press of Glencoe, 1963).

**8.** Clinton Rossiter, *The Supreme Court and the Commander in Chief* (Ithaca: Cornell University Press, 1951); Glendon Schubert, *The Presidency in the Courts* (Minneapolis: University of Minnesota Press, 1957).

**9.** *Universal Camera Corporation* v. *National Labor Relations Board*, 340 U.S. 474, 490–491 (1951). Cf., however, Kenneth Culp Davis, *Administrative Law Treatise* (St. Paul, Minn.: West Publishing Co., 1958), Vol. 4, Sec. 29.04.

**10.** On the enforcement of the Supreme Court's racial integration policies, see Kenneth N. Vines, "Federal District Judges and Race Relations Cases in the South," *Journal of Politics*, XXVI (1964), 337–357, and his "The Role of Circuit Courts of Appeals in the Federal Judicial Process: A Case Study," *Midwest Journal of Political Science*, VII (1963), 305–319; Jack W. Peltason, *Fifty-Eight Lonely Men* (New York: Harcourt, Brace and World, Inc., 1961). On the enforcement of the Court's reapportionment and redistricting policies, see *Congressional Quarterly Weekly Report*, XXI, No. 23 (June 7, 1963), 938–945 (on congressional redistricting), and No. 52 (December 27, 1963), 2258–2263 (on state legislative reapportionment).

**11.** Cf. Vilhelm Aubert, "White Collar Crime and Social Structure," *American Journal of Sociology*, LVIII (1952), 263–271.

**12.** See Chester A. Newland, "Press Coverage of the United States Supreme Court," *Western Political Quarterly*, XVII (1964), 15–36, and his "Legal Periodicals and the United States Supreme Court," *Midwest Journal of Political Science*, III (1959), 58–74.

**13.** Oliver Wendell Holmes, Jr., *Collected Legal Papers* (New York: Harcourt, Brace & Company, 1920), pp. 295–296.

**14.** Cases decided by the Supreme Court in "original jurisdiction" typically involve conflicts of interest among and between state political systems and the national political system, and, although few in number, such cases often raise for decision major issues of public policy. See Lucius J. Barker, "The Offshore Oil Cases," Chapter 7 in C. Herman Pritchett and Alan F. Westin (eds.), *The Third Branch of Government: 8 Cases in Constitutional Politics* (New York: Harcourt, Brace & World, Inc., 1963). Since the Supreme Court has neither the time nor the facilities to conduct trials, it appoints so-called "special masters" to function as the equivalent of *ad hoc* United States district judges, in order to compile a record and to formulate tentative decisions in the form of what are termed "recommendations" to the Supreme Court. An example of such a policy dispute is the allocation of the waters of the Colorado River among the seven states with a primary interest (particularly California, now the most populous state in the union, which for a long time has been absolutely dependent upon imported Colorado water for almost its entire supply). This dispute has been actively under way for over two generations, and the current—by no means the initial—Supreme Court litigation began in 1952. In June 1963, the Supreme Court filed the 101-page report of what doubtless will prove to have been its interim decision, together with various opinions pro and con the accommodation of interests acceptable to a majority of the Court. See *Arizona* v. *California*, 373 U.S. 546 (1963).

**15.** See, for example, *Sacher* v. *United*

*States*, 343 U.S. 1 (1952).
**16.** 374 U.S. 865–866.
**17.** *Ibid.*, p. 870.
**18.** *Wayman* v. *Southard*, 10 Wheaton 1 (1825).
**19.** *McNabb* v. *United States*, 318 U.S. 332 (1943). For a more recent example, see *Jencks* v. *United States*, 353 U.S. 657 (1957). The latter decision was the basis for what is called the "Jencks rule"— that the "right to confrontation" requires the government to produce for inspection by the defense confidential reports to the F.B.I. by government witnesses, concerning the substance of their testimony in criminal trials. The alternative to production of the reports is dismissal of the action.
**20.** Cf. *Weeks* v. *United States*, 232 U.S. 383 (1914); *Wolf* v. *Colorado*, 338 U.S. 25 (1949); *Mapp* v. *Ohio*, 367 U.S. 643 (1961).
**21.** See Fred Kort, "Content Analysis of Judicial Opinions and Rules of Law," Chapter 6 in Schubert (ed.), *Judicial Decision-Making* (ftn. 7, *supra*), and Reed C. Lawlor, "What Computers Can Do: Analysis and Prediction of Judicial Decisions," *American Bar Association Journal*, XLIX (April 1963), 337–344, and his "Foundations of Logical Legal Decision-Making," *Modern Uses of Logic in Law*, III, No. 4 (June 1963), 98–114.

**CHAPTER FOUR**
**1.** "In this country the judiciary was made independent because it has, I believe, the primary responsibility and duty of giving force and effect to constitutional liberties and limitations upon the executive and legislative branches. . . . Suggestions were . . . made in and out of Congress [during its initial session in 1789] that a Bill of Rights would be a futile gesture since there would be no way to enforce the safeguards for freedom it provided. Mr. Madison answered this argument in these words:

If they [the Bill of Rights amendments] are incorporated into the Constitution, independent tribunals of justice will consider themselves in a peculiar manner the guardians of those rights; they will be an impenetrable bulwark against any assumption of power in the Legis-

lative or Executive; they will be naturally led to resist every encroachment upon rights expressly stipulated for in the Constitution by the declaration of rights. [1 Annals of Cong. 439.]
I fail to see how courts can escape this sacred trust." Justice Hugo Black, "The Bill of Rights," *New York University Law Review*, XXXV (1960), 870, 880.
**2.** "Stare decisis is usually the wise policy, because *in most matters it is more important that the applicable rule of law be settled than that it be settled right.*" Justice Louis Brandeis, dissenting in *Burnet* v. *Coronado Oil and Gas Co.*, 285 U.S. 393, 406 (1932). (Emphasis added.)
**3.** Herbert McClosky, "Conservatism and Personality," *American Political Science Review*, LII (1958), 27–45; Milton Rokeach, *The Open and Closed Mind* (New York: Basic Books, Inc., 1960); Hans Eysenck, *The Psychology of Politics* (London: Routledge and Kegan Paul, 1954).
**4.** See Robert G. Scigliano, *The Michigan One-Man Grand Jury* (East Lansing: Michigan State University Governmental Research Bureau, Political Research Studies No. 4, 1957).
**5.** *In re Oliver*, 333 U.S. 257 (1948), and *In re Murchison*, 349 U.S. 133 (1955).
**6.** See "Politics and Criminal Prosecution in New Orleans," Chapter 3 in Kenneth N. Vines and Herbert Jacob, *Studies in Judicial Politics* (New Orleans: Tulane University Studies in Political Science, Vol. 8, 1962), especially pp. 79–80: "The District Attorney's Role in the Criminal Process," and Figure 1 at p. 81.
**7.** See Charles Winick, "The Psychology of Juries," Chapter 5 in Hans Toch (ed.), *Legal and Criminal Psychology* (New York: Holt, Rinehart and Winston, Inc., 1961), pp. 96–120.
**8.** Theodore L. Becker, Donald C. Hildrun, and Keith Bateman, "The Influence of Jurors' Values on their Verdicts: A Courts and Politics Experiment," *Southwestern Social Science Quarterly*, XLV (Spring 1965). Cf. William Bevan, Robert S. Albert, Pierre R. Loiseaux, Peter N. Mayfield, and George Wright, "Jury Behavior as a Function of the Prestige of the Foreman and the Nature of His Leadership," *Journal of Public Law*, VII

(1958), 419–449.

**9.** *The New York Times,* September 6, 1963, p. 59, col. 5.

**10.** See Jerome Frank, *Courts on Trial* (Princeton, N.J.: Princeton University Press, 1950). For an example, see *Sacher* v. *United States,* 343 U.S. 1 (1952), especially the Appendix to the dissenting opinion of Mr. Justice Frankfurter, pp. 42–89.

**11.** Charles Winick, Israel Gerver, and Abraham Blumber, "The Psychology of Judges," Chapter 6 in Toch (ed.), *Legal and Criminal Psychology* (ftn. 7, *supra*), pp. 121–145. See also the bibliography, "Part One: Social Psychology and Judges," in Schubert (ed.), *Judicial Decision-Making* (New York: The Free Press of Glencoe, 1963), pp. 257–261.

**12.** Dorwin Cartwright and Alvin Zander (eds.), *Group Dynamics,* 2nd ed. (Evanston, Ill.: Row, Peterson & Co., 1960), and Robert F. Bales, *Interaction Process Analysis: A Method for the Study of Small Groups* (Cambridge, Mass.: Harvard University Press, 1950).

**13.** See "Cultural Anthropology and Judicial Systems," Chapter 2 in Glendon Schubert (ed.), *Judicial Behavior: A Reader in Theory and Research* (Chicago: Rand McNally & Company, 1964).

**14.** Stuart S. Nagel, "Cultural Patterns and Judicial Systems," *Vanderbilt Law Review,* XVI (1962), 147–157; Richard D. Schwartz and James C. Miller, "Legal Evolution and Societal Complexity," *American Journal of Sociology,* LXX (1964), 159–169.

**15.** *Dennis* v. *United States,* 341 U.S. 494 (1951). The page references in the quotations are from the portions of the record reprinted in the Appendix to Mr. Justice Frankfurter's opinion in *Sacher* v. *United States* (ftn. 10, *supra*).

**16.** Glendon Schubert, *Quantitative Analysis of Judicial Behavior* (New York: The Free Press of Glencoe, 1959), pp. 264–265.

**17.** For a more comprehensive discussion, see "The Publication of Reports of the Supreme Court's Decisions," Appendix A in Glendon Schubert, *Constitutional Politics* (New York: Holt, Rinehart and Winston, Inc., 1960), pp. 703–706.

**18.** *Shaughnessy* v. *United States ex rel. Mezei,* 345 U.S. 206 (1953). But see *The New York Times,* Aug. 12, 1954, p. 10, col. 4.

**19.** *Smith* v. *Baldi,* 344 U.S. 561 (1953).

**20.** *Lynch* v. *Overholser,* 369 U.S. 705 (1962).

**21.** For a more extended discussion of these historical differences and related matters, see Schubert, *Constitutional Politics* (ftn. 17, *supra*), pp. 89–114; the classic historical reference work is Felix Frankfurter and James M. Landis, *The Business of the Supreme Court* (New York: The Macmillan Co., 1928).

**22.** For a celebrated example, see *Rathbun (Humphrey's Executor)* v. *United States,* 295 U.S. 602 (1935).

**23.** *Eisler* v. *United States,* 388 U.S. 189, 196 (1949).

**24.** See Glendon Schubert, *The Public Interest* (New York: The Free Press of Glencoe, 1959), Chapter 4.

**25.** Cf. Ralph K. Huitt, "The Congressional Committee: A Case Study," *American Political Science Review,* XLVIII (1954), 364: "In the price control [hearings by the Senate Committee on Banking and Currency] the senators were not sitting as arbiters of the group struggle, but as participants; it flowed through them."

**26.** Portions of the oral argument in what the editors consider to be the more important cases are published in the Supreme Court Section of *United States Law Week* (Washington: Bureau of National Affairs), and *The New York Times* and other newspapers occasionally report parts of the oral argument in a case.

**27.** See Alexander M. Bickel, *The Unpublished Opinions of Mr. Justice Brandeis* (Cambridge, Mass.: Belknap Press of Harvard University Press, 1957).

**28.** Note, "Evasion of Supreme Court Mandates in Cases Remanded to State Courts Since 1941," *Harvard Law Review,* XLVII (1954), 1251–1259, and Walter F. Murphy, "Lower Court Checks on Supreme Court Power," *American Political Science Review,* LIII (1959), 1017–1031.

**29.** Cf. *Reid* v. *Covert,* 351 U.S. 487 (June 11, 1956), 352 U.S. 901 (November 5, 1956, on petition for hearing), and 354

U.S. 1 (June 10, 1957); or *Cahill* v. *New York, New Haven & Hartford Railroad Co.*, 350 U.S. 898–899 (November 21, 1955), 350 U.S. 943 (January 9, 1956, on petition for rehearing), and 351 U.S. 183 (May 14, 1956).
**30.** Concurring, in *Jewell Ridge Coal Co.* v. *Local No. 6167, United Mine Workers of America*, 325 U.S. 897–898 (1945).
**31.** See *Jones* v. *Opelika*, 316 U.S. 584, 623–624 (June 8, 1942), and *West Virginia State Board of Education* v. *Barnette*, 319 U.S. 624 (June 14, 1943); or see Justice Clark's concurring opinion in *Irvine* v. *California*, 347 U.S. 128, 138–139 (1954), and his opinion for the Court in *Mapp* v. *Ohio*, 367 U.S. 643 (1961).

**CHAPTER FIVE**

**1.** *Santa Clara County* v. *Southern Pacific R.R.*, 118 U.S. 394 (1886); Walton H. Hamilton, "The Path of Due Process of Law," in Conyers Read (ed.), *The Constitution Reconsidered* (New York: Columbia University Press, 1938), p. 181. The point had been argued but not decided during the preceding term, in *San Mateo County* v. *Southern Pacific Railroad Co.*, 116 U.S. 138 (1885).
**2.** Clement E. Vose, "Litigation as a Form of Pressure Group Activity," *Annals of the American Academy of Political and Social Science*, CCCXIX (September 1958), 22, 24–25; Vose, *Caucasians Only: The Supreme Court, The NAACP, and the Restrictive Covenant Cases* (Berkeley and Los Angeles: University of California Press, 1959).
**3.** Cf. John P. Frank, *The Marble Palace* (New York: Alfred A. Knopf, Inc., 1958), pp. 84–94.
**4.** Rodney L. Mott, "Judicial Influence," *American Political Science Review*, XXX (1936), 295–315; Stuart S. Nagel, Sociometric Relations among American Courts," *Southwestern Social Science Quarterly*, XLIII (1962), 136–142.
**5.** See Jack W. Peltason, *Federal Courts in the Political Process* (New York: Random House, 1955), p. 16.
**6.** *Dennis* v. *United States*, 341 U.S. 494, 510 (1951).
**7.** Peltason, *Federal Courts* (ftn. 5, *supra*), p. 72n.20.

**8.** Anthony Lewis, "Legislative Apportionment and the Federal Courts," *Harvard Law Review*, LXXI (1958), 1057—1098.
**9.** Most of Lewis' article, Cox's brief, and the Supreme Court's decision and opinions are reprinted in Glendon Schubert, *Reapportionment* (New York: Charles Scribner's Sons, 1965), Part II.
**10.** *Congressional Record*, 85th Cong., 1st Sess., Vol. 103, Part 12, pp. 16159—16169, especially pp. 16160–16161.
**11.** Chester A. Newland, "Press Coverage of the United States Supreme Court," *Western Political Quarterly*, XVII (1964), 15–36 at 33.
**12.** Stuart S. Nagel, "Judicial Backgrounds and Criminal Cases," *Journal of Criminal Law, Criminology, and Police Science*, LIII (1962), 333–339; John R. Schmidhauser, "*Stare Decisis*, Dissent, and the Background of the Justices of the Supreme Court of the United States." *University of Toronto Law Journal*, XIV (1962), 194–212.
**13.** John R. Schmidhauser, "The Justices of the Supreme Court: A Collective Portrait," *Midwest Journal of Political Science* III (1959), 22–23.
**14.** Schmidhauser, "*Stare Decisis*" (ftn. 12, *supra*), p. 202.
**15.** Schmidhauser, "The Justices of the Supreme Court" (ftn. 13, *supra*), pp. 41–44, 47.
**16.** Stuart S. Nagel, "Political Parties and Judicial Review in American History," *Journal of Public Law*, XI (1963), 340.
**17.** William Howard Taft, for example, is well known both for the great importance that he as President attached to the many appointments that he made to the Court (six in four years) and also for the conspicuous manner in which, as Chief Justice during the 1920's, he beleaguered (in turn) Harding and Coolidge and Hoover with his advice concerning the men who ought to be appointed to the courts. See Chapter 1n.8.
**18.** C. Herman Pritchett, "Division of Opinion among Justices of the United States Supreme Court, 1939–1941," *American Political Science Review*, XXXV (1941), 890–898; Pritchett, *The Roosevelt Court:*

*A Study in Judicial Politics and Values, 1937–1947* (New York: The Macmillan Co., 1948); Louis L. Thurstone and James W. Degan, "A Factorial Study of the Supreme Court," *Proceedings of the National Academy of Science*, XXXVII (1951), 628–635; Jessie Bernard, "Dimensions and Axes of Supreme Court Decisions: A Study in the Sociology of Conflict," *Social Forces*, XXXIV (1955), 19–27; Eloise C. Snyder, "The Supreme Court as a Small Group," *Social Forces*, XXXVI (1958), 232–238; Glendon Schubert, *Quantitative Analysis of Judicial Behavior* (New York: The Free Press of Glencoe, 1959), pp. 77–172; S. Sidney Ulmer, "The Analysis of Behavior Patterns on the United States Supreme Court," *Journal of Politics*, XXII (1960), 629–653. Glendon Schubert, *The Judicial Mind: The Attitudes and Ideologies of Supreme Court Justices, 1946–1963* (Evanston, Ill.: Northwestern University Press, 1965).

**19.** John R. Schmidhauser, "Judicial Behavior and the Sectional Crisis of 1837–1860," *Journal of Politics*, XXIII (1961), 615–638.

**20.** Particularly in regard to ceremonial and some administrative functions, such as presiding over oral argument and when decisions are announced; the preparation of the consent lists; and the preparation of the *per curiam* opinions.

**21.** David J. Danelski, "The Influence of the Chief Justice in the Decisional Process," in Walter F. Murphy and C. Herman Pritchett (eds.), *Courts, Judges and Politics* (New York: Random House, 1961), pp. 497–508.

**22.** S. Sidney Ulmer, "Homeostatic Tendencies in the United States Supreme Court," in Ulmer (ed.), *Introductory Readings in Political Behavior* (Chicago: Rand McNally & Company, 1961), pp. 167–188.

**23.** Schubert, *Constitutional Politics* (New York: Holt, Rinehart & Winston, Inc., 1960), pp. 123–125; John P. Frank, "Harlan Fiske Stone: An Estimate," *Stanford Law Review*, IX (1957), p. 629n.

**24.** S. Sidney Ulmer, "A Note on Attitudinal Consistency in the United States Supreme Court," *Indian Journal of Political Science*, XXII (1961), 195–204 (the political scale); Harold J. Spaeth, "Warren Court Attitudes toward Business: The 'B' Scale," in Glendon Schubert (ed.), *Judicial Decision-Making* (New York: The Free Press of Glencoe, 1963), pp. 79–108, especially pp. 79–84 (the economic scale); Schubert, "The 1960 Term of the Supreme Court: A Psychological Analysis," *American Political Science Review*, LVI (1962), 90–107, especially 97–101 (both the political scale and the economic scale).

**25.** Glendon Schubert, "Policy without Law: An Extension of the Certiorari Game," *Stanford Law Review*, XIV (1962), 284–327.

**26.** See Karl N. Llewellyn, *The Common-Law Tradition: Deciding Appeals* (Boston: Little, Brown & Co., 1960); Richard A. Wasserstrom, *The Judicial Decision: Toward a Theory of Legal Justification* (Stanford: Stanford University Press, 1961).

**27.** Fred Kort, "Content Analysis of Judicial Opinions and Rules of Law," in Schubert (ed.), *Judicial Decision-Making* (ftn. 24, *supra*), pp. 133–197, especially pp. 177–178.

**28.** Fred Rodell, "For Every Justice, Judicial Deference Is a Sometime Thing," *Georgetown Law Journal*, L (1962), 707–708.

**29.** Reed C. Lawlor, "What Computers Can Do: Analysis and Prediction of Judicial Decisions," *American Bar Association Journal*, XLIX (1963), 337–344, especially 343–344.

**30.** *Gideon* v. *Wainwright*, 372 U.S. 335 (1963).

**31.** Joseph Tanenhaus, Marvin Schick, Matthew Muraskin, and Daniel Rosen, "The Supreme Court's Certiorari Jurisdiction: Cue Theory," in Schubert (ed.), *Judicial Decision-Making* (ftn. 24, *supra*), pp. 111–132.

**32.** Glendon Schubert, "Judicial Attitudes and Voting Behavior: The 1961 Term of the United States Supreme Court," *Law and Contemporary Problems*, XXVIII (1963), 100–142 at 137–142; and Schubert, *Judicial Behavior* (Chicago: Rand McNally & Company, 1964), pp. 579–587.

**33.** Ulmer, "A Note on Attitudinal Consistency" (ftn. 24, *supra*); Schubert,

*The Judicial Mind* (ftn. 18, *supra*).

**34.** See Schubert, *The Judicial Mind* (ftn. 18, *supra*), Chapter 6.

**35.** *Edwards* v. *South Carolina,* 372 U.S. 228 (1963). See also *Turner* v. *Memphis,* 369 U.S. 350 (1962) [restaurants]; *Bailey* v. *Patterson,* 369 U.S. 31 (1962) [transportation]; *Garner* v. *Louisiana,* 368 U.S. 157 (1961) [sit-ins].

**36.** *National Association for the Advancement of Colored People* v. *Button,* 371 U.S. 415 (1963); *Gibson* v. *Florida Legislative Investigation Committee,* 372 U.S. 539 (1963).

**37.** *Gray* v. *Sanders,* 372 U.S. 368 (1963); *Wesberry* v. *Sanders,* 376 U.S. 1 (1964).

**38.** John P. Roche, "The Expatriation Decisions: A Study in Constitutional Improvisation and the Uses of History," *American Political Science Review,* LVIII (1964), 72–80; Schubert (ed.), *Judicial Decision-Making* (ftn. 24, *supra*), pp. 55–77.

**39.** *Toth* v. *Quarles,* 350 U.S. 11 (1955); *Reid* v. *Covert,* 354 U.S. 1 (1957); *Trop* v. *Dulles,* 356 U.S. 86 (1958); *Kinsella* v. *Singleton,* 361 U.S. 234 (1960); *Grisham* v. *Hagan,* 361 U.S. 278 (1960); *McElroy* v. *Guagliardo,* 361 U.S. 281 (1960); *Wilson* v. *Bohlender,* 361 U.S. 281 (1960); *Kennedy* v. *Mendoza-Martinez,* 372 U.S. 144 (1963); *Rusk* v. *Cort,* 372 U.S. 144 (1963); *Schneider* v. *Rusk,* 377 U.S. 163 (May 18, 1964); *Aptheker* v. *Secretary of State,* 378 U.S. 500 (June 22, 1964). In the *Schneider* decision, for example, Douglas (speaking for the five-man majority) said: "We start with the premise that the rights of citizenship of the native born and of the naturalized person are of the same dignity and are co-extensive. The only difference drawn by the Constitution is that only the 'natural born' citizen is eligible to be President."

**40.** Cf. *Hurd* v. *Hodge,* 334 U.S. 24 (1948); the only apparent exception is *Bolling* v. *Sharpe,* 347 U.S. 497 (1954).

**41.** Schubert, *The Judicial Mind* (ftn. 18, *supra*), Chapter 6.

**42.** See Schubert, *Constitutional Politics* (ftn. 23, *supra*), Chapter 12.

**43.** *Mapp* v. *Ohio,* 367 U.S. 643 (1961).

**44.** *Ker* v. *California.* 374 U.S. 23 (1963).

**45.** *Griswold* v. *Connecticut,* 33 *U.S. Law Week* 4587 (1965).

**46.** For an excellent discussion see Anthony Lewis, *Gideon's Trumpet* (New York: Random House, 1964).

**47.** *Douglas* v. *California,* 372 U.S. 353 (1963); *Lane* v. *Brown,* 372 U.S. 477 (1963); *Draper* v. *Washington,* 372 U.S. 487 (1963).

**48.** *Torcaso* v. *Watkins,* 367 U.S. 488 (1961).

**49.** *Engel* v. *Vitale,* 370 U.S. 421 (1962); *School District of Abington Township, Pennsylvania* v. *Schempp,* 376 U.S. 203 (1963); *Murray* v. *Curlett,* 374 U.S. 203 (1963).

**50.** *Wilkinson* v. *United States,* 365 U.S. 399 (1961); *Braden* v. *United States,* 365 U.S. 431 (1961); *Uphaus* v. *Wyman,* 364 U.S. 388 (1960).

**51.** *Communist Party* v. *Subversive Activities Control Board,* 367 U.S. 1 (1961).

**52.** *Scales* v. *United States,* 367 U.S. 203 (1961).

**53.** *In re Anastaplo,* 366 U.S. 82 (1961).

**54.** E.g., *Bantam Books* v. *Sullivan,* 372 U.S. 58 (1963).

**55.** *Michalic* v. *Cleveland Tankers,* 367 U.S. 325 (1960).

**56.** *Machinists* v. *Street,* 367 U.S. 740 (1961).

**57.** *Local 357, Teamsters* v. *National Labor Relations Board,* 365 U.S. 667 (1961).

**58.** It should be noted that questions of *national* taxation relate to a different attitudinal variable, which is largely independent of the issues of liberalism and conservatism considered in this chapter.

**CHAPTER SIX**

**1.** Charles Grove Haines, *The Role of the Supreme Court in American Government and Politics, 1789–1835* (Berkeley and Los Angeles: University of California Press, 1944), p. 29, and cf. Chapter 3, especially pp. 78–82.

**2.** John R. Schmidhauser, "Judicial Behavior and the Sectional Crisis of 1837–1860," *Journal of Politics,* XXIII (1961), 628.

**3.** Edward S. Corwin, "The 'Higher-Law' Background of American Constitutional Law," *Harvard Law Review,* XLII (1928–29), 149, 365; Charles G. Haines, *The Revival of Natural Law Concepts* (Cambridge, Mass.: Harvard University Press, 1930); J. A. C. Grant, "Natural Law

Background of the Due Process of Law," *Columbia Law Review*, XXXI (1931) 56.
**4.** Haines, *The Role of the Supreme Court* (ftn. 1, *supra*), pp. 159–165.
**5.** Arnold M. Paul, *Conservative Crisis and the Rule of Law: Attitudes of Bar and Bench, 1887–1895* (Ithaca: Cornell University Press, 1960), pp. 229, 231, 233, 237.
**6.** C. Herman Pritchett, *The Roosevelt Court: A Study in Judicial Politics and Values, 1937–1947* (New York: The Macmillan Co., 1948), pp. 71–81, 270–273, 300–301.
**7.** Finley Peter Dunne, "The Supreme Court's Decisions," in *Mr. Dooley's Opinions* (New York: Russell Pub. Co., 1901), p. 26.
**8.** Paul, *Conservative Crisis* (ftn. 5, *supra*), p. 226.
**9.** W. A. Sutherland, "Politics and the Supreme Court," *American Law Review*, XLVIII (1914), 395.
**10.** Henry F. Pringle, *The Life and Times of William Howard Taft* (New York: Farrar & Rinehart, 1939), II, 967.
**11.** Joseph Alsop and Turner Catledge, *The 168 Days* (New York: Doubleday & Co., Inc., 1938).
**12.** Glendon Schubert, "The Hughberts Game," in *Quantitative Analysis of Judicial Behavior* (New York: The Free Press of Glencoe, 1959), pp. 192–210.
**13.** *Lovell* v. *Griffin*, 303 U.S. 444 (1938); see C. Herman Pritchett, *The Roosevelt Court* (New York: The Macmillan Co., 1948), pp. 93–100 and 293 n.7.
**14.** *Smith* v. *Allwright*, 321 U.S. 649 (1944).
**15.** *Colegrove* v. *Green*, 328 U.S. 549 (1946); *Baker* v. *Carr*, 369 U.S. 186 (1962).
**16.** For an analysis of the work of the district judges, see Jack W. Peltason, *Fifty-Eight Lonely Men* (New York: Harcourt, Brace, & World, Inc., 1961).
**17.** *Cooper* v. *Aaron*, 358 U.S. 1 (1958).
**18.** See the current and recent issues of *Southern School News* and *Race Relations Law Reporter*.
**19.** *Wesberry* v. *Sanders*, 376 U.S. 1 (1964).
**20.** By the spring of 1964, liberal lay Catholic leaders had begun to plead publicly, before convocations of the hierarchy of the American Catholic Church, that the continuation of the parochial school system is undesirable on both educational and economic grounds. There are some evident sociological, psychological, and economic parallels between separate school systems that are segregated on the basis of religion and separate school systems that are segregated on the basis of race.
**21.** It should be understood that this analysis is completely relativistic. We assume that whatever may be the existing state of consensus between the Court and other decision-makers, it is appropriate to speak of greater or the same or a lesser degree of policy agreement than presently obtains, irrespective of the direction of change when either actor assumes a dynamic role. Hence, "absence of conflict" means no further *increase* in conflict between the Court's policies and those of other decision-makers.

**CHAPTER SEVEN**
**1.** Wolfgang Friedmann, *Legal Theory*, 3rd ed. (London: Stevens & Sons, Ltd., 1953), p. 163.
**2.** Alpheus T. Mason, *Harlan Fiske Stone: Pillar of the Law* (New York: Viking Press, Inc., 1956); Charles Fairman, *Mr. Justice Miller and the Supreme Court, 1862–1890* (Cambridge, Mass.: Harvard University Press, 1939); Carl B. Swisher, *Roger Brooke Taney* (New York: The Macmillan Co., 1935); Albert J. Beveridge, *The Life of John Marshall* (New York: Houghton Mifflin Company, 1916).
**3.** Alexander M. Bickel, *The Unpublished Opinions of Mr. Justice Brandeis: The Supreme Court at Work* (Cambridge, Mass.: Harvard University Press, 1957); Walter F. Murphy, "Marshaling the Court: Leadership, Bargaining, and the Judicial Process," *University of Chicago Law Review*, XXIX (1962), 656–663.
**4.** See p. 186n.8.
**5.** Martin Shapiro, "Political Jurisprudence," *Kentucky Law Journal*, LII (1964), 294–295. See also his *Law and Politics in the Supreme Court: New Approaches to Political Jurisprudence* (New York: The Free Press of Glencoe, 1964).
**6.** For a more detailed description of these studies, see the bibliographical

essay by Glendon Schubert, "Behavioral Research in Public Law," *American Political Science Review*, LVII (1963), 433–445. Two recent collections of research studies in judicial behavior are Schubert (ed.), *Judicial Decision-Making* (New York: The Free Press of Glencoe, Volume 4 of the International Yearbook of Political Behavior Research, 1963); and Schubert (ed.), *Judicial Behavior: A Reader in Theory and Research* (Chicago: Rand McNally & Company, 1964).

**7.** Roscoe Pound, "The Causes of Popular Dissatisfaction with the Administration of Justice," *American Bar Association Proceedings*, XXIX (1906), Part I, 395–417.

**8.** Martin Landau, "On the Use of Metaphor in Political Analysis." *Social Research*, XXVIII (1961), 331–353.

**9.** Roscoe Pound, "The Call for a Realist Jurisprudence," *Harvard Law Review*, XLIV (1931), 697–711. Cf. the sympathetic statement by Max Radin, "Legal Realism," *Columbia Law Review*, XXXI (1931), 824–828.

**10.** Karl N. Llewellyn, "Some Realism about Realism," *Harvard Law Review*, XLIV (1931), 1222–1256.

**11.** Karl N. Llewellyn, *The Common Law Tradition—Deciding Appeals* (Boston: Little, Brown & Co., 1960), pp. 508–520 (Appendix B); and see Takeo Hayakawa, "Karl N. Llewellyn as a Lawman from Japan Sees Him," *Rutgers University Law Review*, XVIII (1964), especially 730–734.

**12.** Theodore L. Becker, "Inquiry into a School of Thought in the Judicial Behavior Movement," *Midwest Journal of Political Science*, VII (1963), 255, 264, 254, 262, 263 (emphasis in the original). For a more extended development of this point of view, see Becker's *Political Behavioralism and Modern Jurisprudence* (Chicago: Rand McNally & Company, 1965). For further discussion of the relative predictive capacity of (1) judicial behavioralists and (2) "well informed and legally intuitive constitutional lawyers," see Glendon Schubert, "Judicial Attitudes and Voting Behavior: The 1961 Term of the United States Supreme Court," *Law and Contemporary Problems*, XXVIII (1963),

especially 102–108: "Prediction in Law and Judicial Behavior."

**13.** Shapiro, "Political Jurisprudence" (ftn. 5, *supra*), p. 317.

**14.** Becker, "Inquiry . . ." (ftn. 12, *supra*), p. 261.

**15.** Cf., however, Glendon Schubert, "Civilian Control and *Stare Decisis* in the Warren Court," Chapter 3 in Schubert (ed.), *Judicial Decision-Making* (ftn. 6, *supra*), pp. 55–77, and John R. Schmidhauser, "*Stare Decisis*, Dissent, and the Background of the Justices of the Supreme Court of the United States," *University of Toronto Law Journal*, XIV (1962), 196–212.

**16.** See Fred Kort, "Predicting Supreme Court Decisions Mathematically: A Quantitative Analysis of the Right to Counsel Cases," *American Political Science Review*, LI (1957), 1–12, and Kort, "Content Analysis of Judicial Opinions and Rules of Law," Chapter 6 in Schubert (ed.), *Judicial Decision-Making* (ftn. 6, *supra*), pp. 133–197, especially pp. 179–182.

**17.** E.g., Benjamin N. Cardozo, *The Nature of the Judicial Process* (New Haven: Yale University Press, 1921); Jerome Frank, *Law and the Modern Mind* (New York: Coward-McCann, Inc., 1930); Felix S. Cohen, "Transcendental Nonsense and the Functional Approach," *Columbia Law Review*, XXXV (1935), 809–849; Lee Loevinger, "Jurimetrics, The Next Step Forward," *Minnesota Law Review*, XXXIII (1949), 455–493; Jack W. Peltason, "A Political Science of Public Law," *Southwestern Social Science Quarterly*, XXXIV (1953), 51–56; Victor G. Rosenblum, *Law as a Political Instrument* (New York: Random House, 1955); Clement E. Vose, *Caucasians Only: The Supreme Court, the NAACP, and the Restrictive Covenant Cases* (Berkeley: University of California Press, 1959).

**18.** Shapiro, "Political Jurisprudence" (ftn. 5, *supra*), pp. 302, 297.

**19.** See Charles G. Haines' comments on "The Mechanical Theory," in his "General Observations on the Effects of Personal, Political, and Economic Influences in the Decisions of Judges," *Illinois Law Review*, XVII (1922), 96–116.

20. Jack W. Peltason, book review in *American Political Science Review*, LVIII (1964), 675.

21. Wallace Mendelson, "The Neo-Behavioral Approach to the Judicial Process: A Critique," *American Political Science Review*, LVII (1963), 602.

22. Walter Berns, "Law and Behavioral Science," *Law and Contemporary Problems*, XXVIII (1963), 198. Ulmer's article is "Supreme Court Behavior in Racial Exclusion Cases: 1935-1960," *American Political Science Review*, LVI (1962), 325-330. For further discussion of how the knowledge of behavioral research might aid the practical lawyer, see Stuart S. Nagel, "Testing Empirical Generalizations in Legal Research," *Journal of Legal Education*, XV (1963), 380-381, and Schubert (ed.), *Judicial Behavior* (ftn. 6, *supra*), pp. 458-459.

23. Berns, "Law and Behavioral Science" (ftn. 22, *supra*), p. 195.

24. [Cf. Herbert A. Simon, "The Proverbs of Administration," *Public Administration Review*, VI (1946), 53-67, or see "Some Problems in Administrative Theory," Chapter 2 in Simon's *Administrative Behavior*, rev. ed. (New York: The Macmillan Co., 1957), pp. 20-36.]

25. Shapiro, "Political Jurisprudence" (ftn. 5, *supra*), p. 329.

26. Mendelson, "The Neo-Behavioral Approach" (ftn. 21, *supra*), 593, 603. By "neo behavioralism" Mendelson means "the new psychometric research in judicial decision-making." *Ibid.*, p. 594.

27. Becker, "Inquiry . . ." (ftn. 12, *supra*), p. 265 (emphasis in the original).

28. Berns, "Law and Behavioral Science" (ftn. 22, *supra*), pp. 199-200. For further discussion of the concept of "public good" and of the rationalist and idealist models of judicial decision-making, see Glendon Schubert, *The Public Interest: A Critique of the Theory of a Political Concept* (New York: The Free Press of Glencoe, 1960), pp. 74-78, 123-135.

29. Shapiro, "Political Jurisprudence" (ftn. 5, *supra*), p. 342.

30. *Ibid.*, p. 299, n.11: "Wallace Mendelson has been the most prolific academic proponent of judicial modesty [i.e., restraint] and has issued a very long succession of articles and reviews defending and rationalizing Justice Frankfurter's opinions. For a summary of his views see his *Justices Black and Frankfurter: Conflict in the Court* ([Chicago: University of Chicago Press], 1961)."

31. Mendelson, "The Neo-Behavioral Approach" (ftn. 21, *supra*), pp. 598, 603.

32. Fred Rodell, *Nine Men* (New York: Random House, 1955).

33. Jack W. Peltason, *Fifty-Eight Lonely Men* (New York: Harcourt, Brace & World, Inc., 1961); Kenneth N. Vines, "Federal District Judges and Race Relations Cases in the South," *Journal of Politics*, XXVI (1964), 337-357.

34. Stuart S. Nagel, "Off-the-Bench Judicial Attitudes," Chapter 2 in Schubert (ed.), *Judicial Decision-Making* (ftn. 6, *supra*), pp. 29-53.

35. "[I]f judges are viewed as policy-makers, then it is natural to ask of them as one asks of other policy-makers, how do their individual preferences effect [*sic*] their decisions. The traditional concern with judicial thought meshes nicely with the modern interest in the motivational aspects of political action." Shapiro, "Political Jurisprudence" (ftn. 5, *supra*), pp. 310-311.

36. Cf. Joel B. Grossman, "Role-Playing and the Analysis of Judicial Behavior: The Case of Justice Frankfurter," *Journal of Public Law*, XI (1963), 285-309, and Harold J. Spaeth, "The Judicial Restraint of Mr. Justice Frankfurter—Myth or Reality," *Midwest Journal of Political Science*, VIII (1964), 22-38.

37. See, e.g., Karl R. Popper, *The Open Society and Its Enemies* (New York: Harper & Row, 1963 edition), I, 319: "Plato and Geometry."

38. John P. Roche, "Political Science and Science Fiction," *American Political Science Review*, LII (1958), 1026, 1028.

39. *Ibid.*, p. 1026.

40. Shapiro, "Political Jurisprudence" (ftn. 5, *supra*), pp. 307, 308, 326.

41. Roche, "Political Science and Science Fiction" (ftn. 38, *supra*), p. 1029.

42. Becker, "Inquiry . . ." (ftn. 12, *supra*), p. 262.

43. Reed C. Lawlor predicts correctly a major policy decision of the Supreme

Court in his "What Computers Can Do: Analysis and Prediction of Judicial Decision," *American Bar Association Journal,* XLIX (May 1963), 337–344. Schubert predicted correctly all twenty-two of the Court's reapportionment decisions of the 1963 term: see "Judicial Attitudes and Voting Behavior" (ftn. 12, *supra*), pp. 140–141, for the predictions, and *Judicial Behavior* (ftn. 6, *supra*), pp. 584–586, for the outcomes. Both articles are reprinted in Schubert, "Mathematical Prediction of Judicial Behavior," *ibid.,* Chapter 5, pp. 443–587.

**44.**   Roche, "Political Science and Science Fiction" (ftn. 41, *supra*), p. 1029.

**45.**   Becker, "Inquiry . . ." (ftn. 12, *supra*), pp. 259–260.

**46.**   For a fuller statement of the "facts are facts, and no nonsense about it" point of view, see Wallace Mendelson, "The Untroubled World of Jurimetrics," with comment by Fred Kort and response by Mendelson, *Journal of Politics,* XXVI (1964), 914–928. Mendelson argues that attitudinal scales of judicial votes "ought" to remain invariant, notwithstanding differences in the samples and methods used and the considerable indeterminacy resulting from missing data (due to judicial nonparticipation in the decisions). Evidently, Mendelson's scholarly attitude toward "the facts" of judicial decision-making is just as dogmatic as his attitude toward "the law": cf. ftn. 21, *supra*.

**47.**   See the explicit discussion of this distinction by Fred Kort in "Content Analysis of Judicial Opinions and Rules of Law," Chapter 6 in Schubert (ed.), *Judicial Decision-Making* (ftn. 6, *supra*), pp. 179–180.

**48.**   Louis L. Thurstone and James W. Degan, "A Factorial Study of the Supreme Court," *Proceedings of the National Academy of Science,* XXXVII (1951), 628–635.

**49.**   S. Sidney Ulmer, "Leadership in the Michigan Supreme Court," Chapter 1 in Schubert (ed.), *Judicial Decision-Making* (ftn. 6, *supra*), pp. 13–28.

**50.**   See Clyde H. Coombs, *A Theory of Data* (New York: John Wiley & Sons, Inc., 1964), Chapter 1.

**51.**   Berns, "Law and Behavioral Science" (ftn. 22, *supra*), p. 212. Cf. Julius Stone, "Man and the Machine in the Search for Justice," *Stanford Law Review,* XVI (1964), especially 515–516, 558–559.

**52.**   Theodore L. Becker, "On Science, Political Science, and Law," *American Behavioral Scientist,* VII (December 1963), 12 (emphasis in the original).

**53.**   Pritchett, *The Roosevelt Court* (New York: The Macmillan Co., 1948), p. xi.

**54.**   Jerome Frank, *If Men Were Angels* (New York: Harper & Brothers, 1942), p. 223 (emphasis in the original). On the open political society, see Popper, *The Open Society and Its Enemies* (ftn. 37, *supra*), Vols. 1 and 2.

**55.**   Cf. Herbert J. Storing (ed.), *Essays on the Scientific Study of Politics* (New York: Holt, Rinehart and Winston, Inc., 1962), especially the "Epilogue" by Leo Strauss, and Heinz Eulau, *The Behavioral Persuasion in Politics* (New York: Random House, 1963).

**56.**   Oliver Wendell Holmes, Jr., "Common Carriers and the Common Law," *American Law Review,* XIII (1879), 630–631.

**57.**   Jack W. Peltason, book review (ftn. 20, *supra*), p. 675. See the discussion of the proposition, "On the whole, it is true to say that an umbrella corresponds with, more than it differs from, a blackboard," in James G. March, "Sociological Jurisprudence Revisited," in Schubert (ed.), *Judicial Behavior* (ftn. 6, *supra*), pp. 138–139.

**58.**   "[I]f we turn our attention to the judiciary as a facet in the group struggle and relate the activities of judges to that of other groups, we can begin to develop a political science of public law without trying to 'out-history' the historian, 'outlaw' the lawyer, or 'out-psychology' the psychologist." Peltason, "A Political Science of Public Law" (ftn. 17, *supra*), p. 56.

**59.**   Schubert (ed.), *Judicial Behavior* (ftn. 6, *supra*), p. 13.

**60.**   Becker, "On Science, Political Science, and Law" (ftn. 52, *supra*), p. 12. Becker's plea to get out of the musty old library into the field, where real-life activities are on-going, must be evaluated in the context of his belittling of suggestions that the direct observation of courtroom behaviors might provide an additional source of data worthy of investigation. We should not waste our time and resources, says Becker, in bothering to investigate the possibility that there is any important relationship between what goes on in a courtroom and what judges decide about cases—apparently because his traditionalist concept of "law" precludes the possibility that data about human behavior could affect court decisions. See his "Inquiry . . ." (ftn. 12, *supra*), pp. 256–257.

**61.** Peltason, book review (ftn. 20, *supra*), p. 676.

**62.** Shapiro, "Political Jurisprudence" (ftn. 5, *supra*), pp. 318, 320.

**63.** Herbert Jacob and Kenneth Vines, "The Role of the Judiciary in American State Politics," Chapter 9 in Schubert (ed.), *Judicial Decision-Making* (ftn. 6, *supra*), p. 246. For examples of their own empirical research, see Jacob and Vines, *Studies in Judicial Politics* (New Orleans:

Tulane University, Tulane Studies in Political Science, Vol. 8, 1962); Vines, "The Role of Circuit Courts of Appeal in the Federal Judicial Process: A Case Study," *Midwest Journal of Political Science*, VII (1963), 305–319; Vines, "Federal District Judges and Race Relations Cases," (ftn. 33, *supra*).

**64.** Shapiro, "Political Jurisprudence" (ftn. 5, *supra*), p. 322.

**65.** Leon Mayhew, book review in *American Journal of Sociology*, LXX (1964), 240.

**66.** Shapiro, "Political Jurisprudence" (ftn. 5, *supra*), p. 324.

**67.** In lieu thereof, an elementary exposition of the theory and technique of cumulative scaling of judicial decisions can be found in Chapter 5 of Glendon Schubert, *Quantitative Analysis of Judicial Behavior* (New York: The Free Press of Glencoe, 1959), pp. 269–290.

**68.** William H. Riker, "Voting and the Summation of Preferences," *American Political Science Review*, LV (1961), 900–911.

## BIBLIOGRAPHICAL ESSAY

The literature on courts, judges, and law is of almost boundless proportions. Fortunately, several up-to-date and comprehensive bibliographies are available. Much of the best of the traditional and conventional writings is listed in Henry J. Abraham, *The Judicial Process*, rev. ed. (New York: Oxford, 1962), pp. 329–360. The behavioral work (through 1962) is listed in Glendon Schubert (ed.), *Judicial Decision-Making* (New York: The Free Press, 1963), pp. 257–265, and the most important recent research (since 1955) is discussed in the bibliographical essay by Glendon Schubert, "Behavioral Research in Public Law," *American Political Science Review*, LVII (1963), 433–445. In the present essay I shall guide the reader to a few selected studies which I shall discuss on the basis of their articulation with the text.

### CHAPTER ONE

Three of the most important issues of national domestic policy at the present time are legislative reapportionment, racial integration, and the secular base of public education. All of these issues have been drastically reshaped, since the end of World War II, by judicial policy-making. The historic roots of, and the contemporary socioeconomic and political context for, the judicial policies in regard to these issues are eloquently discussed in Alan P. Grimes, *Equality in America: Religion, Race, and the Urban Majority* (New York: Oxford, 1964).

An excellent general discussion of how systems theory relates to political analysis is William C. Mitchell, *The American Polity: A Social and Cultural Interpretation* (New York: The Free Press, 1962), which was written for undergraduate use. Systems theory is discussed in David Easton, *A Framework for Political Analysis* (New York: Prentice-Hall, 1965).

Two recent books focus upon the boundary relationships between the national judiciary and the Congress, with particular reference to the congressional "backlash" against the Supreme Court's pro-civil liberty policies of the middle 1950's: C. Herman Pritchett's *Congress versus the Supreme Court, 1957–1960* (Minneapolis: Univ. of Minn. Press, 1961) reprints a series of his lectures, while Walter F. Murphy's *Congress and the Court* (Chicago: Univ. of Chicago Press, 1962) is a more detailed study. Glendon Schubert, *The Presidency in the Courts* (Minneapolis: Univ. of Minn. Press, 1957), surveys judicial review of presidential action, while more general questions of "administrative law," especially in relation to the "independent federal regulatory commissions," are discussed from a variety of legal points of view in the collection of readings edited by Samuel Krislov and Lloyd D. Musolf, *The Politics of Regulation* (Boston: Houghton Mifflin, 1964).

The development of the American constitutional system is discussed from a historical point of view in Arthur N. Holcombe, *Securing the Blessings of Liberty* (Chicago: Scott, Foresman, 1964). From a legal point of view, two recent surveys of the American constitutional system are Charles L. Black, Jr., *Perspectives in Constitutional Law* (Englewood Cliffs, N.J.: Prentice-Hall, 1963) and C. Herman Pritchett, *The American Constitutional System* (New York: McGraw-Hill, 1963). The selection of Supreme Court justices, especially in relation to their age, education, and prior experience in public office, is the subject of Cortez A. M. Ewing, *The Judges of the Supreme Court, 1789–1937* (Minneapolis: Univ. of Minn. Press, 1938). Somewhat broader in scope, analyzing social and economic attributes and discussing developments through 1957, is John R. Schmidhauser, "The Justices of the Supreme Court: A Collective Portrait," *Midwest Journal of Political Science*, III (1959), 1–59. The most extensive recent analysis of the political context for Supreme Court policy-making is Glendon Schubert, *Constitutional Politics: The Political Behavior of Supreme Court Justices and the Constitutional Policies That They Make* (New York: Holt, Rinehart & Winston, 1960), especially pp. 1–171.

Two books that stress the public opinion leadership function of the organized legal profession, especially during the formative years of the ABA, are Benjamin R. Twiss, *Lawyers and the Constitution: How Laissez Faire Came to the Supreme Court* (Princeton: Princeton Univ. Press, 1942) and Arnold M. Paul, *Conservative Crisis and the Rule of Law: Attitudes of Bar and Bench, 1887–1895* (Ithaca, N.Y.: Cornell Univ. Press, 1960). An analysis of the contemporary movement to establish, through state legislation, what amounts to a "closed shop" for legal practice, is in Dayton D. McKean, *The Integrated Bar* (Boston: Houghton Mifflin, 1963). Both the political life of the ABA and factors based upon custom in the institutional environment for policy-making by the Supreme Court are dealt with by John R. Schmidhauser in *The Supreme Court: Its Politics, Personalities, and Procedures* (New York: Holt, Rinehart, and Winston, 1960), and by Joel Grossman in *Lawyers and Judges* (New York: Wiley, 1965).

CHAPTER TWO

The most general study of judicial systems in the United States is Lewis Mayers, *The American Legal System*, rev. ed. (New York: Harper and Row, 1964). *Minimum Standards of Judicial Administration*, by Arthur T. Vanderbilt (New York: New York Univ. Institute of Judicial Administration, 1949), is an older but still useful survey of the structure of state judicial systems. Both Mayers and Vanderbilt are concerned with judicial administration from a decidedly legal point of view; two studies by political scientists, of the structure of particular state judicial systems, afford different perspectives: in *Intergovernmental Relations and the Courts* (Minneapolis: Univ. of Minn. Press, 1950), Forrest Talbott analyzes the courts of Minnesota as a problem in public administration, while Kenneth N. Vines and Herbert Jacob discuss selected aspects of the political relationships of Louisiana courts in *Studies in Judicial Politics* (New Orleans: Tulane Univ., Tulane Studies in Political Science, Vol. 8, 1962). An older study, which remains perhaps the best analysis of the courts in a metropolitan area, is Alfred Lepawsky, *The Judicial Systems of Metropolitan Chicago* (Chicago: Univ. of Chicago Press,

1932). Jack W. Peltason's *Federal Courts in the Political Process* (New York: Random House, 1955) is a concise political analysis of the national judicial system, from the point of view of conventional (interest group) theory.

CHAPTER THREE

The overall relationship between the national and the state judicial systems is dealt with only incidentally in a number of good books whose focus is elsewhere, such as Talbott's *Intergovernmental Relations and the Courts* (above) and Frankfurter and Landis, *The Business of the Supreme Court* (below). The tendency of legal scholars has been to concentrate attention upon Supreme Court review of the decisions of the highest courts of the states, as in John R. Schmidhauser's *The Supreme Court as Final Arbiter of Federal-State Relations* (Chapel Hill: Univ. of N.C. Press, 1958).

There is also a dearth of quantitative analyses of the functions of the national judicial system. The editors of the *Harvard Law Review* publish annually (November issue) some summary statistics on the Supreme Court's disposition of its workload for the term ending in the previous June. There are also, of course, the official reports, such as the *Annual Report of the Director of the Administrative Office of the United States Courts* and the *Annual Report of the Attorney General of the United States*, published by the Superintendent of Documents and by the Department of Justice, respectively; unfortunately, the data they present are in a form designed for lawyers and budget officers, rather than social scientists. The only good study concerned with Supreme Court supervision of lower courts, both national and state, from a political and administrative rather than a legal point of view is Felix Frankfurter and James M. Landis, *The Business of the Supreme Court* (New York: Macmillan, 1928). Although it is a valuable historical analysis, the Frankfurter and Landis book is now out of date with regard to such matters as the Court's dockets, jurisdictional decision-making, and formal and informal rule-making as means of supervising lower courts. A more recent discussion of the Court's workload and summary (including jurisdictional) decision-making is in Glendon Schubert, *Quantitative Analysis of Judicial Behavior* (Glencoe, Ill.: The Free Press, 1959), Ch. 2.

Turning to qualitative analyses of the national judicial system, we are confronted with a superfluity of commentary. The overwhelming tendency among law professors has been to justify the policy-making function of the national courts. Two particularly articulate statements of this sort are Paul A. Freund, *On Understanding the Supreme Court* (Boston: Little, Brown, 1949) and Alexander M. Bickel, *The Least Dangerous Branch: The Supreme Court at the Bar of Politics* (Indianapolis: Bobbs-Merrill, 1962). Political scientists, on the other hand, have tended to view judicial policy-making as a brake upon the wheel of progress, and their skepticism has been reflected in such studies as Alpheus T. Mason, *The Supreme Court: Instrument of Power or of Revealed Truth, 1930–1937* (Boston: Boston Univ. Press, 1953) and Robert A. Dahl, "Decision-Making in a Democracy: The Role of the Supreme Court as a National Policy-Maker," *Journal of Public Law*, VI (1957), 279–295.

**CHAPTER FOUR**

A general discussion of adjudication procedures, written for undergraduate social science majors rather than for law students, is political scientist C. Gordon Post's *An Introduction to the Law* (Englewood Cliffs, N.J.: Prentice-Hall, 1963). Also intended for a lay audience is lawyer Delmar Karlen's *The Citizen in Court: Litigant, Witness, Juror, Judge* (New York: Holt, Rinehart and Winston, 1964). Four law professors have edited a collection of articles and court opinions that exemplify the legal approach to judicial decision-making procedures: Carl A. Auerbach, Willard Hurst, Lloyd K. Garrison, and Samuel Mermin, *The Legal Process: An Introduction to Decision-Making by Judicial, Legislative, Executive, and Administrative Agencies* (San Francisco: Chandler, 1961). For a socio-psychological approach to the same subject, see Hans Toch (ed.), *Legal*

*and Criminal Psychology* (New York: Holt, Rinehart and Winston, 1961), Ch.1–7.

Trial courts are the particular focus of Jerome Frank's *Courts on Trial: Myth and Reality in American Justice* (Princeton: Princeton Univ. Press, 1950). Frank, who was a leading "legal realist" during the 1920's and 1930's, was an appellate judge but never a trial judge; Karl N. Llewellyn, another leading realist who was a law professor but never an appellate judge, has provided a treatise on appellate courts: *The Common Law Tradition: Deciding Appeals* (Boston: Little, Brown, 1960). A standard work on adjudication procedure in criminal cases is Lester B. Orfield, *Criminal Procedure from Arrest to Appeal* (New York: New York Univ. Press, 1947), and a more recent book, which empathizes with criminal defendants, is Arnold S. Trebach, *The Rationing of Justice: Constitutional Rights and the Criminal Process* (New Brunswick, N.J.: Rutgers Univ. Press, 1964).

Arthur T. Vanderbilt provides a general, elementary, lawyer-like discussion in *Judges and Jurors: Their Functions, Qualifications and Selection* (Boston: Boston Univ. Press, 1956). Two books on the more specialized subject of grand juries are Robert Scigliano's excellent political analysis of *The Michigan One-Man Grand Jury* (East Lansing: Mich. State Univ., Governmental Research Bureau, 1957) and Richard D. Younger's historical survey, *The People's Panel: The Grand Jury in the United States, 1934–1941* (Providence, R.I.: Brown Univ. Press, 1963).

**CHAPTER FIVE**

There are several excellent case studies of the political sources and consequences enveloping a particular litigation. One such study, by a political scientist, emphasizes the political aspects of group activity in the sponsorship and management of a series of litigations involving the enforceability of restrictive racial covenants in real estate sales: see Clement E. Vose, *Caucasians Only: The Supreme Court, the N.A.A.C.P., and the Restrictive Covenant Cases* (Berkeley: Univ. of Calif. Press, 1959). A more recent book, written by a journalist who customarily covers the Supreme Court for *The New York Times,* narrates the tale of how an individual outcast influenced the constitutional policy governing indigent appeals from criminal convictions in the state court systems: Anthony Lewis, *Gideon's Trumpet* (New York: Random House, 1964).

Although they do not classify and report the relevant information systematically, the numerous judicial biographies are an excellent source of data on judicial attributes. Among the best are Albert J. Beveridge, *The Life of John Marshall* (New York: Houghton Mifflin, 1916); Charles Fairman, *Mr. Justice Miller and the Supreme Court, 1862-1890* (Cambridge: Harvard Univ. Press, 1939); and John P. Frank, *Justice Daniel Dissenting* (Cambridge: Harvard Univ. Press, 1964). Not all great justices (if we accept as our criterion of "greatness" the consensual judgment of constitutional historians) have been the subject of great biographies, nor are the best biographies necessarily about the most famous justices. A series of article-length biographies of a dozen justices appears in each of two symposia: "Studies in Judicial Biography," *Vanderbilt Law Review,* X (1957), 167–413, and Allison Dunham and Philip B. Kurland (eds.), *Mr. Justice,* rev. ed. (Chicago: Univ. of Chicago Press, 1964). Another series, thirty-eight much briefer sketches of Supreme Court justices, can be found in Rocco J. Tresolini, *American Constitutional Law* (New York: Macmillan, 1959), pp. 633–659. Special bibliographies on judicial biography have been published in Abraham, *The Judicial Process* (above), pp. 341–344; Holcombe, *Securing the Blessings of Liberty* (above), p. 178; and John R. Schmidhauser, "The Justices of the Supreme Court: A Collective Portrait," *Midwest Journal of Political Science,* III (1959), 50–57.

There is an increasing literature on the subject of policy conversion as a process, as the attention of behavioral research scholars has focused upon the human factors in judicial decision-making. Especially influential upon research and teaching by political scientists have been two books by C. Herman Pritchett, *The Roosevelt Court: A Study in Judicial Politics and Values, 1937–1947* (New York: Macmillan, 1948) and *Civil Liberties and the Vinson Court* (Chicago: Univ. of Chicago Press, 1954), which are about the attitudes of Supreme Court justices. Sociologist Edward Green has surveyed a much larger group of trial judges of the Philadelphia criminal courts, in relation to differences in their sentencing behavior: *Judicial Attitudes in Sentencing* (New York: St. Martin's Press, 1961). My own book *The Judicial Mind: The Attitudes and Ideologies of Supreme Court Justices, 1946–1963* (Evanston, Ill.: Northwestern Univ. Press, 1965) is a study of the relationships among judicial attitudes, voting behavior, social and political and economic ideologies. The prediction of judicial decisions (votes, opinions, and policy outcomes) is discussed in Ch. 5 of my *Judicial Behavior* (above).

Policy norms are the subject of an immense literature, since this is the subject to which traditional legal scholarship long has largely been confined. That type of analysis is well represented by two books by political scientists: Edward S. Corwin, *The Constitution and What It Means Today,* 12th ed. (Princeton: Princeton Univ. Press, 1958) is the magnum opus of the scholar who was dean among constitutional lawyers for almost two generations; a much briefer version of the same material, intended for beginning students, is Edward S. Corwin and Jack W. Peltason, *Understanding the Constitution,* 3rd ed. (New York: Holt, Rinehart and Winston, 1964). The same subject is viewed from a political rather than a legal point of view by many other commentators. Typical of the more popular type of critique of the Court's work is Rosalie M. Gordon's *Nine Men Against America: The Supreme Court and Its Attack on American Liberties* (New York: Devin-Adair, 1958). Miss Gordon writes as a conservative who dislikes the liberal thrust of the Court's policy-making during the middle 1950's, but most of the time the shoe has been on the other foot, as exemplified by Drew Pearson and Robert S. Allen, *The Nine Old Men* (New York: Doubleday, 1936). For a scholarly critique with a sympathetic attitude toward the Court's contemporary policy line, see C. Herman Pritchett and Alan F. Westin (eds.), *The Third Branch of Government: 8 Cases in Constitutional Politics* (New York: Harcourt, Brace & World, 1963).

Bernard Taper, *Gomillion versus Lightfoot: The Tuskegee Gerrymander Case* (New York: McGraw-Hill, 1962) provides an exceptionally well-written account of the background of one of the Court's decisions involving the social issues of racial and voting equality. Victor Rosenblum's *Law as a Political Instrument* (New York: Random House, 1955) supplies an analysis of case materials with which students can trace the development of norms, through policy-making by the Supreme Court, in regard to both a political issue (racial segregation in public transportation and public education) and an economic issue (national and state regulation of milk marketing).

CHAPTER SIX

The standard history of the Supreme Court was written by a lawyer with a conservative orientation: Charles Warren, *The Supreme Court in United States History*, 3 vols. (Boston: Little, Brown, 1922–1923). An alternative interpretation, written from the point of view of the denouement of American progressivism, is provided in James Allen Smith, *The Growth and Decadence of Constitutional Government* (New York: Holt, 1930). More radical views are expressed by Gustavus Myers in his *History of the Supreme Court of the United States* (Chicago: Charles H. Kerr, 1925), which employs a crude version of Marxism to reinterpret the Court's decisions as made with a view to the justices' personal profit. Equally radical is William W. Crosskey's *Politics and the Constitution in the History of the United States* (Chicago: Univ. of Chicago Press, 1953), which purports to demonstrate semantically how the vast majority of Presidents, congressmen, and Supreme Court justices have misunderstood the "true" meaning of the constitutional document. Fred Rodell's *Nine Men: A Political History of the Supreme Court from 1790 to 1955* (New York: Random House, 1955) is a

liberal critique of what has been most of the time a rather conservative group of lawyer-politicians.

There are also many historical studies of the periods in terms of which Ch. Six analyzed changes in the development of constitutional policy by the Supreme Court; indeed, Robert G. McCloskey's *The American Supreme Court* (Chicago: Univ. of Chicago Press, 1960) corresponds, in its chapter organization, to that classification; Ch. 5 and 6 are particularly valuable for the period of conservatism. Charles Grove Haines, *The Role of the Supreme Court in American Government and Politics, 1789–1835* (Berkeley: Univ. of Calif. Press, 1944) is the leading work on the Marshall Court. For the Taney Court, see Charles Grove Haines and Foster Sherwood, *The Role of the Supreme Court in American Government and Politics, 1835–1864* (Berkeley: Univ. of California Press, 1957). Alpheus T. Mason's *The Supreme Court from Taft to Warren* (Baton Rouge: La. State Univ. Press, 1958) focuses upon the transition from modern conservatism to modern liberalism. James E. Clayton's *The Making of Justice* (New York: Dutton, 1964) is a case study of the 1962 term of the Court.

There is an extensive literature on judicial review, activism, and restraint. Charles A. Beard thought that he had settled once and for all, more than half a century ago, the controversy over the intent of the framers regarding the Supreme Court's power of judicial review, when he published *The Supreme Court and the Constitution* (Englewood Cliffs, N.J.: Prentice-Hall, 1962 ed.); this edition also contains an extensive bibliography on judicial review. Charles Grove Haines' *The American Doctrine of Judicial Supremacy*, rev. ed. (Berkeley: Univ. of Calif. Press, 1932) is a historical analysis of the developmental use of judicial review by American courts. Robert H. Jackson's *The Struggle for Judicial Supremacy* (New York: Knopf, 1941) is a briefer and less scholarly but well-written account that focuses upon the Supreme Court and especially upon his own battles—as Roosevelt's Solicitor General during the height of the legal attack upon the New Deal—

with the Hughes Court. The continental divide between modern conservatism and liberalism in the Court's use of judicial review is the Court-packing episode of 1937, a detailed journalistic account of which is provided in Joseph Alsop and Turner Catledge, *The 168 Days* (New York: Doubleday, 1938).

Contemporary controversy over judicial activism and restraint in general, and in the use of judicial review in particular, is reflected in a bifurcation of professional opinion between law professors and political scientists. Most law professors identify with the courts and justify the good (i.e., liberal) works produced by contemporary Supreme Court policymaking: see, for example, Eugene V. Rostow, *The Sovereign Prerogative: The Supreme Court and the Quest for Law* (New Haven: Yale Univ. Press, 1962) and Charles L. Black, Jr., *The People and the Court: Judicial Review in a Democracy* (New York: Macmillan, 1960). Most political scientists, on the other hand, identify with legislatures and tend to view judicial policy-making as a perversion of the democratic process, even when it may be used—temporarily, no doubt—to accomplish such desirable goals as racial integration and legislative reapportionment. This point of view is well expressed by Wallace Mendelson in *Justices Black and Frankfurter: Conflict on the Court* (Chicago: Univ. of Chicago Press, 1961) and by Charles S. Hyneman in *The Supreme Court on Trial* (New York: Atherton, 1963).

CHAPTER SEVEN

Wolfgang Friedmann's *Legal Theory*, 4th ed. (London: Stevens, 1960) is a standard text on jurisprudence, by a law professor, that emphasizes the work of scholars from continental European and English-speaking countries. Fred V. Cahill, Jr., *Judicial Legislation* (New York: The Ronald Press, 1952) is written by a political scientist and focuses upon American legal theory. Richard A. Wasserstrom, *The Judicial Decision* (Stanford: Stanford Univ. Press, 1961), is an attempt by a professor of legal philosophy to explain judicial decision-making on

the basis of deductions from a formal, logical model; such endeavors no longer are common. The most popular book on sociological jurisprudence is Benjamin N. Cardozo's *The Nature of the Judicial Process* (New Haven: Yale Univ. Press, 1921). On realist jurisprudence, consult Jerome Frank's *Law and the Modern Mind* (New York: Coward-McCann, 1930), which brought Freudian psychology to the attention of the legal profession, and Karl N. Llewellyn's valedictory, *Jurisprudence: Realism in Theory and Practice* (Chicago: Univ. of Chicago Press, 1962), a selection of his articles over a period of four decades.

The conventional literature on the judicial process is mostly a product of political scientist' writings since World War II. The underlying objective of their approach is to bring courts and judges within the scope of political analysis, as exemplified by three collections of readings: Walter F. Murphy and C. Herman Pritchett, *Courts, Judges, and Politics: An Introduction to the Judicial Process* (New York: Random House, 1961); Robert Scigliano, *The Courts: A Reader in the Judicial Process* (Boston: Little, Brown, 1962); and John R. Schmidhauser, *Constitutional Law in the Political Process* (Chicago: Rand McNally, 1963). Much of the material in the above readers relates to the Supreme Court, and Loren P. Beth has summarized this part of it in *Politics, The Constitution, and the Supreme Court* (Evanston, Ill.: Row, Peterson, 1962), which includes a useful series of partially annotated chapter bibliographies.

Much of the recent research in judicial behavior is published or reprinted in three books: Hans W. Baade (ed.), *Jurimetrics* (New York: Basic Books, 1963; initially published as the Winter 1963 issue of *Law and Contemporary Problems*, XXVIII); Vol. 4 in the International Yearbook of Political Behavior Research, *Judicial Decision-Making* (New York: The Free Press, 1963) a book I edited that consists of original research studies; and *Judicial Behavior: A Reader in Theory and Research* (Chicago: Rand McNally, 1964), which I edited also. Several articles on judicial behavioral and related research appear in the symposium "Frontiers of Legal Research," *American Behavioral Scientist,* VII:4 (December 1963), 3–55. See also the special supplement to the above issue of the journal: Rollo Handy and Paul Kurtz, *A Current Appraisal of the Behavioral Sciences,* Sec. 4, "Political Science: Jurisprudence" (Great Barrington, Mass.: Behavioral Research Council, 1963).

In regard to the projects for student research, see the following sources for elementary instruction in case analysis of legal doctrines: Elmer E. Schattschneider, Victor Jones, and Stephen K. Bailey, *A Guide to the Study of Public Affairs* (New York: William Sloane, 1952), Ch. 9, "How to Read a Judicial Decision"; Robert S. Hirschfield, *The Constitution and the Court* (New York: Random House, 1962), pp. 221–239; and Auerbach, *et al., The Legal Process* (above), pp. 12–15, 43–65. For instruction in the field research methods of interviewing and direct observation, see any social science research manual (e.g., William J. Goode and Paul K. Hatt, *Methods in Social Research* [New York: McGraw-Hill, 1952]). On the theory and method of correlating judicial attributes and attitudes, and the design of appropriate research projects, see two articles by Stuart S. Nagel: "Testing Relations between Judicial Characteristics and Judicial Decision-Making," *Western Political Quarterly,* XV (1962), 425–437, and "Testing Empirical Generalizations in Legal Research," *Journal of Legal Education,* XV (1963), 365–381.

**INDEX OF CASES**

CANISIUS COLLEGE LIBRARY
KF8700 .S241 c. 1
Judicial policy--maki

3 5084 00052 0687